THE ART OF JAPANESE MANAGEMENT

Richard Tanner Pascale
Graduate School of Business, Stanford University

Anthony G. Athos
Graduate School of Business Administration, Harvard University

ALLEN LANE

ALLEN LANE
Penguin Books Ltd
536 King's Road
London SW10 0UH

First published in the U.S.A. by Simon and Schuster 1981
First published in Great Britain by Allen Lane 1982

ISBN 0 7139 1459 9

Printed in Great Britain by Billing & Sons Ltd
London, Guildford & Worcester

IN MEMORY OF
G.P.J. AND F.J.R.

Acknowledgments

WE ARE grateful and indebted to many people who helped us make this book possible. The large number who influenced our thinking is perhaps best suggested by our footnotes. While it would be impossible here to convey the impact all these many teachers have had on us, we do wish to thank them one and all. We know how important they have been to us, and we are deeply grateful.

More directly, the book has gained immeasurably from the encouragement and counsel of Thomas P. Rohlen, an anthropologist who has worked and lived inside a Japanese company in Japan. Rohlen is one of America's foremost authorities on Japan, and his insights into the nature of Japanese management led us beyond the usual clichés. He helped us particularly with the material on Matsushita presented in Chapter Two, and offered extensive advice on Chapters Five and Six.

Ann Carol Brown, a professional manager and former organizational consultant, was continually involved during the writing of the book. She not only kept us aware of the managerial realities of daily work and the accompanying managerial experiencing, she also played a central role in developing the sections on performance appraisal and power.

Noriko Kameda, a management consultant who has studied and worked in both the United States and Japan, assisted us continually through many drafts. She was important in explaining the meanings of Japanese concepts and their application in the workplace. And she also contributed much to the chapter on Matsushita.

William G. Ouchi served as a collaborator during the recruitment phase of the study of Japanese and American firms. Subsequently, Mary Ann Maguire served as co-researcher during the actual field research phase. She contributed discipline, insight, and an unfailing sense of humor.

Others in Japan were extraordinarily generous in furthering our understanding of Japanese organizations. Richard E. Dyck served as our liaison with Japanese companies. His helpfulness was exceeded only by his patience with our learning process. Taizo Ueda, a senior member of the Honda Motor Company, significantly furthered our understanding by his insights into Japanese enterprise. Kenji Takayama and Scott S. Tani of the Matsushita Electric Company made the chapter on their company possible through their arrangements and support. Takayoshi Shinjo, a successful businessman strongly anchored in Japanese traditions, invited Richard Pascale to live with his family during an important part of the research in Japan. In his home, and with the aid of Yumiko Shinjo, countless hours were spent discussing the philosophy that underlies all other aspects of Japanese organizations. In the Shinjo home, we experienced a view of Japanese life that proved as intellectually priceless as it was personally meaningful.

The conceptual foundation of the book, "The 7-S Framework," as well as the notion of "the excellent company" were in large part outcomes of a substantial investment by McKinsey & Company in applied research over the past three years. This research, with which the authors were closely associated, is itself an example of the kind of collaboration explored in later pages, and we are deeply indebted and grateful to our colleagues in the firm.

Initially Tom Peters and Jim Bennett of McKinsey set out to review the entire literature and current thought about organizational effectiveness. They concluded that the emphasis upon strategy and structure had gone beyond the point of diminishing returns, and that other factors were also critically important and deserved more explicit attention. Notably, they argued within McKinsey that the impact of management style, systems and, importantly, management's guiding concepts, while not ignored by researchers or executives, was not yet sufficiently understood or appreciated. Peters pointed out in a working paper on "excellent companies" that firms so designated explicitly managed a wider range of variables than other companies.

At that point, Bob Waterman, a McKinsey director with long experience as an organizational consultant joined the project. He found Peters' and Bennett's basic thinking fit his experience, but discovered that their ideas were very difficult to convey persuasively to a wider audience of consultants and executives steeped in the strategy-structure emphasis. He invited Athos and then Pascale to join the project as consultants. Athos had long been interested in the source and impact of higher-order meanings generated within some organizations, and intrigued by the relationship of top executive values and style with those meanings. Pascale had been for years conducting comparative research of American and Japanese companies, which led him increasingly to focus his attention upon the kind of additional variables Peters and Athos were exploring. Both Athos and Pascale had been teaching in graduate business schools for many years and they were asked to help develop the McKinsey team's thinking in such a way that the resulting ideas would be not only more conceptually advanced but also more effectively communicable.

At a series of meetings in June 1978 involving the authors, Waterman and Peters, Athos proposed that the variables so far being discussed needed to be organized into a conceptual scheme so that their interrelationships might be emphasized, and so that the "fit" among the variables might be better understood. He suggested that "guiding concepts" be renamed "superordinate goals" and proposed a "5-S" framework of strategy, structure, systems, style, and superordinate goals. He and Pascale persuaded Waterman and Peters to use such alliterative labeling, arguing that its advantages for learning outweighed its lack of sophistication. At that time Peters and Pascale suggested another variable was needed, one that had to do with timing and implementation. Athos and Pascale proposed calling it "sequencing."

Since that series of meetings, several separate but related efforts have advanced all our thinking on the 7-S Framework which is used in this book and which is being widely discussed and applied by managers all over the world.

Bob Waterman took the lead in gaining acceptance of the Framework within McKinsey and with outside corporations, and he published an article "Structure Is Not Organization" (which is referred to in Chapter Two). Tom Peters suggested adding the variable "Skill" to the framework to include the notion of "organizational capability" that Waterman had long emphasized. Peters was also increasingly aware that "sequencing" just didn't "fit" with the rest of the variables.

Meanwhile, Athos and Pascale began using the Framework in their classes at Harvard and Stanford, and in their own consulting work. Athos, building on the prior work of Chuck Gibson in Harvard's Program for Management Development, refined his thinking about Style and Superordinate Goals with his middle-manager students. Pascale found the Framework useful in teaching his MBA students at Stanford and in advancing his grasp of the Japanese-American comparisons with which he was struggling. Both found the Framework at that point "taught" very promisingly.

McKinsey launched a series of workshops for their own consultants and clients, to which Pascale contributed as a teacher and participant. These workshops also developed further understanding of the Framework and its applications as well as of the idea of the excellent company. For example, Julian Phillips of McKinsey, who joined the workshop effort early in its progress, argued vigorously for replacing "sequencing" with staff." Since everyone was having trouble with sequencing it was easy to drop. And since Peters was proposing that "people" and "power" needed somehow to be included (Athos was adding "aggregates of people" at Harvard), it was also possible to agree that Staff was an addition which resolved various concerns. Thus, the final 7-S Framework came into being.

Peters and Waterman have since increasingly taken the 7-S Framework outside their firm in many presentations to corporate groups, and intensified their research into excellent companies. Over seventy such companies have now been studied by McKinsey using the 7-S Framework, and their research continues.

The collaboration among us has been long and fruitful, and we are very grateful to McKinsey & Company, and especially to the people mentioned above. Without their persistence, commitment and creativity, a major part of what this book may contribute would not exist. Our respect and affection for them equals our gratitude.

Many people have read and commented on drafts of the book. Among them are Kyoshi Ikemi of the Honda Motor Company, academic colleagues Alexander George and Aaron Wildavsky, Tom Decker of Wells Fargo Bank, Timothy Blodgett and Allison Graham. There are those who helped us refine our thinking via consulting, particularly four clients: Wells Fargo Bank, the Coca-Cola Company, Touche Ross & Company, and the Harvard Community Health Plan. Then too we owe special thanks to the editors at Simon and Schuster, particularly Alice Mayhew.

Finally, we would like to thank Marilyn Rose, Laurie Yadon, Cynthia Ward and Kay Smith who typed the many drafts and retained their sense of humor after ours was gone. And we express our gratitude to the Harvard Graduate School of Business Administration and the Stanford Graduate School of Business for their encouragement and support.

ANTHONY G. ATHOS
Annisquam, Massachusetts
February 1981

RICHARD T. PASCALE
Pescadero, California
February 1981

Introduction

THIS IS an important book. Its importance derives from both its timing and its contents. We are, I believe, at the beginning of a period where significant new research into the practice of management is essential. The academic journals, the business press, and the popular media have all recently speculated on the managerial causes of weak competitive performance by American enterprise. Top managements, the business schools that train them, and the consultants who advise them have all been faulted for a destructive preoccupation with analytical technique—too narrow in its conception and too short term in its application. The United States securities markets have also been cited as an institution that reinforces and accentuates these preoccupations.

Just at the moment when these criticisms are beginning to be heard—and taken seriously in some quarters—Richard Pascale and Anthony Athos have written a book that may be both a landmark in its perception of what has gone wrong with American management and a compass to guide new research in managerial thinking.

The weaknesses in American management that have been at fault in our declining international competitiveness have not been so much an over reliance on analysis and technique as a failure to fit the application of technique into a broader, more complete, and more coherent concept of what enables organizations to perform in a superior way and to endure over time. The authors present such a concept, called the 7-S model. The model represents a simple but powerful insight into what makes enterprise succeed. My firm, McKinsey & Company, has worked with this model extensively in serving our clients. Indeed several of our partners participated in the formulation of the 7-S concept with Athos and Pascale. Our practical experience with it confirms its validity.

In describing the 7-S model, Pascale and Athos do not disparage the analytical methodologies that have been developed, taught, and applied during the last three decades. These methods have contributed importantly to the formulation of business strategies, the development of effective organization structures, and the definition of useful systems for managing businesses large and small. About this there is no doubt. But the authors present a framework of management that blends thinking about style, skills, staff, and superordinate goals with notions of strategy, structure, and systems into an interdependent, reinforcing network. It is the absence of, or conflicts within, this complete network, the authors argue, that accounts for weak corporate performance. This point is made and illustrated with numerous examples and comparisons between Japanese and American management practices.

By broadening our perspective, by demonstrating the value of truly integrated thinking and behavior, by underscoring the importance of a total and balanced view of management's job, by taking us back, in effect, to managerial basics, Athos and Pascale have done practitioners of management a great service and have provided their academic colleagues with a bounty of ideas for future research.

It seems likely to me, for example, that this book will stimulate new thinking about the nature of and effect on performance of superordinate goals—the shared values and beliefs that bind together the fabric of all successful, enduring corporations. Beyond that it can be expected that much more reseaach will develop in the other so-called soft S's: staff, style, and skills. We understand far too little about each of these areas. But where we are truly ill-equipped is in having sufficient theory and supporting empirical evidence of the kind introduced by the authors—theory that describes the wholeness of management. We badly need more ideas, more thinking, more explanations for how enterprises work and prosper and fail. I think the reader will find that Pascale and Athos have made an impressive contribution to our understanding and that this book will provide an important stimulant to research that will lead to even deeper understanding in the future.

D. Ronald Daniel, Managing Director
McKinsey & Company, Inc.

Contents

Chapter One

The Japanese Mirror

LONG BEFORE the century of Columbus, man had developed the skills of seamanship and sailcraft. When the sailors of that time looked out upon the seas, what they *saw* was a flat surface and not surprisingly, when cartographers ran out of known world before they ran out of parchment, they inscribed the words "Here Be Dragons" on the ominous blankness. Then came Columbus. As he watched sailing ships disappear over the horizon, he noticed that they didn't just "disappear," but that the hull always disappeared first, then the sails, and finally the tip of the mast. In very pragmatic, operational terms, Columbus *saw* the oceans differently.

Man is limited not so much by his tools as by his vision. Historians tell us that the notion of the earth as round had been discussed for five hundred years before Columbus' time. What Columbus did was to translate an abstract concept into its practical implications. He bet something on all the speculation and his own observations (and came back from the New World convinced that he had been to the other side of the sphere). He was only half right in distance, but 100 percent right in opening up new navigational possibilities. Columbus' accomplishment, once accepted, enabled mankind to use the existing skills of seacraft for vastly greater undertakings. Analogously, these chapters are not an assault on the existing tools of management, but upon the Western *vision* of management which circumscribes our effectiveness.

A great many statistics testify to Japanese economic prowess and to the decline of America's industrial standing. Indeed, the numbers are shocking. But the real challenge, as was true of the sailors before Columbus' voyages, is not to be so overwhelmed by the seeming immensity of what lies before us that we are defeated by our *assumptions* about the problem. Rather, taking heed from Columbus, we need a different understanding of the problem which permits us to cope better with it. That is what this book is about.

We tend to be blind to our own assumptions when we are locked inside them. One way of breaking out of this prison of perception is by contrasting our assumptions with those of other cultures. Japan is a natural candidate. With a very different historical, cultural, and religious tradition, she has demonstrated considerable prowess as a highly sophisticated industrial power.

In 1980, Japan's GNP was third highest in the world[1] and, if we extrapolate current trends, it would be number one by the year 2000.[2] A country the size of Montana, Japan has virtually no physical resources, yet it supports over 115 million people (half the population of the United States), exports $75 billion worth more goods than it imports, and has an investment rate as well as a GNP growth rate which is twice that of the United States.[3] Japan has come to dominate in one selected industry after another—eclipsing the British in motorcycles, surpassing the Germans and the Americans in automobile production, wresting leadership from the Germans and the Swiss in watches, cameras, and optical instruments, and overcoming the United States' historical dominance in businesses as diverse as steel, shipbuilding, pianos, zippers, and consumer electronics.[4] Today, Japanese wages are slightly higher than those in the United States, and the cost of doing business in Japan—with imported raw materials, expensive real estate, and crowded highways—is decidedly higher.[5] American executives complain of extra costs that stem from occupational safety regulations and pollution controls. While initially lagging, Japan's standards in these areas are now among the most stringent in the world.[6] Some of us rationalize the disparity by emphasizing the problems stemming from the Arab oil crisis of 1974. While all other industrialized democracies have experienced inflation and a decline in productivity growth as a result of higher petroleum costs, Japan, which imports all of its oil, has maintained a very low rate of inflation, has increased productivity, and has by most accounts proven a more competitive trading partner in the past five years than ever before.

Despite the advantages of a homogeneous population, and those related to culture to be explored herein, there is no simple way to dismiss Japan's success. If anything, the extent of Japanese superiority over the United States in industrial competitiveness is underestimated. Japan is doing more than a little right. And our hypothesis is that a big part of that "something" has only a little to do with such techniques as its quality control circles and lifetime employment. In this book we will argue that a major reason for the superiority of the Japanese is their managerial skill.*

One's first reaction to statistics about Japan's productivity and performance is often denial, and then a shrug of helplessness. The differences seem large and the task of "becoming more Japanese" seems impossible. But the striking finding of the research on which this book is based is that many of our most skilled American managers, and many of our most outstanding companies, do things that are surprisingly similar to what the Japanese do.[7] Our problem today is that the tools are there but our "vision" is limited. A great many American managers are influenced by beliefs, assumptions, and perceptions about management that unduly constrain them.

Our managerial "set" is being challenged persistently on

---

*Over the past six years, thirty-four firms were studied and provided the empirical basis for this book. These firms were: automotive (Ford Motor Co., Honda Motor Co., Toyota, and Nippon Denso); light manufacturing (New Hampshire Ball Bearing, Fafnir Bearing [division of Textron], NTN Bearing, Nippon Miniature Bearing, Talon [Zippers, division of Textron], and YKK [Zippers]); retailing (J. C. Penney and Shirokiya department stores); food processing (Lee and Perrins and Kikkoman); consumer and industrial electronics (Zenith, Admiral, SONY, Matsushita Electric Co., NCR, Texas Instruments, IBM, and Fujitsu); aircraft manufacturing (Aerocommander [division of Rockwell International] and Mitsubishi Aircraft); motorcycles (Harley Davidson [division of AMF] and Kawasaki); banking (Wells Fargo Bank, Bank of Tokyo, and Mitsubishi Bank); transportation (United Airlines, TWA, and Japan Airlines); conglomerates (ITT and Litton, also the divisions of AMF, Rockwell International, and Textron, as noted above).

three fronts. First, we are challenged on the frontier of managerial *practice*, where even bigger doses of what we already do well yield diminishing returns. Something more is needed to get our organizations to run effectively. Second, we are challenged by shifting values within our society which lead people to expect different things from organizations and to seek different meanings from work itself. And, third, the competition is killing us.

The principal objectives of this book can be stated simply.

First, regardless of society or culture, mankind has discovered only a limited number of tools for making organizations work. Of these, some tend to be overused and others underemployed. Given the magnitude of the task of running large organizations, we need to get all the use we can out of all the tools available.

Second, managerial reality is not an absolute; rather, it is socially and culturally determined. Across all cultures and in all societies, human beings coming together to perform certain collective acts encounter common problems having to do with establishing direction, coordination, and motivation. Culture affects how these problems are perceived and how they are resolved. Societal learning also establishes horizons of perception. Thus, our second objective is to point out our managerial blind spots related to American culture and society.

Third, firms which perform well year after year, whether Japanese or American, tend to have a lot in common. It is easier to grasp what certain American companies are doing right by first understanding their Japanese counterparts. In part, this is because the subtleties are easier to discern when thrown into cross-cultural relief. In addition, some of the most important things that high-performing American companies do differently from many other U.S. firms are somewhat disguised to conform to conventional expectations. Our third objective is to consider what outstanding U.S. companies do differently and to point to the implications for other American firms.

Let us briefly consider how we got where we are. The first organizations of consequence in the West were governmental, religious, and military institutions. From these, our first concepts of leadership, the chain of command, coordination, control, and functional specialization were formed. The Roman Empire and the Catholic Church were particularly influential. First, they experimented—not altogether successfully—with decentralization, as this was an inescapable consequence of their great geographical dispersion. Second, in an effort to harness the centrifugal forces of decentralization, they established innovative control systems that sought to impose uniform creeds of belief, cults of membership, and codes of behavior. The Church had a major advantage: As Western culture's major custodian of man's relationship to God, it commanded a special place in Western societies. It served their highest-order aspirations and thus could rally support and lay claim to man's loyalties. Initially, it sought worshipers; later, it sought revenues and the manpower to build cathedrals, extend the faith, administer property, field armies, and wield secular power. These demands were accepted for many centuries as appropriate, given the central role the Church played in society.

By the fourteenth century, the Roman Empire was long gone but the Church remained—as the single, dominant organization in European societies.[8] The scope of activities, however, simply outdistanced its capacity to sustain them when in that century, and the next two, the meaning it provided dimmed because of corruption within and challenge without. The ensuing turmoil permitted the gradual emergence of nation-states with governments capable of providing many social and military services. And, as it turns out, these outcomes of the Middle Ages greatly affected how Westerners view organizations today.

In contrast to China or Japan, Western society evolved *separate* institutions with *separate* spheres of influence: the Church emerged as custodian of man's faith and spiritual life while governmental and then commercial institutions were given the role of providing for man's worldly existence. Not unexpectedly, Western organizational theory evolved to legitimize this duality as a natural state of affairs. Machiavelli in the sixteenth century was one of the first to consider management as a function separate from moral law.[9] He advanced an amoral theory for governing organizations.

The coming of the machine age was the next major event in shaping Western views of man, organization, and society. The Industrial Revolution, with its invention of mass production, diminished the importance of the skilled trades and the social affiliations obtained through them. The emergence of the concept of "factors of production" (land, labor, and capital) had revolutionary implications for the Western view of humankind. Humans (the labor content) were no longer an inextricable part of the organic whole of society. Rather, the person, as laborer, became an objectified and standardized component of the production process. Not surprisingly, this view of "labor" tended to divorce man as a social and spiritual being from his "productive" role at work. Correspondingly, this reaffirmed the lingering lesson of the centuries that one's spiritual and social life should reside *outside* the workplace. This concept has persisted in Western thinking to this day and, as we will see, it is one of the sources of our present problem.

Industrialization in the eighteenth century fostered a great many large enterprises whose complex and diverse activities made even more thoughtful organization necessary. Max Weber's writings after this period described the ascendancy of the "bureaucratic institution."[10] Weber espoused the view that the bureaucratic form was superior to all others—as indeed it was to the alternatives at hand. One result of Weber's influence is that the factors he used to discuss organization—size, complexity, formalization, and centralization—remain today principal dimensions along which we still think about organizational designs.

The large corporation began to emerge as a dominant organization in society around the turn of this century.[11] As the West tended to lead the rest of the world in spawning such enterprises, it is not surprising that so-called *modern* management, as *we* know it, is largely a Western creation. The scope of activity of these large and diverse enterprises required tiers of management and delegation of authority. But how could those without ownership be trusted? Nearly half a century was needed for the concept of professional management to establish itself.

How would these new "professionals" manage? The principal problems facing them were and are (1) how to organize efficiently and delegate responsibilities, and (2) how to reward and motivate employees, as well as how to control resources and ensure results. The way in which management solves these problems in a society is a measure of the society itself. The principal difference between Eastern institutions and those in the West is that ours turned to organizational structure and formal systems to cope with these challenges. In contrast, Eastern institutions, while until recently advancing more slowly in thinking about organizational forms and formal systems, paid much more attention to social and spiritual means. Early Chinese and Japanese institutions employed a great deal of coercion. Ideologies bound people to organizational aims, and the latter invariably relied heavily on sanctions of threat or terror. Members were recruited at an early age and molded in a way that marked their personalities for life. It was felt that no large-scale organization could be efficient without such strict arrangements.[12] Of course, somewhat similar arrangements were used in the West and supported by the outside spiritual organizations, for the most part.

Gradually, both Eastern and Western organizations came to exercise influence with less overt coercion, in part because society itself, through governmental units at many levels, had taken on a much larger role in readying individuals for organizational life. Centuries ago, it was the organization that had to teach its members the significance of punctuality, the concept of ownership, sanctions against thievery, the importance of consistent and reliable job performance, and permissible ways of handling conflict. (In recent years, some U.S. corporations have returned to these tasks to bring some of the urban "underclass" into the work force.) Today these very considerable tasks are largely accomplished by society long before its members enter the work force. However, because Eastern societies were so populous, and because spiritual, public, and private matters were so integrated, their organizations tended to regard the task of control in the context of the *whole* of human needs, rather than as a more narrow transaction between labor and capital. They were generally more sophisticated than the West in utilizing social and spiritual forces for the organization's benefit, and in accepting the responsibilities to their employees that went with such broad influence.

A developing society requires departure, change and novelty in language, in concepts, and in ways of doing things. There has to be creative movement, at least at fairly frequent intervals. A society in a changing environment is doomed if it does not produce "managerial" innovations which break inherited molds of perception, old patterns of behavior, and prior expressions of beliefs and values. As we review our stock of business innovations in the period of dramatic change since World War II, we observe a troubling disparity. While our technological advances have been tremendous and our formation of capital enormous, Western organizations run themselves in 1981 in much the same way as in 1940. There is still a troublesome tension between boss and subordinate, and between the firm and the public good, broadly defined. There are still negative attitudes toward necessary collective efforts, notably toward meetings and activities with outside groups. We still esteem the tough, individualistic, and dominating

U.S. leadership ideal that prevailed in past centuries. To be sure, changes have taken place. New attitudes in society at large have somewhat rounded the edge of traditional authority and command. Decentralized organization has become commonplace, aided by computer-augmented control systems that make diversity more manageable. Organizations are less openly autocratic. But our view is that contemporary values and beliefs about how to run organizations are remarkably similar to those of fifty years ago. Our world has changed, our society has changed, but our assumptions about management have ominously stayed much the same.

At this point one might ask: But is ineffective management really our problem, rather than such factors as instabilities in world markets, uncertain oil supplies, changing labor attitudes, low capital formation, and interference by government? Here we must acknowledge a bias—that management is the problem and that more effective management is pivotal to improving our lot. Clearly, management doesn't operate in a vacuum. But it is the task of management to cope with such factors in a positive and imaginative way—and our best managed American and Japanese companies regularly do so and prove that it *can* be done. Without denying the reality and importance of such problems, we will focus here on what inhibits many American executives from dealing with them more effectively. And we will argue for fuller use of more of the levers available to managers, notably those not yet "culturally available" to many.

Today world competition poses an organizational challenge that cannot be met simply by technology or financial resources. Technological innovations and resource allocation are outcomes of *human* processes. Our success is not inevitable. Our ability to compete rests on our ability to organize human beings in such a way as to generate opportunity and results, rather than impasses, stagnation, bureaucracy, and wasteful friction. Some of our best organizations do very well. But a preponderance of American companies seems bound by a managerial scope that limits their potential significantly. There is no reason to expect that old approaches will prevail. We have little reason to continue to be smug about past accomplishments. The present rebukes us too much.

Are we still pragmatic enough to learn from others? "Yankee ingenuity" borrowed wholesale from European industrialized nations and adapted technologies and organizational forms to fit U.S. needs. Today we borrow Japanese and German technical know-how in building new cars as we try to close the gap created by their headstart in that market. But technology, technique, and innovative ways of *thinking* move across national boundaries more readily than ways of perceiving, believing, and behaving. We face a tough task in changing how we manage because we are a large part of the problem. We must change who we *are,* as well as what we do.

Let us avoid false expectations. We may not expect to borrow wholesale and directly from the Japanese. But, by the same token, societies can and do borrow from one another. The Japanese have been extremely effective in borrowing from us in areas in which we excel. They did not become Americanized in the process any more than we need to become Japanized. They took the best that the United States had to offer which could be transplanted in the East and used it. Our task is the same: to take the best of the Japanese way of managing and translate it so that our managerial traditions are enlarged. We can't ape the Japanese system. But we can incorporate some of their approach, which will strengthen our areas of weakness.

The task we propose is not easy. We Americans take for granted as "natural" many ways of interpreting organizational experience which are, in fact, cast in our distinct cultural molds. We are urging that we unlock these molds. In doing so, we will move from a world we know to one less familiar. Along the way, we may challenge some valued Western "truths" and come to question some prior interpretations of our managerial experience. Being discomforted to some degree is part of any learning process. It can be quite marked, of course, when we are learning something new about ourselves. Such discomfort results from holding onto hard-won ways of being in the world and is a mark of integrity as much as resistance.

One day a famous Japanese business executive paid a visit to a well-known Zen master to discuss Zen's relevance to management. Following Japanese etiquette, the master served green tea. When the cup of the visitor was full, the master kept pouring; the tea overflowed. The executive was startled. "The cup is full; no more will go in." Said the master, "Like this cup, you are full of your own thoughts. How can I show you Zen unless you first empty your cup?"

Let us proceed, then, noting how hard it is to "empty one's cup," even if one wants something else poured into it.

Chapter Two

The Matsushita
Example

ALONG WITH five other giants in its industry (General Electric, Siemens, ITT, Phillips, and Hitachi), the Matsushita Electric Company (pronounced Ma-TSU-shi-ta) ranks among the fifty largest corporations in the world.[1] Its products are sold under the brand names National, Panasonic, Quasar, and Technics. The phenomenal growth that has enabled Matsushita to rank so highly is itself impressive. But when we consider its deliberate development as a tightly knit subsociety, its comfortable fit to its nation's culture and values, and its equally deliberate achievement of an ongoing effectiveness that seems very likely to persist beyond the departure of its founder-builder, we can see that it is not just relatively short-term financial success that is impressive. Matsushita has become a great corporation that makes more than money, and is likely to go on doing so, for it has become an organizational system that meets the needs of its society, its customers, its executives, and its employees, and it is "programmed" to adapt as may be necessary to changes that may come. This is an extraordinary achievement that

28

cannot be accomplished in a few years by a CEO who defines his goals as short term and primarily financial. To build a great corporation anywhere takes a long time and involves complex goals that meet the needs of many human groups, while honoring the values of its culture. That some great U.S. corporations have done so is cause for cheer, and we will discuss them later in the book. For now, let us explore Matsushita.

The factors that have contributed to Matsushita's growth and current position as a leading enterprise shed a great deal of light on the art of Japanese management in action. Matsushita's success cannot be explained simply by the tired clichés that so often excuse us from examining critically the success of Japanese companies. Matsushita is not especially noteworthy for its "consensus decision making" and "bottom-up communication." Nor is Matsushita synonymous with "Japan, Inc." The firm has never had the financial nurturance of a zaibatsu. Nor, as a consumer goods manufacturer, has the firm ever been a targeted priority of the Japanese government, provided with special protection and economic support. Matsushita's success has been won in large part through the use of managerial tools that we think of as "invented" in the West. In fact, Matsushita has often beaten us at our own game. These factors make Matsushita of particular relevance to Americans.

Founder Konosuke Matsushita was a commoner who started as an apprentice in a bicycle shop earning twenty-five cents a day.² As the news of Thomas Edison's remarkable discoveries filtered its way to Japan, Matsushita was inspired by the possibilities of a new industry. He left his secure job and set out on his own. His first product was a double outlet adapter, molded in his living room. The product screwed into light sockets, permitting the one-outlet Japanese houses to double their capacity—with room for a lightbulb and an extra electric appliance. The year was 1918. Within a decade, Matsushita Electric Company had emerged as a leader of the fledgling appliance industry. It still is, and Konosuke Matsushita, now eighty-six years old, is still with us, although largely in retirement as of this writing.

Strategy[3]

Matsushita consistently violated the strategic rules by which Japanese business was played. Instead of using the Matsushita name (as was customary in Japan), he introduced the *National* name brand and promoted it vigorously through advertising; instead of dealing through existing networks of independently owned manufacturers' reps (which still are the dominant distribution system in Japan today), Matsushita created his own channels of distribution and went directly to the retailers; instead of an arm's-length relationship with them, he offered trade financing and forged a close and continuing partnership. Matsushita pioneered the introduction of installment sales and the use of point-of-purchase displays in retail outlets. In summary, not only was his marketing strategy innovative, but many of its principal features were nothing short of revolutionary in his time.

The second element of the Matsushita strategy gave explicit recognition to the importance of market share. As soon as higher production volumes generated cost savings, these were passed on to the customer via reduced prices. In the 1930s, the conventional wisdom was for manufacturers to recoup their investments as quickly as possible by lowering production costs but holding prices as high as possible. Matsushita, inspired by Henry Ford's pricing strategy for the Model T, grasped the concept of aggressively pursuing market share, gaining economies through manufacturing experience, and lowering price, thus establishing barriers to entry for competitors who found the small margins unattractive. Matsushita went a step further than Ford in articulating this approach as a fundamental tenet of his product market strategy across all product groups—a strategy that has been pursued to the present time.

The third element of Matsushita's strategy is followership. From the outset, Matsushita did not attempt to pioneer new technology but emphasized quality and price. His second product—a bullet-shaped bicycle lamp—used styling as well as quality and price to identify itself in the marketplace; it became the most popular product of its kind and time. To this day, Matsushita rarely originates a product, but always succeeds in manufacturing it for less and marketing it best. One has only to contemplate the ongoing battle for dominance in videotape recorders to witness a current example. SONY not only pioneered this technology but had established its brand name *Betamax* as synonymous with the videotape recorder. Given SONY's initial leadership in this market, one might have thought that its position was unassailable. But in a pattern that has worked hundreds of times over past decades, Matsushita looked for a means to leapfrog competition. Market surveys indicated that consumers wanted longer (4- to 6-hour) video capacity versus the 2-hour capacity for Betamax. Matsushita designed a more compact VTR system that met this need and was highly reliable, and priced the product 10 to 15 percent below the Betamax. Today Matsushita, selling under the Panasonic and RCA labels, manufactures two out of every three videotape recorders sold.[4]

At the heart of Matsushita's followership strategy is production engineering. An executive from RCA states, "If you watch where Matsushita puts its resources, their success through followership should come as no surprise. They have 23 production research laboratories equipped with the latest technology available. Their concept of 'research and development' is to analyze competing products and figure out how to do better."[5] Matsushita has consistently invested 4 percent of sales in R&D, of which the major portion goes to production engineering. In 1980, that amounted to $400 million!

Matsushita's underlying strategic assumption is that profits are linked to growth and that investments which promote growth will eventually pay off in profits *over the long term*. Matsushita's performance under a wide variety of economic circumstances tends to give credence to the validity of these beliefs. Year after year over the past two decades, Matsushita's growth rate has equaled or surpassed that of all of its global competitors. There is a seesawing contest between Matsushita and General Electric for first place among the giants in terms of profit as a percent of sales and profit as a percent of assets employed.[6] Matsushita's 4.2 percent net income as a percent of sales in 1979 was equal to GE's and nearly double that of Siemens or Phillips.[7] In the same year, Matsushita's sales per employee were better than double those of any competitor (including GE, Siemens, ITT, Phillips, and Hitachi), underscoring the extraordinary efficiency of its production operations. Today, Matsushita is the largest manufacturer of electrical appliances in the world.[8]

Organizational Structure

The second major factor in Matsushita's success concerns the structure of the organization itself. The firm has always been at the leading edge of organizational innovation. In the period 1933–36, paralleling Pierre Du Pont's efforts to develop the divisionalized organization in the United States, Konosuke Matsushita and his controller Arataro Takahashi were evolving a similar concept in Japan.[9] Matsushita (with only 1,600 employees at the time) conceived of divisional organization as a means of keeping things small and entrepreneurial. During this period, Matsushita was engaged in manufacturing radios and other small consumer appliances. What attracted him to the divisional approach was not only the advantages of increased organizational clarity and control (which appealed to Du Pont and subsequently to Alfred Sloan) but also, and particularly, the *behavioral* advantages of the arrangement. Each division could be set afloat, each ship to its own hull. Division managers would thus be motivated to keep a sharp eye on the marketplace as surely as a ship's captain watches the weather.[10]

In Matsushita's view, there were four factors that motivated his organizational innovations of the 1930s:[11] first, he wished to establish independent managers and distinct product categories whose performance could be measured clearly; second, as a result of their self-sufficiency, managers would be driven to establish a strong consumer orientation (a factor which Matsushita viewed as a key to success); third, through this arrangement, he sought to gain the advantages of smaller companies—particularly flexibility. Finally, the divisions, Matsushita reasoned, would evolve specialized expertise and their managers would become seasoned much more rapidly. Thus, the divisional system would serve to train a cadre of general managers who would be needed as the company grew.

Matsushita realized that there were also inherent disadvantages of this system. As the divisions became independent, they would tend to move centrifugally away from central control, and there would be difficulties in promoting interdivisional cooperation. Also, highly specialized divisions might not have the perspective or strength to cope with major threats to a whole product group. Matsushita thus counterbalanced his strong thrust toward decentralization by centralizing four key functions, which remain to the present day. First, he created a cadre of controllers reporting to headquarters and a comprehensive centralized accounting system; second, he instituted a company "bank" into which divisional profits flowed and from which divisions had to solicit funds for capital improvements; third, he centralized the personnel function. Matsushita viewed people as *the* critical resource of his company. To this day, no employee above a junior high school graduate is hired without central personnel prescreening. All managerial promotions are carefully reviewed by headquarters as well. Fourth and finally, Matsushita centralized training. As will be discussed in a later section, all Matsushita employees flow through a basic training system that includes a heavy emphasis on Matsushita values.[12]

As Matsushita's organizational structure evolved, he alternatively added and subtracted company-wide functions such as R&D centers and centralized production engineering. In 1953, he organized his divisions into product groups with division managers reporting vertically to the president of Matsushita and horizontally to their group vice presidents, who served as specialists with detailed knowledge on a whole family of products. This concept of having two bosses was anathema to managers of his day. Matsushita reckoned, however, that we all grow up under two bosses—a mother and a father—and that it is the nature of life to have to juggle the complexities that arise from such arrangements. Here was the makings of a matrix organization, perhaps ten years ahead of its widespread appearance in the United States.[13]

It might be noted at this point that we as Westerners tend to congratulate ourselves for having pioneered most of the major breakthroughs in managing large organizations. Much of this is deserved. It should also be acknowledged, however, that the ideas may be invented simultaneously in a number of places. We would do well to make less of East–West polarities and instead take note of how excellent business organizations throughout the world cope with the tradeoffs between complexity and efficiency. In this respect, Matsushita enjoys its place among the major innovators.

The Unresolvable Conflict

Matsushita was among the first to recognize that centralization versus decentralization is an unresolvable conflict, and that great organizations must have both.[14] Thus, despite the extraordinary efficiency of his divisionalized system, Matsushita continually tinkered as a way of ensuring his organization's vitality. Yasau Okamoto, an authority on Matsushita, writes: "When we look at the overall characteristics of Matsushita's structure, we see decentralization and centralization revolving in a kind of spiral. That is to say, it's not that decentralization replaces centralization and then reverses itself again, but rather that the two forms of organization swing back and forth in an ever more complex marriage."[15] According to Okamoto, between 1945 and 1952, responding to postwar confusion and recession, Matsushita dismantled his divisional organization and strongly centralized under his own authority. At one point in this period, he ran the Advertising Department *personally* in addition to being the CEO.[16]

Why? In the recessionary postwar economy, Matsushita believed that the firm needed to stimulate consumer confidence in the future as well as demand for new products through advertising. By the early fifties, these problems had passed. In the period 1953–55, with competition increasing, Matsushita perceived a need to respond flexibly on many fronts at once. This gave rise to a period of decentralization, instituting independent product groups and adding separate marketing, administrative, and R&D functions.[17] The period 1955–60 saw another swing toward recentralization—a period of high growth and penetration of international markets. Then came the early sixties and another period of recession and stagnation. This time, Matsushita decentralized to give more initiative to the field; for the first time, each product group was given full responsibility for its marketing and sales activities. This thrust continued through 1973, with the gradual elimination of headquarters staff. With the onset of the oil crisis and the stagnation of the mid- and late seventies, the trend moved back again toward more centralized control.

Thus, Matsushita contrives to shift its organizational structure to meet the environmental challenge. As this account suggests, Matsushita's conception of organizations was always fluid.

He never took his organizational charts too literally, and built in safety valves to make them human. For example, his controllers and other headquarters staff were always referred to as "coordinators." To further harness line/staff tensions, he insisted on the location of staff controllers within the factories they served—not isolated at the head office.

As the organization evolved, so, it seems, did the founder prepare the firm for his succession. In 1959, at the age of sixty-five, Matsushita established a three-person Executive Council, which met daily and handled major decisions. One of its members was in charge of short-term strategy and domestic operations; another (Controller Takahashi) was charged with finance, accounting, and international operations; Matsushita retained primary responsibility for long-term strategy and the authority of final decision maker.[18] Over the next ten years, Matsushita played a more or less active role—sometimes remaining relatively uninvolved for periods of as long as a year, then reappearing when crisis occurred. By 1971 he resigned as president and assumed the title of chairman. He commented: "A danger arises when firms outgrow the generation that founded them. There is a tendency to depend too much on the founder, and I have felt of late that our management had not operated smoothly. I have a fear that our organization is looking too much to one man. Therefore, I have decided to resign so that my successors can be cultivated."[19] In the position of chairman, Matsushita adopted a grandfatherly role. But in 1977, in the face of environmental difficulties, he emerged again to reshuffle senior management, having been convinced that the man he had earlier appointed as president (his adopted son) was not capable of handling the job.[20] Promoting his son to chairman, the founder adopted the title of honorary chairman. Now, at age eighty-six, he is once again relatively inactive. Four years have passed since his last significant intervention. Perhaps the organization is ready?

Systems

Organizational structure provides, at best, the skeleton of an organization. The muscle and vital organs derive from other sources. The various *systems* that managers employ to move information around in organizations, make decisions, and implement change are, we believe, management's most powerful tool for expressing how it wants an organization to work and what they want to accomplish. There are the "hard copy" systems involving reports and computer printouts containing written words and numbers. There are also a host of other systems such as meetings and those routines that are concerned with how information is shared, how conflict is handled, and how decisions are made.

The various systems that constitute an organization's vital arteries are comprised of routine processes and mundane details. Systems are hard to get excited about. But while they are not chic or pretty, they are powerful. States McKinsey director Robert H. Waterman, "It is the systems of an organization—far more than the yearly announcements of strategy and periodic revisions to the organization chart—that communicate down the line what senior management really cares about." Feeding the management information system consumes an enormous amount of time. In the process, systems condition directly how we spend our time and how we focus our energies.

Matsushita pioneered his effective financial control system and borrowed his planning system from Phillips, the Dutch electronics manufacturer.[21] These two systems work together to give coherence and direction to his far-flung empire. The planning system is simple but powerful. Every six months, each division manager is asked for three plans. The first is a long-term, five-year plan, which is updated as new technologies and environmental events alter the division's future. The second plan is a midterm two-year plan, which begins to put into operation how the division will translate its long-term strategy into new plant capacity and into specific new products. Neither of these two plans is intensively reviewed by top management, although they do receive considerable attention from the group side of the matrix hierarchy.[22]

The division manager's most significant submission in the planning process is what is known as the "Program for the Next Six-Month Operating Period." In this plan, the division lays down month-by-month projections for production, sales, profits, inventory, accounts receivable, personnel requirements, quality control targets, and capital investments. When a variance occurs, a task force drawn from the division manager's staff and his quasi-independent controllers digs into the matter quickly.[23] In many firms, operational plans break down because the identified steps and the established milestones are not concrete and therefore are not measurable. Another source of problems arises when those targets that are established and measurable are not tied meaningfully to major strategic objectives. The Matsushita system suffers from neither of these deficiencies. A former IBM executive comments: "The planning system is beautiful—at least on a par with IBM's. It is very detailed and pragmatic. When a manager's six-month operating plan asserts he is going to increase capacity by *x* units and sales by *y* dollars per year, they nail it down every step of the way—when he's going to hire salesmen, who needs retraining, what production equipment goes on order, and how long it takes to debug the assembly line. There are few bald assertions; it's very, very carefully done."[24]

Recalling Matsushita's strong desire to cultivate and maintain an entrepreneurial fervor among its divisions, one might properly ask whether the structured planning approach (and detailed accounting systems which track results against plans) is not overly burdensome. A senior manager of Matsushita's Electric Range Division offers this interesting reply: "It's important to begin by acknowledging that the Japanese tend to be extremely literate with numbers—far more so than most American businessmen I've met. Too much has been made of the vagueness of our verbal language. We compensate for this with a facility at the 'numbers language.' To be sure, it's a rigorous system. But because I believe, and my seniors believe, that I should be running my division, I treat the control system process like some people treat their morning jog. It's rigorous exercise but it makes me stronger."[25]

The division manager puts his finger on what we will witness again and again in Matsushita. Through a variety of factors ingrained in the Matsushita style, its underlying values, and the way it indoctrinates its personnel, the entrepreneurial spirit remains. How this is preserved will be described subsequently—and it gets to the heart of what makes Matsushita special. Matsushita fosters autonomy and provides enormous incentive for group and individual performance. But in combination with a variety of forces that sustain entrepreneurial vitality, Matsushita exercises extraordinarily tight control over a few variables. The planning process, and in particular the six-month operating plan, are taken very seriously. Group marketing managers exert influence to ensure that the sales targets are ambitious enough. Production Engineering, one of the bastions of strength of Matsushita, presses divisional managers to remain at the state of the art in plant efficiency and to set ambitious production and quality control targets. The pressures are not too numerous. They are focused, persistent, and powerfully motivating. Everyone understands that the indicators will be tracked monthly against plan and reviewed scrupulously for variances. Performance will be judged and rewards bestowed accordingly. A senior manager of the Refrigerator Division makes these comments: "Working here is like being on one of your professional American football teams. You have multiple 'bosses' there, too—a line coach, a backfield coach, maybe even a doctor and trainer. You also have films that you carefully review after each game to spot the discrepancies between intended plays and the actual execution. Athletes perform under these conditions because everybody's objective is to win. Here at Matsushita we feel similarly. We disagree sometimes, of course, but just as on your football teams, when there are conflicts we work out adjustments and accommodations. You come out with a better team as the result." [26]

Matsushita's handling of one of its relatively recent U.S. acquisitions is revealing. When the firm acquired Motorola's aging television plants for $50M in 1974, many expected a human relations miracle. [27] After twelve months on the job, the new division manager was up to his *obi** in problems—an aging work force, poor morale, terrible quality problems, internecine strife among managers, and a loss of $19M per year. Some of his first moves were predictable. He sent key executives off to Japan for training, interposed Japanese "consultants" to work behind their American counterparts (and gracefully get things on track), instituted weekly meetings of all departments, created task forces, and tried to focus on key problems and get information flowing. So much for the things that stereotypes would lead us to expect. He also began slashing costs, furloughed all production employees for one month, forced early retirements, demoted redundant supervisors, eliminated cost-of-living increases, and dismissed one third of management. [28] Listen to the words of the Japanese senior manager in charge: "Motorola is a particularly big problem. We sent a team of the American executives to Japan and they came back with grand ideas about needing to reorganize and change our strategy. They need to be more pragmatic. We need better quality control.

---

*An *obi* is worn about the waist of a kimono like a belt.

We need proper profit analysis. We need proper control of piece goods and finished goods inventory. These are things you don't need to be Japanese to notice, but they weren't being done. I call it common sense. As you know, it is our style to try to solicit suggestions from below. But when the suggestions are not forthcoming, we go top down."[29]

The statement was made in December 1974. Six years later, morale was high, quality was up, the plant was profitable and humming smoothly. But what ticks like a Seiko watch today is the result of comprehensive attention to *all* the management variables. We might be tempted to think that because the Japanese value teamwork and harmony and human relations, they can't play hard ball. One generation of employees of the former Motorola plant can testify that they can. What our stereotypes really reflect is not *their* reality, but how *we* think—and our tendency to think either/or. Indeed, close observers of professional team sports in America will agree that to win consistently, everything has to be right, *including* teamwork, but not at the sacrifice of training, recruitment, or the other disciplines.

Financial Controls and Accounting

The planning process, especially the detailed six-month plans, establish the targets against which performance can be measured. The other necessary half of the process is the elaborate system for monitoring results and spotting difficulties. Shortly after founding the company, Mr. Matsushita recruited an executive with exceptional skills in finance and accounting to complement his own skills in marketing and general management. Arataro Takahashi was to become his alter ego.[30] Together, they pioneered the world's first profit center.

A highly focused managerial information system reports on a dozen key indicators of divisional performance on a monthly basis. Even before the days of computers, Takahashi succeeded in having each division's monthly operating results within a few days after the end of the month. Such punctuality permitted the head office and the divisions to flag discrepancies and take prompt action—despite the organization's growing size. The second feature of Matsushita's system was its transfer pricing arrangements. These permitted any division to buy externally if it could obtain better prices on the outside. This "real market test" has remained a cornerstone of Matsushita's financial system to this day. Matsushita expects every division to be self-sufficient within five years and strongly resists subsidizing losing operations.[31]

Matsushita required that each autonomous division pay 60 percent of its pretax profits to the head office. These funds covered the costs of financial administration personnel, Product Group Management, R&D, and Production Engineering, as well as providing the head office with the equity base for its venture capital fund.[32] Matsushita has always insisted on a very lean, line-oriented head office staff. Today, with over 200,000 employees (87,000 in Japan, 30,000 overseas, and the balance in non-wholly-owned subsidiaries), the Matsushita group head office staff totals only 3,500 professionals.[33] The remainder of a division's profit (about 40%) belonged to the division and was spent on such things as facility updating and expansion, production engineering, and "self-renewal," that is, bringing in a new generation of products to replace the older ones. An American executive managing a U.S. subsidiary had these interesting comments: "A big factor in Matsushita's ability to sustain its entrepreneurial flavor over the years has been its willingness to allow divisions to retain a substantial portion of their profits for reinvestment. You can't imagine how hard managers will work when they know they're responsible for their own destiny. In America, we've become infatuated with this 'portfolio concept' in which certain divisions are 'harvested' and their resources shifted to more promising 'stars.' We think those ideas are simplistic. Of course, Matsushita has the ability to shift resources into new areas, using the 60 percent of income it receives from divisions. But the principal fallacy of the portfolio concept is that all that frequently stands between a division being viewed as a cash cow or a star is management's creativity in seeing how to reposition their products in tune with the marketplace. Matsushita gives the divisions a major responsibility for doing that—and spurs them on with a lot of additional help and pressure from the product group specialists."[34]

At the front line of the financial control system are the controllers. Each is assigned to one of nearly 100 operating divisions scattered throughout the world; only 100 remain at head office. As noted earlier, the quasi-independent controllers are housed inside the divisions to which they are assigned.

The tightrope act of performing credibly for two masters

requires a skilled cadre. They are taught to avoid pressing the division managers with advice, but to provide them with a facts base that speaks for itself. In part, their job is made easier by a head office senior management group which is renowned for its ability in monthly reviews to get beyond the figures and come to grips with the underlying problems.

The controllers are viewed as general managers in training, and as such they are expected to develop a managerial point of view. As added incentive, controllers are evaluated not just by what they expose but also on how well the division does. It is not surprising that controllers are carefully chosen from each year's crop of new recruits and receive special training. "A controller," said one veteran, "must have clean hands, a hard mind and a warm heart."[35] Another described his role this way: "We are rarely viewed as watchdogs—partly because Matsushita's comprehensive system encourages a very open operation. A great many things— the published monthly performance reports, peer review meetings of division heads, the involvement of marketing and production engineering coordinators from the group offices—all create an environment of knowledge of what's going on. Takahashi's information system works so well that there is little payoff concealment. As a result, the controller isn't set up like a head office spy who's going to 'leak' something. We act more like a wife in the traditional Japanese household. Like the wife, we work largely outside the public view but keep tabs on the finances and remind the division head how things are doing."[36] (Note, in passing, the surprising image of "wife" used by a controller to describe himself, which would be close to unthinkable in most American corporations. As we will discuss later, traditional U.S. gender differentiation imposes either/ors that importantly influence how we look at things.)

The success of Matsushita's system is suggested by the record during the period up to Matsushita's retirement as chairman in 1973. Between World War II and 1973, sales in constant dollars multiplied over 4,000-fold; profits increased at an even greater rate.[37] Despite considerable diversification and enormous increase in size, product complexity, and geographical dispersion, Matsushita increased efficiency substantially.[38]

As we probe more deeply into how such an achievement was possible, several additional factors come to light. In the words of the managing director of a major subsidiary, "We don't use numbers as gears to drive the system; we use the individual. Of course, the numbers help to keep track of his performance and spot problems; we need such controls to operate effectively. But fundamentally, Matsushita believes that people can be trusted. However, our control system provides the guidelines to prevent ruinous mistakes. On highways in Japan we have 'crash rails' to prevent those speeding in one direction from swerving into an oncoming lane. Matsushita's financial 'crash rails' serve the same purpose."[39]

From the outside, the Matsushita approach appears more onerous—at least to some. One senior executive from the Japanese automotive industry states: "Matsushita has a great many accountants and finance experts wandering around in the subsidiaries. It's a very severe control system."[40] A senior partner from Touche Ross, Tokyo, adds: "There are a great number of Japanese firms that are remarkably close to the American model —Matsushita, YKK, SONY and Honda, to name a few. Their control systems are very tight and they are more bottom line oriented. This is probably the wave of the future. But don't forget that we, too, have our traditional firms—like Nippon Steel and Sumitomo Chemical. A lot of Japanese stereotypes tend to be drawn from these traditional organizations."[41]

Other Features

Other elements of Matsushita's financial control system remain to be discussed. The first is the venture capital fund, and the second is the system of meetings through which performance is reviewed. The head office places a portion of the 60 percent contributed by the divisions into the "Matsushita Bank," as it is called. Matsushita uses these resources to finance new ventures, and the divisions can borrow from it. Divisions are not allowed to hold their own bank accounts, except to handle day-to-day business transactions. Even the 40 percent which the division keeps must be held by the head office (where it earns interest for the division) until the time comes when the division wants to invest it. If a division requires a float from headquarters, it is expected to settle accounts by the end of the month. Similarly, it is mandatory that divisions have no accounts payable outstanding beyond 30 days, and collections are expected to be made within the same time frame. If a division must borrow from the head office, it is charged a very substantial interest fee (2% above prime). If the division is performing poorly and senior management believes that management is at fault, an even higher "punitive" interest fee may be assessed.[42] Enormous pressure is then applied to control capital overruns: Matsushita, as it is said, runs a very tight ship.

Divisional Performance Reviews

The inner workings of the financial controls come into sharpest focus during the monthly and quarterly reviews. Here we catch a glimpse of the less quantitative side of Matsushita's systems and an insight into its style. At the end of each month, each division's performance data go to the executive vice president of finance with explanations attached for each variance from the six-month operation plan. The next step involves the division manager and his team spending several days at headquarters going over each item in great detail. When senior management meets with the division, the plans are reviewed again, this time in a more hospitable atmosphere.[43]

The principal criteria of management efficiency imposed on divisions are ability to stay on plan, sales and market share increases, recovery of accounts receivable, and inventory turn.[44] Matsushita's management is known for long-range evaluation. If times are bad, senior management may ask close questions, but what really counts is that you're trying your best and doing as well as anyone in your market. But Matsushita is no soft touch. The chairman talks openly about "transferring poor performers to other spots in the organization where their talents would better fit the circumstances."[45] This remedy is applied frequently enough to carry meaning. Division managers who aren't performing simply don't last in those positions very long.

Division managers also attend quarterly peer reviews, at which their summary operating results are shared in front of one another. Divisions are grouped into A, B, C, or D classes; the A (outstanding) divisions make their presentations first, the D's last. In the words of one in attendance, "There is little need to expose people in public. Where your division stands in the ranking and whether you're moving up or down the list is a powerful motivator. No one individual or division is cruelly singled out or openly embarrassed in these meetings, but every division implicated in a poor quarterly performance leaves determined not to face that embarrassment again."[46]

We have discussed the various financial and planning systems at length. One additional system of note involves Matsushita's elaborate sales network. Among the Japanese, Matsushita is perhaps most famous for its exclusive wholesale distributorships, which give it enormous might at the retail level. Through this operation, the company deals through three kinds of retail outlets: (1) those partially or wholly owned by Matsushita; (2) those owned privately but dealing exclusively with the Matsushita brands; and (3) those retailers who carry competing goods as well as the company's. As a basis for comparison, Matsushita has 21,000 exclusive outlets in Japan compared to SONY's 1,000.[47]

Matsushita's sales force and sales executives are monitored through prospect lists and yield statistics almost as exacting as those used on the production floor. Like Procter & Gamble and IBM, Matsushita also has an elaborate network of customer clubs to keep itself informed of the needs of those who use its products and to solicit their ideas on improvement. The firm leaves no stone unturned when it comes to reaching the marketplace. Its sales organization is supported with an advertising budget of $100 million per year, the largest of any company in Japan.[48]

In fact, the most important aspect of the Matsushita sales "system" is the zealous personal attention Matsushita gives to the customer. In Mr. Matsushita's words, "Our social mission as a manufacturer is only realized when products reach, are used by, and satisfy the customer. . . . It is therefore vital for an enterprise to have the quickest possible information on what the customer is asking for. We need to take the customer's skin temperature daily."[49] Matsushita salesmen recite market share statistics for their own products and their competitors with the facility that American salesmen recite football scores on Monday morning. Matsushita expects even his senior executives to make visits to retail outlets frequently.

To Americans, the remarkable quality about the web of Matsushita's organizational matrix and its sales, production, and financial controls may be that it is not viewed by those who work within it as oppressive. Consider this sample of quotes from a number of Matsushita division managers:

"We do have some regulations in the corporation," observes

a general manager of the Radio Division, "but I've internalized them to the point that they are hardly necessary. The head office doesn't second guess our management programs very often. We don't feel we always have to get approvals for what we are doing here. Certainly, there are occasions when we ask for advice by inquiring, 'We have just designed such-and-such a product. Do you think it makes sense?' Some time ago, the chairman proposed that we design a radio to sell for Y2,000 ($6.00), assuring us that if we did so, he would buy 100,000 sets. For two or three years we did nothing about it. Once we produced it, we sold over a million units of that product line. Sometimes opinions come down from the top, even if we do not ask for them. But we freely exchange opinions and ideas around here, regardless of rank relationships."[50]

The general manager of the Electric Range Division states: "I often go to see the directors of finance, sales, and personnel divisions, too, on appointments made one or two days ahead. Our talks usually last something like 30 minutes. In addition, we have a monthly management seminar, where we communicate with the chairman, president, executive vice president, and so on. At coffee breaks, we exchange information with those who are attending."[51]

Finally, a comment from the general manager of the Television Division: "One day, Chairman Matsushita said to us, 'I'm going to retire from the operation front and be a consultant. If you have anything on which you want my opinions, feel free to see me.' I was the third or fourth to pay him a visit. After listening attentively to my ideas, he criticized our advertising pamphlets and TV commercials and said, 'You should have more talks with the group people. But don't forget that you are the one to make decisions.' "[52]

The remarkable quality of these quotes is that division managers reflect rather uniformly their notion that they are indeed fairly autonomous entrepreneurs. They recognize the existence of others in the organization, but give little hint of being oppressed or interfered with. One might expect, as a result, that the head office staff and group executives would therefore feel less influential. This, too, appears not to be the case. These individuals seem to take pleasure in exerting their influence while preserving the divisions' independence. Magic? Certainly, Matsushita's capacity to sustain this paradox cannot be understood by examining its structure and systems alone. We turn, therefore, to two highly significant parts of the puzzle—Matsushita's style and his underlying organizational philosophy.

Style

There are several distinct themes to Konosuke Matsushita's personal style. The first is his intensely "hands-on" approach. Consistent with his desire to instill an entrepreneurial spirit in the organization, Matsushita, and his alter ego, Takahashi, established a style of management that was small-business-like in a number of respects. Both seemed to have an inexhaustible appetite for information. To this day, each can peruse lengthy reports and columns of numbers with an instinct for the relevant.

Both men are famous for telephoning their executives in the field at all times of the day or night, and it is unusual if the president doesn't talk in person, or by phone, with each division manager every day or two. Inevitably, it is said, these senior managers in turn put their finger on key areas or point to some unnoticed market potential. Both men exhibit an approach to management that involves its getting into the factory, into the field, and out with the customer. Matsushita executives are noted for spending less time in their offices. The firm stresses the importance of spending a lot of time in the marketplace.

Our discussion of Matsushita style might strike some readers as a departure from the frequently cited descriptions of Japanese senior managers who sit calmly above the field of battle. It is not that this portrait is altogether untrue of Matsushita, but that it is partially incorrect. Indeed, the "ideal" Japanese leader sits solidly and stoically above the fray, whereas the American ideal is often younger, kinetic, a go-getter. Matsushita's own style blends the two. He once observed: "When you have 100 employees, you are on the front line and even if you yell and hit them, they follow you. But if the group grows to 1,000, you must not be on the front line but stay in the middle. When the organization grows to 10,000, you stay behind in awe and give thanks."[53]

As noted earlier, during the sixties and seventies, Mr. Matsushita adopted a more hands-off managerial role as he sought to develop the next generation of leadership. But as crises arose, he was back into the thick of things with a fury. Takashashi, ten years

Matsushita's junior, remains one of the firm's principal trouble-shooters. Although he is a corporate counselor of the company, major difficulties in a division bring Takahashi into the heart of the issue—probing, asking tough questions, putting a finger on the trouble spots. "But the curious twist to these senior management interventions," says one Matsushita division manager, "is that they never quite seem like inquisitions because you feel senior management is doing it to train you, to build your competence for the day when they will no longer be around. A fundamental tenet of Matsushita is 'to develop extraordinary qualities in ordinary men.' This underlying goal interjects human objectives into troubleshooting sessions that might otherwise appear harsh and cold-blooded." [54]

Matsushita understands that a manager's behavior is a powerful form of symbolic communication to people down the line, telling them what he really cares about. [55] Matsushita's key to success has been his ability to get to the employee seven levels down and motivate *him* to decide energetically and creatively to pursue the organization's objectives. Style is a crucial vehicle for this purpose. The Matsushita organization passes down war stories and sagas which exemplify the values of the firm. There is the story about how Matsushita stepped into the electric fan crisis of 1964, cut two stages out of the distribution process, and saved enough to provide for rebates for retailers to get the product moving again. [56] There was the episode during the 1970 recession when Takahashi shifted assembly-line workers to door-to-door selling to bring down inventory and cut costs. [57] In these and many other such accounts, there is a singular theme: Matsushita management is tough-minded, pragmatic, and energetic. "At the heart, our style at Matsushita," said one executive, "is to get to the problem and fix it. Problems are expected to be isolated at the level where they occur. Our Matsushita culture strongly endorses the executive who takes initiative. Senior management's behavior strongly reinforces this approach; their example is a model for how the division manager should be thinking every day. This is not a company where detailed remedies flow down from above." [58]

Another feature of the Matsushita style is its pragmatic approach to conflict. Again, contrary to Japanese stereotypes, there is a lot of competition and latent conflict in Matsushita, particularly as divisions (such as radio and tape recorders) vie to develop products that overlap one another's turf. The firm's venture capital committee witnesses many disagreements when competing divisions request resources for such products. Here, again, we see a fine blend of what we would label characteristically Western and Eastern approaches. As Matsushita and Takahashi are both rather direct, their approach has seeped into the culture of the company. Yet discussions, though intense and focused, give rise to very little open interpersonal conflict. Matsushita executives were puzzled when we asked about "having fights with other divisions." One manager explained it this way: "We disagree like husbands and wives do in a healthy marriage (or the way close business partners might when they have worked together many, many years). We have conflict without conflicting. Our underlying premise is that in life we will make adjustments. And by 'adjustment' we presuppose that the parties will fundamentally strive to pull together rather than push apart."[59]

A product group general manager lends further insight: "When two divisions are competing to make the same new product, I often get involved. I listen to both and usually the facts favor one division or the other. We all try to get these facts out on the table and let reason speak for itself. We build 'acceptance time' into these discussions. By that I mean that people need time to accustom themselves to new ways of thinking about things. We press—but we always try to allow people to come around to a point of view in their own way."[60]

"Acceptance time" is a powerful antidote to conflict in Japanese organizations. The things a person believes in are often more important belongings than physical possessions. People die for their central beliefs as well as for their important possessions. Even less compelling beliefs reach back into a person's past and forward into his future. When new ideas or facts come along, however compelling they may be, it is felt that people need time to let go gradually of the old before they can accept the new. Despite the pressures and intensity, acceptance time is built into the Matsushita way of doing business.

"We must create the right climate to get people ready for new technology," says the managing director of Production Engineering. "You can't *force* people to accept your ideas—we try insofar as possible to expose them gradually and win their acceptance."[61] These remarks coincide closely with a quote from Chairman Matsushita: "When I meet with my managers it is seldom formal. We communicate knee to knee. A crucial element is their independence, so, however pointed my question and direct the implications, I refrain from giving orders. We must respect the pride of different individuals and honor the traditions of their companies."[62]

Spiritual Values

"Spiritual" is an unlikely term in a narrative of corporate life. Yet nothing less suffices to capture the strong belief system that underlies Matsushita's philosophy. Some of the perplexing near contradictions of the Matsushita style become more understandable as we explicitly consider the values which underlie them. It is difficult, for example, to reconcile how senior management criticism can be perceived as "training"; how the firm can transfer its poor performers and develop "character" rather than demoralization. It is puzzling to witness a firm of such insistent efficiency, yet hear key executives speak of acceptance time and their desire to "win people over."

Any human organization must inevitably juggle internal contradictions—usually between the imperatives of efficiency and the countervailing human tradeoffs. Perhaps the phenomenon of "spirituality" evolved as a means of making sense out of these inescapable dilemmas—between the individual and society, between man and efficiency. For Matsushita, the roots of his approach were specifically religious. In 1932, as the world recession deepened, Matsushita encountered a religious movement in Japan which had gained wide appeal and grown rapidly.[63] The experience impressed Matsushita deeply. "It comes clear to me," he wrote, "that people need a way of linking their productive lives to society."[64] Matsushita reconsidered his organization's purpose in this light. What emerged was a management philosophy tying business profitability to the social good in a kind of Darwinian paradigm. "A business should quickly stand on its own," said Matsushita, "based on the service it provides the society. Profits should not be a reflection of corporate greed but a vote of confidence from society that what is offered by the firm is valued. When a business fails to make profits it should die—it is a waste of resources to society. A firm should not adopt a paternal attitude toward its failing divisions and subsidize them."[65]

At first encounter, we skeptical citizens in a time of government bailouts find such a rationale for profitability somewhat artificial and contrived. A Matsushita executive offers this explanation. "When you think about it unideologically, societies give rise to organizations which serve their needs and societies reward them for this service. Many Westerners tend to smirk at the higher purposes to which Japanese organizations avowedly dedicate themselves and assume that these calls to higher values are just thinly disguised manipulation. But when one of your organizations—like IBM, for example—*really* gets its members to 'think,' or to believe, that 'IBM means service,' it is no longer an ad slogan. It becomes a belief system for thousands of people who work for that company—a human value beyond profit to which their productive lives are dedicated. No less is true for the business philosophy of Matsushita."[66]

The Matsushita philosophy provides a basis of meaning beyond the products it produces. Matsushita was the first company in Japan to have a song and a code of values. "It seems silly to Westerners," says one executive, "but every morning at 8:00 A.M., all across Japan, there are 87,000 people reciting the code of values and singing together. It's like we are all a community."[67] Matsushita foresaw that a lifetime's organizational experience shapes one's character indelibly. It was unthinkable, in his view, that work, which occupies at least half of our waking hours, should be denied its powerful role. The firm, therefore, had an inescapable responsibility to help the employees' inner selves. This responsibility could best be realized by tying the corporation to society and the individual by insisting that management serve as trainers and developers of character, not just as exploiters of human resources. Some Western minds will find these ideas at best remote, at worst delusive. But such a connection between philosophy and hardheaded business objectives is one that the Japanese take as natural. One observer notes that Matsushita provides two distinct kinds of training. One is basic skills training, but the second and more fundamental one is training in the Matsushita values.[68] These values are inculcated through a long apprenticeship across one's career. The newly hired are exposed to them continually. As a member of any working group, each person is asked at least once every other month to give a ten-minute talk to his group on the firm's values and its relationship to society. It is said that nothing is so powerful in persuading oneself as having to persuade others.

Matsushita has long employed this technique of "self-indoctrination." Subordinates may be asked to consider a proposal they have set forth in light of the values of Matsushita. And everyone has heard and reheard the famous words of the founder: "If you make an honest mistake, the company will be very forgiving. Treat it as a training expense and learn from it. You will be severely criticized (read: dismissed), however, if you deviate from the company's basic principles."[69] The basic principles, beliefs, and values of the firm are as follows:

BASIC BUSINESS PRINCIPLES
To recognize our responsibilities as industrialists, to foster progress, to promote the general welfare of society, and to devote ourselves to the further development of world culture.

EMPLOYEES CREED
Progress and development can be realized only through the combined efforts and cooperation of each member of our Company. Each of us, therefore, shall keep this idea constantly in mind as we devote ourselves to the continuous improvement of our Company.

THE SEVEN "SPIRITUAL" VALUES
1) National Service Through Industry
2) Fairness
3) Harmony and Cooperation
4) Struggle for Betterment
5) Courtesy and Humility
6) Adjustment and Assimilation
7) Gratitude

These values, taken to heart, provide a spiritual fabric of great resilience. They foster consistent expectations among employees in a work force that reaches from continent to continent. They permit a highly complex and decentralized firm to evoke an enormous continuity that sustains it even when more operational guidance breaks down. And when we compare Matsushita with American firms of the same age—firms that were born in the 1920s such as General Motors, American Telephone and Telegraph, Westinghouse, and RCA—it is difficult to find many that have sustained their original vitality. Any inquiry into how Matsushita has sustained itself while so many others have fallen behind must surely turn to its value system as a central ingredient in its success.

The director of a major Matsushita subsidiary comments: "Matsushita's management philosophy is very important to us. It enables us to match Western efficiency without being one bit less Japanese. Perhaps the ultimate triumph of Matsushita is the balancing of the rationalism of the West with the spiritualism of the East."[70]

Staffing Policies and Staff Development

Matsushita's concerns with style and spiritual values are firmly embedded in the people who comprise this extraordinary company. From the outset, Matsushita believed that an enterprise as a whole was no better than the people in it. He characterized the organization's role as being like the hoops around a barrel. Without the hoops, the individual staves are all slightly different, causing the barrel to leak. Through the discipline of the hoops, he said, the individual parts come together to fulfill their intended purpose.

There are several noteworthy aspects to Matsushita's staffing practices, and the first has to do with the extraordinary training and mentoring process through which new recruits are molded. An obsessive concern for training is, in fact, a distinctly Japanese quality. Virtually every one of the over 200,000 employees who work for the Matsushita group or its affiliates has been through a substantial training experience. All Matsushita professionals—whether engineers, accountants, or salesmen—begin with the basics of the business. Each spends six months selling or working directly in a retail outlet. Each also spends time performing routine tasks on an assembly line. And, as noted earlier, during the introductory years, each new recruit comes to learn the "Matsushita way" from which little deviance is tolerated.[71]

It should be noted here that Matsushita's seemingly doctrinaire approach is not unlike that practiced by several outstanding firms in the United States. McKinsey & Company's Paul Kraus comments: "At P&G, Sears and IBM, they make the system work by running it something like the Army. If you get out of step, they come after you. They hire young people at twenty-one who are open and malleable and they only start them at the bottom. They bring them up to believe in the system and to abide by its rules. The distinctiveness of our really outstanding firms is their obsessive attention to these details. Over a period of time, those who stay come to be part of a separate culture in which shared understandings act as a great facilitator in getting business done."[72]

As noted earlier, Matsushita's training system indoctrinates the young powerfully. Courses include sessions on company organization, financial systems, and, of course, Chairman Matsushita's philosophy. The messages start to come clear and early. On-the-job exposure to the disciplines of sales and production establish unambiguously where competence begins. What counts at Matsushita, they learn, is knowing the customer and getting marketable products to the point of sale at minimum cost. At each step of the promotional ladder, managers and supervisors receive additional training—each time including doses of the Matsushita philosophy and refresher experiences in retail outlets and production.

In the 1930s, as Matsushita was creating his autonomous divisionalized structure, he anticipated the difficulties of achieving company-wide integration as well as product line differentiation. He instituted an extremely important vehicle for fostering a company-wide perspective: the Matsushita program of job rotation. Each year, 5 percent of Matsushita employees (comprised of one third managers, supervisors, and workers, respectively) rotate from one division to another. Rotated employees are permanently assigned to their new division until their next promotion occurs.[73]

As a general proposition, Matsushita has proven incredibly adept at perpetuating its aggressive strategy and corporate values for a period of over sixty years. Part of this arises from the strong imprint of the Matsushita style. Part of it derives from the firm's spiritual fabric, which provides a kind of secular "religious system" that keeps the organization's members believing in the same things and marching in the same direction. (For a firm of over 200,000 people, there is an extraordinarily high degree of shared understanding as to what really counts.) Part of it occurs through the training programs just described. Values are meticulously imparted to each successive generation of management. Part of it results from the seemingly well-engineered withdrawal of Mr. Matsushita and Mr. Takahashi, who move into semiretirement and back again, each time withdrawing more completely and for longer periods. Finally, Matsushita promotes managerial continuity through long job tenure. Lifelong employment plays a major role here. It provides a cadre of managers tried and tested over twenty or thirty years of service—a highly reliable resource to carry the firm's traditions forward. But lest we leap too readily upon this ingredient as a cultural excuse for Matsushita's success, many American firms also have a long-tenured corps of managers and key blue-collar personnel. (The average job tenure of American managers in our study was over twenty years.) More is involved than lifetime employment alone.

The Personnel Department of Matsushita, as noted earlier, reviews divisional hiring decisions involving all personnel above a junior high school level of education. It also tracks carefully the top two or three managers in each division and requires a standardized six-month performance evaluation of them. This pool is considered the high-potential corps. Consistent with Matsushita's "extraordinary results from ordinary men" maxim, the firm makes no particular effort to draw this cadre from the elite universities —any more than IBM or P&G make a particular effort to recruit their managers from the more famous American business schools. Malleable recruits, who are more receptive to socialization, are assumed to make better bets than their more "elite" counterparts.

Matsushita managers are strongly encouraged to spot the talent and potential within the ranks and put the right man in the right place. "Don't judge the personalities of people but their performance," the chairman frequently says. "A manager should learn a subordinate's potential from a number of directions," he cautions, "in order to arrive at the right direction on how to apply his potential in the most effective way."[74] In many firms, such statements are platitudes—but seasoned Matsushita hands insist that this instinct for training and developing people (the extraordinary from the ordinary) is a deeply held value.

Yet for all its commitment to "self-actualizing" its employees, Matsushita is extraordinarily performance oriented. As noted earlier, while Matsushita doesn't fire people, it regularly rotates those in trouble into other jobs. The erring executive is more likely to be asked to engage in self-reflection and come up with his own ideas where he might fit into the organization better, and to be shunted around until he finds a role where maximum use can be made of his potential.[75] "Managing around here isn't all positive reinforcement," says one managing director. "We manage severely when reject rates are up."[76] Occasionally, knuckle-rapping occurs. But it is always positioned as developing the errant manager and training him for the future. Matsushita's "training outlook" is not a charade. Criticism is viewed at Matsushita as one of the disciplines of personal development.

At Matsushita, performance is rarely sacrificed to seniority. After fifteen years of service (a period long enough to ensure that everyone is firmly socialized into the company), promotion criteria weigh performance with seniority. From this juncture on, the firm does not hesitate to promote young men to key posts over their seniors. The president of Matsushita Electronics, Saburo Matsumoto, had a banking background and was helpful in solving the firm's financial headaches in the fifties. But he lacked a marketing orientation and could not inspire his subordinates to meet the challenge of the sixties. He was replaced by a younger, more dynamic executive. Similarly, in 1977, the chairman promoted a relatively young fifty-seven-year-old executive over two dozen of his seniors to an important post on the executive committee.[77] In Matsushita's words, "Keeping the wrong man in the wrong place puts an obstacle in the way of success for any business."[78] In 1979, an outstanding forty-nine-year-old division general manager was given a seat on the board.[79]

Matsushita's belief in developing people reaches into the rank and file as well. He enjoys taking visitors through his plants, pointing to a worker at random and saying, "There is one of my best managers."[80] He works on the philosophy that a lot of "little" brains are superior to a few "big" brains when it comes to making organizations work properly. As a result, there is an active program that solicits employee recommendations. Matsushita views employee recommendations as instrumental to making improvements on the shop floor and in the marketplace. He believes that a great many little people, paying attention each day to how to improve their jobs, can accomplish more than a whole headquarters full of production engineers and planners.[81]

Praise and positive reinforcement are an important part of the Matsushita philosophy. In 1979, Matsushita received over 25 suggestions per employee (some divisions averaged over 60 per employee); each was ranked on a scale from grade number one (outstanding) through nine. Monetary and group rewards are given. Approximately 90 percent of these suggestions receive rewards; most only a few dollars per month, but the message is reinforced constantly: "Think about your job; develop yourself and help us improve the company."[82] The best suggestions receive company-wide recognition and can earn substantial monetary rewards. Each year, many special awards are also given, including presidential prizes and various divisional honors.

Many Japanese firms have suggestion programs and most view them as vital to success. Matsushita not only rewards suggestions but maintains statistics on the number and quality of suggestions from each division. These are viewed as excellent measures of employee morale.

Employees aren't viewed as "participating" in management, but their opinions are sought. The company's books are open to the union, and the union is directly consulted by each division in preparing its six-month operating plan. "This is a remarkable company," states an electrician at Matsushita's Puerto Rican TV assembly plant. "When they first came, we were initially struck by their production control system and the singular importance of achieving results. What helped the transition was that they sent 100 workers to Japan to see how plants worked there. It all seemed remote but gradually the improvements have been implemented here. Work simplification through improved product design has cut our quality problems. They have an open door to management and really encourage suggestions. Every morning we have meetings at the beginning of the day and we all recite the seven values of Matsushita. It seemed silly at first but you really understand why the company does things when you grasp its philosophy. This was a sloppy, losing operation before they acquired it. When they came in, they said they wanted to turn a profit within three years, and—by God—we made it. It tends to bear out your faith in this company's approach."[83]

Skills

As noted earlier in this chapter, it is difficult in a Japanese organization to separate the individual from the organization. Yet as we have followed the way in which the institution of the Matsushita Electric Company has evolved, we gain some insight as well into the skills of the founder. Perhaps most salient among them is his astonishing versatility, at times intensely hands-on and involved, at other times aloof and grandfatherly. We note his drive for facts, his versatility with numbers, and the readiness with which he adopted Arataro Takahashi as his controller and alter ego. Yet we also see his deep imprint in the Matsushita spiritualism, and there is abundant evidence of his trust in instinct in many of his most pivotal management decisions. Matsushita seems to combine the gifts of many men, and it is difficult to single out any individual Western manager who combines these qualities. Perhaps it would not be too great an overstatement to suggest that in the person of Konosuke Matsushita the Japanese have a managerial genius of world caliber. In one man was combined the managerial gift of Alfred Sloan and the marketing instincts of General Robert E. Wood of Sears. Indeed, historians may one day view Matsushita as one of the greatest managers of our century.

The various factors we have discussed all contribute to Matsushita's unique competence as a competitor in the marketplace. The firm's skills emerge as byproducts from the extraordinary and consistent ways in which the parts of the organization all join together. Its organizational structure is reinforced by its system; these in turn gain enormous support from the Matsushita style, spiritual values, and staffing policies. Matsushita, interweaving human values with hard-edged efficiency, has created an organization of astonishing resilience and vitality. Perhaps Matsushita is like an army—in the best sense. Through the extraordinary inter-consistency between strategy and skills, it is able to replicate itself, generating new autonomous divisions with something approaching the precision with which the DNA chain can replicate human cells in creating new life.

We have traced the arts of Japanese management as practiced by one of Japan's most successful enterprises. Let us now contrast what we have learned with a comparable success story in the United States.

Chapter Three

An American Contrast

HAROLD S. GENEEN managed International Telephone and Telegraph for nearly two decades, and by his retirement in 1979 his name was famous among American executives. He was often associated with words like genius, ambitious, tough, powerful, demanding, and successful. In many ways he was an archetype of a certain kind of American boss, a type respected by many businessmen. (A recent article, "Ten of America's Toughest Bosses," illustrates that the archetype is far from dead.)[1] His success at meeting bottom-line goals was remarkable, and over two decades he fashioned ITT into precisely the kind of company that would meet those goals. But, as we will see, the costs to other people were considerable, the firm may not have always served the values of society at large, and the end result could not long withstand his departure. He had not built a *great* corporation that achieves multiple goals and persists successfully. He had built a profitable corporate entity that apparently was dependent upon himself. That, of course, was no small achievement. It was, however, in the perspective of this book, one that not only was of limited value, but dramatically illustrates an American approach to management that we believe partly accounts for our present trouble.

ITT was stagnating when Geneen became the chief executive officer in 1959. Annual sales were $765 million, mostly from a world-wide communications-related business held in loose rein.[2] Under Geneen's leadership, ITT diversified, acquiring over 150 companies. By the time Geneen retired in 1979, it was the world's largest conglomerate, with annual revenues in 1977 exceeding $11.8 billion, and employing over a third of a million people in 93 countries. Moreover, Geneen's nearly two decades of leadership were accompanied by dramatic improvements in the ratio of sales to assets. That ratio increased from .82 in 1959 to 1.14 sales/assets ratio in 1979.[3] In these terms, ITT gets more leverage than most companies in America. To a very great degree, these achievements are traceable to one man who not only increased the ITT empire tenfold, but welded it together as a coherent and efficient corporate machine.

At first glance, the comparison of ITT with Matsushita is an imperfect one. While the two firms share a common base in the electrical and electronics fields, ITT is a highly diversified conglomerate whereas Matsushita, with a few exceptions, has concentrated on its electrical and electronics core. While the two firms are very much alike in total revenues ($11.8 billion for ITT, $10 billion for Matsushita), ITT with 350,000 employees is somewhat larger than Matsushita and its affiliates whose total work force numbers over 200,000. But statistical comparisons somewhat miss the point. The reason for the contrast is that Konosuke Matsushita and Harold Geneen each represent at least one prototype of managerial excellence in their respective cultures. Over Geneen's two decades of leadership at ITT, he was, in the words of the New York *Herald Tribune,* "lauded by many as the master corporate manager."[4] Indeed, if we were to use the coverage Geneen received in financial and business publications as an index of his notoriety as a manager, he ranks at the forefront, just as Konosuke Matsushita ranks at the forefront among Japanese. We may, of course, quarrel with the correlation of media notoriety and managerial excellence. But the contrast is based *not* on "managerial excellence" per se, but on the fact that a sufficient number of people within their respective cultures saw them as "great managers." They came to stand out and served as a powerful example for others. Geneen may frighten us at times, but some things he did seem to us interesting managerial possibilities, and others may wish to emulate them. We don't want to use Geneen as a straw man to shoot down. Further, we must note at the outset that one characteristic of American organizations in general is that the personalities of our CEOs stand out—they leave a personal imprint—whereas in the Japanese organizations even the strongest managers such as Mr. Matsushita tend to blend in with the institution. Thus, when we examine Matsushita Electric Company we are drawn inevitably to the features of the organization whereas in examining ITT we are drawn just as inevitably to discuss Harold Geneen. With these caveats, we will examine how ITT, under Geneen, worked as a tightly managed company. In both a cultural and an interpersonal sense, *both* Matsushita and ITT are extremes. But from the contrast we may gain some insight useful to us.

Let us consider the principal elements of Geneen's approach and compare them with what we have observed at Matsushita. "Geneen, like General Patton, understood what it meant to wear two pistols," one ITT old-timer recounts. "When Geneen first took over this company, he needed to let people know he was the boss, that he was the man in charge. He did this by calling them up at odd hours, by asking someone about 'item 3' in his report, by demonstrating his total recall of facts and figures. In Europe he insisted that people at meetings address themselves by first names, even though the custom in Europe had always been to use last names. Phone calls in the middle of the night can really encourage people to do their homework—and the word gets around. And it should be remembered that Geneen does his homework more thoroughly than anyone else. He is really well prepared."[5]

Geneen's behavior and the tension he created produced intense competitive pressures which drove the executives of his organization relentlessly. In some ways, his method of management was traditional. As we also saw at Matsushita, ITT developed a powerful central management group, semiautonomous divisions, and a highly refined subsystem of goals and controls. The head of each division was responsible in detail for all aspects of his operation, and was constantly scrutinized by top management. In Geneen's words, the system emphasized "comprehensive analysis covering (each division's) policies and plans as to sales, returns, and capital requirements for five years ahead." In addition, Geneen adds, "there are internal controls, monthly management reviews, constant pressures, and samplings to measure progress."[6] It is the latter part of Geneen's formula that provided the thrust of his competitive approach.

There were important and interrelated elements in Geneen's management approach. The *first* was his quest for "unshakeable facts." To ensure that he got those facts, the *second* revolved around an elaborate design of checks and balances (1) using staff as a parallel and independent source of information from the line, and (2) permitting overlapping delegations of authority among and between line and staff functions. Note a slightly different twist to the "coordinators" we saw in Matsushita: the emphasis at ITT was on "checks and balances." The *third* aspect of Geneen's approach centered on his use of large structured meetings as the focal point of his decision-making process—another difference from Matsushita's. Endowed with higher than usual tolerance for conflict, Geneen made his meetings face-to-face confrontations in order to ensure the reliability of his information and to test the soundness of proposals.[7] This got most of the "true facts" on the table. *Fourth,* and serving as a fine-tuning device to hold the system together, Geneen imposed a variety of rewards and pressures to ensure his total command. Geneen played a central role in his management design. By enforcing his primacy, he sought to ensure that his subordinates' loyalty to ITT's goals took precedence over their competition with one another, and over any temptation to conceal some important truth concerning the enterprise to protect someone.[8] Together, these management methods served Geneen very effectively.

The Search for "Unshakeable Facts"

First, consider Geneen's drive for facts. Like Mr. Matsushita, Geneen had an extraordinary ability to retain information. Unlike Mr. Matsushita, the exploits of his memory were more central to his legend—and a major source of his power. With a photographic memory and a speed reading ability, he astounded subordinates with his capacity to go back years and remind them of every capital request and forecast they had made.[9] To the onlooker, Geneen appeared to retain everything. Not only his desk, but the *floor* of his office, was piled high with reports. He seemed to read and remember it all. (And those piles, to all who heard of them, were symbolic communications about the boss' drive for facts.)

Quest for the facts may have been an obsession with Geneen, but it was the core of his management method. "It is very hard to make decisions," he once said, "and most companies make decisions on a mountain of facts which are not facts."[10] To avoid the pitfall, Geneen developed an extraordinary ability to ferret out the "unshakeable facts" about a division or a product, uncovering layers of "false facts" before he reached the truth.[11]

In 1965, Geneen wrote a terse memo to his subordinates on the subject. "Effective immediately, I want every report specifically, directly, and bluntly to state at the beginning a summary of the unshakeable facts. . . . The highest art of professional management requires the ability to smell a real fact from all others—and moreover, to have the temerity, intellectual curiosity, guts and/or plain impoliteness if necessary to be sure what you have is indeed what we will call an *unshakeable fact*."[12] In Geneen's view, an unshakeable fact is something hard and indisputable; at minimum, it is the firsthand opinion of an expert, based on the most current information. One newly hired aide said, "If you offered Geneen an opinion based on feeling, you were dead."[13] Much of the spirit of ITT management is built on the search for unshakeable facts.

As was the case at Matsushita, a highly detailed planning and control system provided Geneen with the facts in a variety of ways. Managers annually submitted thick and precisely documented five-year and one-year plans. Weekly, monthly, and quarterly reports measured progress against these plans. A typical report by a division head contained ten pages of numbers and ten to twenty pages of supporting documentation explaining variances and red-flag items.[14] Thus, the planning process nailed down a manager's commitment and the reporting system measured the degree to which that commitment was fulfilled. "One of Geneen's greatest secrets," says one manager, "was that he got you to put your neck on the line saying that if we do this, we'll increase our business by 25 percent and profits by 12 percent. Then he kept track of how you were progressing and if you were not running according to plan, you had better be prepared to have a good reason why not and a good suggestion about how to get things back on track."[15]

Unlike Matsushita, who chose to withdraw gradually over his tenure, Geneen remained in the thick of things until the day of his retirement. He liked to get his hands on the raw data and was wary of too much distillation by his staff. "There are lots of things I don't need to know," he explained, "but I don't know what they are till afterward."[16] Geneen did not like to see final proposals until he had identified the direction in which he wanted to move. And, once set on a course, Geneen expected his subordinates to go to great lengths to bring a plan to fruition. He did not like "no" for an answer.

Each month Geneen read all the monthly reports, which filled a book ten inches thick. Armed with this information, his notes scribbled in red in the margins, Geneen came well prepared to meetings, always probing for weak spots.[17] Said one aide, "You spent endless time preparing for these meetings because you knew he would ask about the unexpected. If you floundered, he would pick it up."[18] "Geneen's gift," comments one former subordinate, "wasn't just his capacity to review all elements of a business, but his knack for knowing *when* to pursue something and *how deep* to pursue it. Geneen seemed to have an automatic sensor which told him when he was getting flaky answers."[19]

When Geneen detected trouble, he moved in fast and demanded the details. "You could almost call it management by detail," one Geneen executive says. "There were more problems— some quite minor—solved at Geneen's level in ITT than any other large company I know of."[20] His questions went far beyond the balance sheet; he probed into marketing, research and development, and so on.

Geneen has been criticized for this meticulous attention to detail, for meetings that dragged into the night in which facts were discussed, argued over, examined, and reexamined.[21] Grueling yes, boring frequently; but Geneen got results. People developed an obsession to secure a solid base of unshakeable facts upon which decisions were made.

There were, of course, costs. Certain kinds of corporate decisions require leaps of faith. Interestingly, neither Matsushita nor ITT has excelled in major breakthroughs in basic or applied research. There are no tales in these tightly controlled firms of inventive heroes who courageously stuck to one product like Xerography or Polaroid cameras until faith was rewarded.[22] At ITT perhaps the precondition of unshakeable facts made impossible the suspension of disbelief necessary to pursue such inventive crusades.

There were other costs as well. Subordinates who are driven to establish the certainty of their facts and meet their plans occasionally transgress the boundaries of normal business conduct to ensure that events will happen as they predicted.[23] It is this latter phenomenon that periodically leaves ITT with an image of having gone too far and acted ruthlessly. Perhaps one drawback of such an all-encompassing system is that it becomes a universe even more obsessed with itself than most organizations. Said one former executive, "There were times when I had the distinct impression that to Harold Geneen the external environment was seen primarily as an 'input' to the ITT system."[24] (Contrast this with Matsushita, where the firm was seen as a servant of society.)

Staff Checks and Line Balances

Geneen's concern for the accuracy of the "facts" fostered a variety of devices that ensured rigorous cross-checking. While Geneen recognized the interdependence of himself and his subordinates, he actively guarded against what he saw as overdependence by triangulating every piece of advice with independent data. "Geneen didn't mistrust people in a misanthropic sense," says one senior-level manager. "But he did mistrust a single source."[25] Geneen disliked relying on one perspective as the means for giving him the whole picture. He believed that people have different points of view and that it is dangerous to listen to a small coterie. To manage effectively a conglomerate of the size and complexity of ITT, Geneen believed a CEO needs multiple sources to know what's really going on.[26]

Both Matsushita and ITT go to great lengths to ensure the validity of information. And both firms are extraordinarily efficient at accomplishing this. But for reasons connected with Matsushita's *style*, his *staffing* policies, and his *values* (stressing such things as "training ordinary men to be extraordinary" and "serving society"), the Matsushita organization avoids knife-edged tones.

The cutting edge of Geneen's system of checks and balances was designed into the organizational structure itself. Like many large firms, ITT was organized into a classic matrix. But closer scrutiny reveals uniquely Geneen innovations. While the managers of ITT's subsidiaries reported up the line to Geneen, their controllers reported *directly* to the ITT chief controller in New York, and only in an advisory way to their own chief executive. Thus, if a subsidiary controller thought his boss' budget forecasts were not soundly conceived, he was required to disclose that to headquarters.[27]

Geneen's chief controller, Herb Knortz, was an accountant of legendary thoroughness. At the apex of the financial control system, he checked all the movements of inventories, payables, and receivables, and detected the first signs of incipient losses, excessive stocks, or unprofitable products.[28] One observer says, "In a true sense, the chief controller was the third eye of Geneen. If you really saw how the controller's office worked, you'd realize that being an ITT line manager was like living in a room that's bugged, with a closed-circuit television all around you, and with a bug up your ass!"[29]

ITT's Personnel Department also bore the unique Geneen stamp. In many firms, "personnel" is the term applied to low-voltage matters such as dispensing paychecks and monitoring enrollment in pension plans. In contrast, at ITT the Personnel Department had a great deal of status. It differed from its counterpart at Matsushita, which tended to focus heavily on training, indoctrination, and management development. At ITT the department's primary emphasis was an elaborate system of employee evaluations and bonuses, which Geneen used as powerful management tools. There were about 500 people in ITT's bonus group, which included staff as well as line managers.[30] Each staff executive had specific performance objectives and his bonus was pinned to achieving them. The public relations bonus, for example, might be based on increasing positive public awareness of ITT by five percentage points; a member of the industrial engineering staff might be rewarded in proportion to the cost savings he could eke out of the line activities he monitored.[31]

In addition to managing the bonus program, the Personnel Department was given an important role in screening the managers ITT hired. ITT places high stakes on its 200 top executives. They, in turn, are drawn from a pool numbering about 2,500, which comprises the managerial foundation of the company.[32] Few of this pool had been with ITT for a long period. Management talent tended to be purchased from the marketplace and "plugged" into the organization where it was needed, rather than nurtured and carefully "socialized" as at Matsushita. Any manager hired from outside or promoted into ITT's core group was given a psychological interview and a battery of tests which assessed intellectual abilities and a range of personality traits. "What it was really about," observed one executive, "was a getting-along-with-Geneen test. They looked for independent thinkers (with good reasoning ability) and for other key traits such as being a self-starter and exhibiting controlled aggressiveness."[33] Other important dimensions were whether or not a managerial candidate was inclined toward hyperbole (a surefire source of trouble with Mr. Geneen) and whether he tended to be defensive when confronted with negative reactions (which managers who worked for Geneen were certain to encounter from time to time).

Before a candidate entered the company or moved up, he spent a full day being interviewed and tested by the Personnel staff. While Personnel rarely exercised an outright veto, no one as a general rule was promoted or transferred within the ITT system without a favorable review by the Personnel Department. One experienced executive said, "The Personnel Department doesn't exactly probe into your personal life but with the psychological tests and performance reviews, they sure kept close tabs on you."[34] Detailed printouts on all managers were available; yearly performance appraisals were categorized by pay grade and computerized. This gave top management an inventory of all managers in the company, ranked in order of the composite score of their previous performance ratings.

In addition to the major staff functions of controller and Personnel, ITT, like Matsushita, employed another staff activity of importance—the product group manager. Amidst the blizzard of dotted-line relationships in ITT, this third staff element played a vital role in Geneen's concept of ensuring parallel sources of information. Geneen used product group managers to divide the world-wide job of product planning and marketing along such lines as telecommunications, avionics, consumer products, and so on. These men were "officially" only staff men who could not give orders to operating people. They could merely offer recommendations. But, above all, the product group manager provided Geneen with an independent product perspective. Whereas controllers were attuned to financial things and Personnel was oriented toward tracking and evaluating people, Geneen's free-wheeling product managers were able to cross the traditionally formidable channels of "line expertise" with their own indepen-dent bridge of information. Every week produced reams of data on each of ITT's operating units. This permitted every product manager to know what was going on in Brussels, in Brazil, in Singapore. Armed with these reports, the product manager would ask key questions: "Are there better places to put these resources than in this particular business?" "Are we investing in a product whose life cycle is nearing its end?" "Without the reports and this staff input," said one former product group manager, "Geneen couldn't possibly have gotten through the line manager's justifica-tion by himself."[35]

And so it went—each of the elements of the organization viewing, analyzing, and reporting what was going on from its van-tage point. When there were differences, Geneen was sure to hear about them. Conflict flowed to the top, where Geneen wanted it. "On every manager and every operating unit of the company we got four or five inputs," said the senior vice president of corporate development. "The problems couldn't fail to surface."[36]

In Geneen's words, "Anybody on the staff can go anywhere in the company to ask questions. If he has criticisms, he must bring them up with the plant manager. There's none of this hidden-ball stuff. If they can't agree, they go up the ladder. . . . By operating this way, we cut through three layers of management. At other firms, everyone is careful about their recommendations, and then committees consider them, and reports are filed and discussed. By the time a proposal reaches the top guy, he doesn't know what it means. I get closer to problems by eliminating the layers of man-agement. Everyone is involved in our discussions and we thrash out the problems together. . . .[37] It's results I'm after. I'm no lais-sez-faire, let-me-know-how-things-are-in-six-months manager. I want to know what's going on."[38]

Augmenting Geneen's system were intelligence squads called "task forces" or "action assignments." These teams slashed across the entire company and were created whenever a problem (or the suspicion of a problem) arose. Sometimes two or three different task forces were established to study the same problem or to supply a solution. "Task forces were deadly," commented one highly successful ITT alumnus. "They could really hurt you. They intruded with all the power of the head office wrapped around them. Task forces usually had a charter and you could bet that their leader wasn't going to go back to New York empty-handed."[39]

Line Versus Staff

Inescapably, the interlinking of Geneen's personal style and systems created tensions between line and staff. In contrast to Matsushita, division managers at ITT were seen to lead a challenging and precarious existence. They were important, to be sure, but not powerfully independent, because they were part of a highly integrated system. No manager at ITT operated alone; each knew that the parallel channels of information would make sure that everything about his operation was known. As at Matsushita, there were strong incentives for an ITT manager to come forward on problems himself. If he did not, and the hints of problems began to surface, teams of accountants and product line staffs and special task forces would swarm from New York. "Our multiple reporting system," observed one senior staff executive, "and our system of checks and balances tend to keep people on their toes. You knew that if you didn't pick up a problem, someone else would, and most people would like to be first in being on top of things. There was a large incentive at ITT to get on top of problems early. The motivational properties of our system were many faceted but the overall impetus was toward everyone getting the information and staying on top of it so they wouldn't be shown up."[40]

This point of view represents the staff position. Contrast it with the line perspective and we've captured a tension that distinguishes ITT sharply from Matsushita—a tension that Geneen expertly maintained. "It was a tattle-tale system," says a former division manager. "Staffs wanted to tell the boss something before you did, and half the time they exaggerated problems to make themselves look good. But if you had a serious operating problem, there was no percentage in hiding it. They would find you out. If you didn't practice open disclosure, you simply didn't survive."[41] "It was not a good company," says another, "for people who liked a structured world. You may have thought you were in charge of something, but you would soon find out that there were two or three other men working on the same thing. Some guys just couldn't live in that kind of system. The individual entrepreneur, for example, felt that too many people would get involved in the act here, that there was too much consultation."[42] This was the essence of Geneen's system of management. Implicit in it was that no man was given full responsibility for anything; and the more senior the manager, the more he was subject to inspection, checking, and cross-checking. This was the system that produced "the facts" in Geneen's leather-bound monthly report.

One former product group manager, having come up through the line, traced the source of tension between line and staff to the bonus system. "It was a very important incentive," he acknowledged. "It was 30 percent or more of your salary in senior positions, and even at lower levels it was a sign of being in the 'inner circle.' The problem was that putting staff on individual performance bonuses resulted in their spending a lot of time justifying their existence. They were always trying to prove what they had done in order to look good in their reports—demonstrating how many costs they cut, profits they gained, line management errors they corrected. Needless to say, this created an adversary relationship with the guys on the line and it encouraged a lot of competition rather than mutual support. And these adversary relationships were not localized around one or two troublesome individuals, as you might find in almost any company; it was a pervasive quality of the whole line/staff relationship. The reward system drove that kind of behavior."[43]

One might ask how people at ITT "beat the system." One former ITT executive provided this answer: "Since a line manager could not easily conceal anything under the ITT system, he fared better by bringing problems forward and getting everyone to help with them. About the best way to 'beat the system' was to work with the system. I suppose it's sort of a misnomer to call this 'beating the system' when it involved playing the game precisely as Geneen wanted it to be played."[44]

Despite the company's internal pressures and drawbacks, ITTers have much to say that is good about Geneen's methods. One top-ranking ITT executive says, "What was great about Geneen's approach was that the relevant people were informed. When disagreements arose over policy or courses of action affecting the company, the facts were available to hash them out." Says another, "I didn't feel the ultimate handling of problems was different here than at other major American firms I had worked for. But the reporting system brought up problems to the surface sooner; in fact, it brought problems to the surface that might not have surfaced at all in many other companies."[45]

Meetings: The Acid Test

A crucial synthesis of Geneen's organizational structure and systems, his staffing policies and personal style, was brought into sharp focus at his meetings.

In a locked room high up in the Manhattan headquarters of International Telephone and Telegraph Corporation, fifty executives sit around two long, felt-covered tables. There from all over the world, they are reporting to Geneen, who sits at the center of a table. "John," says Geneen, speaking to one of the executives, "what have you done about that problem?"

John speaks into the microphone in front of him. "Well, I called him, but I couldn't get him to make a decision."

"Do you want me to call him?"

"Gosh, that's a good idea. Would you mind?"

"I'll be glad to," says Geneen. "But it will cost you your paycheck."

"Never mind," says a flustered John. "I'll call him again myself."[46]

Altogether, Geneen and his top executives spent over three months each year in meetings.[47] Why so many? Might not the same results have been achieved by reports? Not in Geneen's view—for it was the pressure-cooker atmosphere of the face-to-face sessions that sifted out the unshakeable facts and distilled them into sound and implementable decisions.

Geneen's meetings were interrogatory, even adversarial. The general manager's report had already been written and everyone was assumed to have studied it. The meeting was really held to identify new problems and to update. And note the symbolism. Geneen's meetings employed a psychology quite similar to the show trials that we have seen used increasingly in many countries in recent years. The use of the microphone and the formality of the "green felt" setting amplified a *personal* confrontation (which most bosses would handle privately with a subordinate) into public spectacle. As with show trials, Geneen was then able to exploit the leverage of example; he influenced the onlooker as powerfully as he did the individual in the hot seat. Fear of humiliation is a powerful motivator. After a few such drills, managers came to meetings well prepared, and they acted differently on the job before they came if they possibly could.

Part of what made Geneen's system work was fear. Fear of *individually* being caught uninformed, of being "humiliated" in meetings, of being "punished." We saw something similar at work in Matsushita in the desire of division managers to avoid being ranked "class D," that is, in a *group* that was symbolically labeled but not directly attacked. Nonetheless, fear did not seem to be simply a negative emotion; it added incentive to do what would reduce it.

It is often said that positive motivations are more powerful than negative ones, but in management systems that are so tightly designed that there is no escape, negative motivations are equally powerful. One of the reasons conventional wisdom places emphasis on positive motivation is that we rebel against the thought of the sort of system that would be necessary to make negative motivations work. We think immediately of an Orwellian "Big Brother" world, of prisons and asylums where there is total control. Or of those situations in which the victim is so terrorized that he identifies with the aggressor (like Patty Hearst) or so dependent that he romanticizes the aggressor (like some student–teacher relations).

As the line manager made his presentation, there was not only Geneen to be feared, but the staff as well. Here again there is a contrast to Matsushita, whose staff worked behind the scenes and talked of such things as building acceptance time into efforts to influence division managers. "For a guy in serious trouble," recalls one former ITT group executive, "it was like watching a wounded rooster in a barnyard being picked to death by the others. If Geneen zoomed in on a guy, that was the cue for the staff to follow suit. Then he would sit back and watch. A lot of four-letter words were used. It could get pretty rough sometimes."[48]

A staff member might have interrupted a managing director's presentation at a typical session. He might want to know why a subsidiary wasn't buying parts from other ITT firms, rather than from outsiders. Geneen would sit back in his blue swivel chair and listen to the exchange. Once the point had been made, he would cut the talk short and assign someone to study the matter. The presentation would move on.[49] It should be noted, in fact, that most of these exchanges, however blunt, were handled professionally. They centered on substance, not on personalities. As one executive stated: "It was like a tennis match; you could play an aggressive game with your opponent but still have a relationship with him when the game was over."[50] From the line managers' vantage point, they were nevertheless sufficiently unsettling to have some side effects. "Experienced line managers formed a pretty close alliance," comments one. "We really felt bad when somebody got worked over. As a result, we generally avoided washing our dirty linen at these meetings. Inasmuch as possible, we brought up our disagreements with one another afterward. It sort of became a club: 'us' versus 'the rest of those bastards.' "[51] But note, they did surface their disagreements with each other and work them out. They confronted problems and did not avoid them. And in their private way of doing this, they diminished the tendency toward depersonalization that a "substantive" attack can produce when one's *personal* reaction is supposedly irrelevant, and gave each other at least some emotional support. They couldn't beat the system, but they *could* grouse about it together.

Geneen could sit for 12 hours. In meetings with U.S. subsidiary managers in New York, the process took two days. The meetings in Brussels involved 30 to 50 companies, and they lasted one week.[52] The control that Geneen exerted at these meetings was crucial. He kept them from bogging down in rhetoric, setting the example by keeping his remarks always relevant. Undoubtedly, it spared ITT many of the pitfalls of long and large meetings. There is always the danger of the "meeting specialist" who is adept at presentation.[53] The requirement that detailed reports be submitted beforehand made the presentation less important. Even smooth promoters had trouble making their "pitch" because they were interrupted constantly with questions. Geneen made short work of slick presentations. "Throw away the speech and just tell us about it," he would say.[54] Above all, at the conclusion of a presentation, Geneen made the synthesis. He had an extraordinary ability to keep all aspects of a problem in his head at the same time.

Geneen valued his meetings, the chance to watch faces, to listen. "You can tell by the tone of a voice if a fellow is having a problem he hasn't reported yet," Geneen once observed. "By insisting on 'real time' communication as well as written reports, I can ensure frankness."[55]

Almost all chief executives employ meetings, but few companies focused on them as well as ITT. "Every week," recounts one recent participant in a general managers' meeting, "Geneen received among the reams of reports a list of contracts ITT bid upon and the awardee. If we lost the bid, we listed the competitive price. At one meeting, Geneen questioned a line manager whose division had lost a bid on a telephone system. 'Why is the cost per line for this telephone system 50 percent higher than our competition?' Geneen asked. General Manager: 'Because the original design was gold plated.' Geneen: 'Well, where did the original design come from?' G.M.: 'We got it from another ITT subsidiary.' Geneen: 'Why did you buy off on their design?' G.M.: 'That's what the technical specs said to do.' Geneen: 'Why didn't you check on the technical specs?' G.M.: 'Time constraints.' Geneen: 'B.S. What really happened?'

"What came out of this conversation," the observer concluded, "was that the general manager's engineers had taken the design from the other ITT subsidiary all right, but they had elaborated on it. The result was that the cost went way up. So what initially looked like a design problem was in fact a management problem. And that general manager went away with a clear understanding that he needed to ride herd on his engineers and not let them embellish designs and make ITT less competitive."[56]

"The overall outcome of these discussions," explained one veteran, "was that if the general manager was not talking straight, Geneen kept digging for the facts and the facts kept mounting. Eventually they mounted up so high against you that the facts served to get the whole truth out."[57]

Problems were not always resolved at the meetings, but when an unresolved question was raised and it was clear that something needed to be done, an "action assignment" was made. People were assigned specifically to work on a particular problem within a limited time. The action assignments drove the follow-ups of ITT's meetings.

We have described several important aspects of Geneen's management system: a foundation for decision making built on unshakeable facts; an intricate web of checks and balances built into organizational structure and rewards and punishments that ensured the veracity of these facts, all culminating in face-to-face meetings which served as the locus of the decision-making process. The process generated heat—but also information and sound decisions. However wearing the competing channels of information might have been on some people, it must be acknowledged that Geneen's system was demonstrably effective in achieving organizational goals.

Incentives and Costs

There are additional aspects to the meshing of Geneen's intricate machinery. Positive incentives, as discussed in an earlier section, included big bonuses, and, in some cases, Geneen's personal attention. As also noted, for some, the disincentives had equal power. As at Matsushita, low achievers were exposed at meetings— though more personally and blatantly. If that didn't work, Geneen didn't just transfer them, as at Matsushita; he fired them. "We supported our managers constructively," Geneen said, "and if support wasn't enough, we used discipline."[58]

ITT's parallel system incurred certain costs. One manager commented, "First, we had a larger staff at headquarters than many companies. Secondly, our system demanded time and a lot of hard work. ITT would have been an easier place to work in without these pressures. But this system made very real energy demands on key staff and line people and it paid them well for it."[59] Here we note another difference between the ITT system and that of Matsushita, where the head office staff was kept much smaller.

As many of the executives we have quoted indicated, tensions between line and staff were both a driving force for disclosure and a potential source of wasteful conflict. The Matsushita system did not generate this conflict; Geneen did—but he was able to harness such tensions for productive purposes and to some degree control their destructive byproducts. Remarks by line managers suggest how close to the surface some of the line/staff antagonisms could be. "The unfortunate side of ITT," says one former senior manager, "was that the staff had authority without responsibility. Some of them really reveled in self-importance. Few managers in the field liked the staff around because, if you succeeded, they'd take credit, and if you failed, it was all yours. But the saving grace of it all was Geneen—for, despite the staff and the reports, he cared about one thing above all others—the bottom line. In the final analysis, it was those *results* that counted, so you kept people informed, absorbed staff incursions rather than fighting them, and kept producing results. As long as you did that, no one laid a hand on you."[60] Note again how the avoidance of punishment is mentioned, and how the image suggests violence.

Matsushita made much of the bottom line, and he attempted to tie it to social goals and to serving people. The bottom line at ITT was Geneen's exclusive focus. He believed that a CEO can get his organization to do only one or two things at a time. If a manager has one goal, then chances that he will be able to define what he wants and get people to understand it and achieve it are much greater. A two-goal focus is possible when the goals are complementary. But if a manager's goals are contrasting (e.g., "productivity" and "people"), the result is usually to soften the emphasis on both. Single-goal focus makes it easier to accomplish some things.

Geneen was extremely accessible. As at Matsushita, any manager could get to the top; there was no palace guard. But Geneen's availability carried equal demands on his executives' time. "The first requirement of a senior executive," Geneen observed, "is instant availability. He must put his firm above his family; he must be prepared to go anywhere at any time, or simply to wait around in case he is needed."[61] Geneen, who lived six blocks from his New York office, sometimes worked until midnight—and departed with three big briefcases of reading material. He returned again in midmorning, with the material read. "After a while," said one senior executive, "I just canceled my social life." Executives were expected to leave a phone number where they could be reached twenty-four hours a day, seven days a week.[62]

Geneen worked on a different clock from most. He got in at 10:00 A.M. and stayed most often until ten or eleven o'clock at night.[63] His top managers were expected pretty much to be around when he was. He came in on Saturdays and Sundays, and that was expected of other executives in the office of the president. Those who remained at ITT accepted this as the way the company worked.

Geneen expected his subordinates to assign ITT matters their highest priority. Those who did not honor this fell by the wayside. Of one man, Geneen said: "He put himself above the company." Of another: "He moved to the suburbs"— implying too much concern with family life. Geneen has said, "If I had enough arms and legs and time, I would do it all myself."[64] He meant it. His subordinates were seen as less reliable extensions of himself.

Understandably, ITT under Geneen developed the reputation for being a tough place to work. Turnover figures are hard to come by, but one former ITT executive who was present during the 1974 recession reported that ITT fired 400 of its 2,500 managers.[65] During a major shakeup of ITT's European subsidiaries in 1978, just prior to Geneen's retirement as chairman of the board, some former executives estimate that ITT had reduced its staff there by 40 percent.[66] In fairness, it should also be added that many executives who stay with ITT are proud of their company and proud of working for Geneen. One said: "Hire the right kind of aggressive managers who are dedicated to their work—and ITT's reward was the satisfaction one gets from working for one of the best managed firms in America. True, the pressure keeps you on your toes—but for many of us there was something exhilarating in that. One wonders, in fact, if there weren't many outside ITT who wouldn't have gladly traded their boredom for a high-pressure atmosphere that demanded excellence."[67]

"I believe Geneen changed," reports another senior ITT manager. "The Geneen of the seventies was mellower than the Geneen of 1959 and he was also smarter. His system of cross-checks was set up in the 1960s period. He'd see a problem in 1960 and get angry when he picked up a flaw in a man's thinking and he'd really get upset that the man hadn't seen it himself. In 1960, his thought was that the man was derelict in his job. Before he retired as CEO, Geneen understood that that man had a lot of other things on his mind. He was more tolerant and less judging."[68]

"Geneen paid his managers more," said one manager, "maybe 10 to 12 percent more than was the going industry rate. He made certain that the guys who ran the operations were well compensated, not only in terms of salary and bonuses, but in terms of other perquisites such as cars and secretaries."[69] "He was very people-conscious," says another manager. "While he was not particularly skillful at dealing with people himself, he insisted on getting good people around who were, and the rewards reflected his willingness to compensate for some of the rigors of working for him."[70]

One of the most challenging problems for great organizations is management transition. At Matsushita, there seemed to be a grand design. We noted the extensive socialization of managers over long periods, the tendency for Mr. Matsushita and Takahashi to retire and then return in periods of crisis, although each time they withdrew for longer periods. We noted how the spiritual values of the organization, notably the development of people, acted as a kind of "magnetic north," pointing everyone in the same general direction. At ITT, it is hard to see such forces at work. Geneen was a one-man show and he ran it brilliantly—but it was hard to see beyond his tenure. He had difficulty dealing with his own discomfort with a strong number two man. He drove away potential successors. Since *Fortune*'s 1966 feature article on ITT, observers scrutinized ITT's executive ranks for Geneen's likely successor. Names like Westfall, Perry, Lobb have come and gone. The striking fact was not that the observers guessed wrong but that those viewed as Geneen's most valued subordinates one year were no longer with ITT the next. Most left well below retirement age. One senior executive said, "Strong people like Geneen did not choose to work for a Geneen over a long period of time. Such was the case with our top European manager who left to become CEO of Revlon."[71] ITT made periodic attempts to designate successors, but none exhibited Geneen's gift for grasping details while at the same time not losing sight of the big picture. A case in point was ITT meetings during Geneen's absences. "They were a joke," said one observer who summarized the views of many. "No one did anything; no one pushed. We all knew there would have to be an 'instant replay' when Geneen returned."[72] "He was like de Gaulle," said one top manager with a sigh; "no one could replace him but someone had to succeed him."[73]

At the age of sixty-eight, under pressure from the board to relinquish operating control, Geneen appointed a successor as CEO. Geneen remained the chairman. Within twenty-eight months, Geneen replaced him with another man supposedly more to his liking.[74]

Following Geneen's retirement in 1979, ITT's fortunes substantially declined: while it ranks eleventh in sales volume and twelfth in assets among the Fortune 500, it has dropped to 435 in terms of net income as a percentage of sales.[75] ITT's return on stockholder equity in 1979 ranked even lower at 451.[76] In its European operations, ITT incurred an $84 million loss in 1979 and the liquidation of the firm's food, drug, and cosmetics operations.[77] ITT has also shut down its consumer electronics appliance plants in France, Germany, and Britain.[78]

What Makes a Great Manager?

It is difficult to step back from such a remarkable man and his management methods to develop an initial understanding of the general managerial implications that can be drawn from his specific case. Whether you judge his genius as malign or benign, whether you would have liked to work for him or not, the "unshakeable fact" remains that Geneen—and the at times extreme contrasts between ITT and Matsushita—can teach us something important.

A first observation is that what makes both Matsushita and Geneen's ITT tick is that all the managerial pieces fit together. ITT's behavioral *skills* and Geneen's competitive *style* were beautifully integrated with the kind of executive *staff* he recruited, the sort of management operation *systems* he utilized, the form of organizational *structure* he instituted, the *strategy* for ITT he employed. ITT had no spiritual values like Matsushita; it did attach *significant* value to the notion of unshakeable facts. The "fit" among all these aspects of Geneen's managerial approach was snug; it led to extraordinary results.

Geneen's personal *skills* were regarded by many as truly remarkable. His amazingly accurate memory, his capacity to process vast amounts of information, his ability to attend to detail without losing sight of the big picture, his gift of interrogation, his stamina in the face of long meetings (indeed, seven-day work weeks), his ability to use nonverbal data to "read" people, his capacity to confront problems and people—these were all clearly important in ITT's functioning. Without these skills, the organization's mechanisms could not have been fashioned, nor could the organization itself have functioned as intended.

Geneen's personal *style* can also be described as attentive, committed, determined, pragmatic, forceful, and disciplined. Negatively, it can be called obsessive, compulsive, domineering, perfectionistic, paranoid, and even addictive. His managerial approach had powerful effects on others, and the labels they used to characterize these *patterns* in his behavior, and thus his values and beliefs, were often charged with emotion.

His belief that executives would dissemble, that they would hide unpleasant truths—indeed, prefer half truths a lot of the time—is not, however, rare. His wish that he could do all the jobs himself is also not unheard of. His valuing what he believed was "good for ITT" above most other values would be recognized by subordinates of some other "tough" bosses as familiar. What is to a degree unusual was that Geneen did not seek just to diminish what he deplored; he sought to eliminate it. This driving will to determine the behavior of his subordinates in the service of his values toward his goals was single-minded—and, of course, importantly dependent on his own unusual skills.

Given his skills and style, it is not surprising that he made unshakeable facts the rallying cry of his organization. It became one of the values that all accepted (or faced censure of varying severity). The "bottom line" of actual against plan was probably another significant value. Since there was no effective way to resist, it follows that over time a natural selection would result in an executive staff that fit him. Others would not join ITT in the first place, or would not survive if they did.

His use of staff departments to "check and balance" line departments was integral to organizational structure and in the managerial systems that supported this structure. Local controllers who reported directly to the head office, personnel selection of executives, and the like, all forced decisions and behavior that fit Geneen's intention. That intention, of course, was to grow a multinational conglomerate via acquisition, and that *strategy* or goal was such that his preferred management practices were one effective way to control such a huge and varied company. And at the center of the whole thing sat Geneen, watching for evidence someone wasn't doing what *he* would do if he were there.

The striking differences between Matsushita and ITT lay not so much in the strategy of these two organizations as a whole, for in large part they were quite similar. The distinctions are certainly not a result of the matrix-type organizational structure that was nearly identical in both companies. Nor did the real differences reside in the systems—at least, in the formal hard copy systems, which in each case involved detailed planning and financial reports with a highly operational focus. These first three factors are insufficient to explain the differences we have seen. The real differences lay in the other elements—the management style, the staffing policies, and above all the spiritual or significant values—and, of course, the human skills to manage all of these.

It might help to visualize at this point the seven elements we have been using to understand better both Matsushita and ITT.

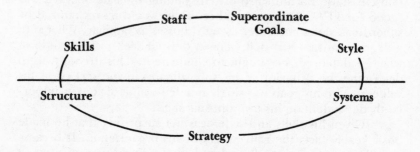

Let's review briefly what the terms mean. *Strategy* pertains to a firm's plan of action that causes it to allocate its scarce resources over time to get from where it is to where it wants to go. *Structure* refers to the way a firm is organized—whether it's decentralized or centralized, whether it emphasizes line or staff—in short, how the "boxes" are arranged. *Systems* refers to how information moves around within the organization. Some systems are "hard copy" types—computer printouts and other ink on paper formats that are used to keep track of what's going on. Other systems are more informal—like meetings. These three elements —*strategy, structure,* and *systems*—are probably quite familiar to most readers.

The other four factors are what we call the "soft" S's. *Staff* pertains *not* to staff in the line/staff sense, but to demographic characteristics of the people who live in an organization. Are they "engineering types," "used car salesmen," "M.B.A.s," "computer jocks"? *Skills* refers to those things which the organization and its key personnel do particularly well—the distinctive abilities that truly set them apart from competition. For example, as an organization Procter & Gamble is skilled at marketing; its management is skilled at sustaining the institution's vitality and maintaining an environment that continually provides new, viable consumer products to replace older ones. It should be noted that skills apply on

THE SEVEN S's

Strategy	Plan or course of action leading to the allocation of a firm's scarce resources, over time, to reach identified goals.
Structure	Characterization of the organization chart (i.e., functional, decentralized, etc.)
Systems	Proceduralized reports and routinized processes such as meeting formats.
Staff	"Demographic" description of important personnel categories within the firm (i.e., engineers, entrepreneurs, M.B.A.s, etc.). "Staff" is *not* meant in line-staff terms.
Style	Characterization of how key managers behave in achieving the organization's goals; also the cultural style of the organization.
Skills	Distinctive capabilities of key personnel or the firm as a whole.
Superordinate Goals	The significant meanings or guiding concepts that an organization imbues in its members.

both the organizational and interpersonal level. We will have much more to say about this element in later sections.

Two final factors require definition. *Style* refers to the patterns of behavior of the top executive and the senior management team. For example, Geneen and his team had a tough, facts-oriented style. Style also refers to that of the organization as a whole. Clearly, Matsushita has a different style from ITT. *Superordinate goals* (which include the spiritual or significant meanings and shared values of the people within an organization) refer to the overarching purposes to which an organization and its members dedicate themselves. These are rarely bottom-line secular goals like growing x percent a year or obtaining y percent return on investment. Rather, this factor pertains to values or goals that "move men's hearts" and that genuinely knit together individual and organizational purposes.

As noted earlier, American managers tend to overfocus on the "hard" elements. In part this may stem from the attention academics have paid to these same variables. Some of the best work done in business schools in recent decades has been in advancing our understanding of the "cold triangle" of strategy, structure, and systems. Each one and the relationships among the three are particularly susceptible to analytical, quantitative, logical, and systematic investigation. In short, "science" of one kind or another, rigorous observation and conceptualization—*thinking*, if you prefer—were required. That's what business schools value. That's how professors get rewarded. And that's what fits our culture's central beliefs about managing. It's no surprise that such an approach dominates curricula in business schools.

Of course, there were some all along who "felt" this was "all wrong." They advanced the case of the four "soft" elements in various ways, and with varying degrees of success. But, as is often the pattern in our culture, this group saw their interests as an "either" to the dominant group's "or." The "tough-minded" disdained the "soft-hearted" ("unscientific" was their most restrained abuse); the latter somewhat less confidently disparaged the former ("inhuman" was a favorite epithet). Each tended to act as if their own preference was central, the others' peripheral. Each seemed to believe God was on their side. It seemed for a while that each was driving the other to further extremes. The tiresomely pedantic intellectual techniques ultimately developed by one group rivaled the undisciplined, anti-intellectual, emotionally excessive "experiences" of the other. This dichotomization recently has softened. But in the meantime a generation of managers has been educated in apparently opposed camps, and too few have managed their own successful synthesis. Most stayed in the "hard-headed" camp, as that was what corporations clearly rewarded (if one was not too obvious about it).[79] The few who went with the other side ended up in one or another "nurturant" roles. Whether formally in Personnel or not, they made a great show of whatever quantitative support they could muster for their cause.

Far more important, we think, than the unwitting contributions of academics to our dilemma, and the unfortunate criteria by which corporations reward their graduates, is the fact that our culture itself impedes the kind of synthesis the Japanese manage so well.

These U.S. cultural givens include some central assumptions and perceptions about:

1. The nature of the human condition, in particular those conditions of ambiguity, uncertainty, and imperfection[80] which must be addressed by managers.
2. The nature of human beings, in particular the split between the person as object (i.e., interchangeable unit of production) and the person as subject (i.e., the unique, whole human being) within the corporation.
3. The nature of relationships, in particular in reference to issues of dependence and independence in corporate life.
4. The nature of leadership, in particular those behavioral skills and patterns of behavior which encourage others to identify with corporate goals.
5. The nature of significant or spiritual meanings, in particular those beliefs which guide behavior within companies and give meaning beyond exchange of time and effort for money and power.

One can see clearly the great difference between Mr. Matsushita and Mr. Geneen in the ways they "thought" about human beings in reference to the subject/object dichotomy. Geneen seemed to regard other people as objects to be used to achieve his purpose, while Matsushita seemed to regard them as both objects to be used and subjects to be honored in achieving his and their purposes. When Geneen found an executive wanting, the man was humiliated or fired. When Matsushita made a similar discovery, the man's group was marked as ineffective and he was reassigned, even demoted, and the opportunity for the individual to grow from the experience was stressed. These are very different approaches indeed. But the Japanese way makes possible great corporations that successfully persist in harmony with their culture's deepest values. The American way often does not. And the problems that result eventually make our largest companies less competitive and effective, eventually candidates for government help or protection, or petitioners in bankruptcy courts. In short, the four "soft" elements can no longer be regarded as frosting on the corporate cake. They are indispensable parts of any corporate commitment to long-term success. In the rest of this book we will enlarge on this theme, in the hope that U.S. executives may see more clearly what really stands in the way of developing our grasp of the four "softer" elements—style, skill, staff, and superordinate goals. Further, it will explore the *interrelationship* of *all* seven variables so as to facilitate thinking that relates operational techniques to the real requirements of individuals and their companies. That's not as attractive perhaps as a simple, all-purpose prescription. But general panaceas have the half life of a celebrity, and while they may please superficially, they don't satisfy deeply in the long run.

Chapter Four

Zen and the Art of Management

TAKEO FUJISAWA, cofounder of Honda Motor Company, once observed that "Japanese and American management is 95 percent the same and differs in all important respects."[1] In the next two chapters, we are going to delve into certain of these "5 percent differences," by Mr. Fujisawa's estimate, but as we proceed we must be mindful of his paradox. If we overindulge in the exotic, we will lose sight of a central lesson of the ITT–Matsushita comparison: namely, that these two organizations do a great many things alike. Indeed, while Matsushita was not as heavy-handed as Geneen, we noted a hard-minded emphasis on the bottom line, pressures for divisions to produce profits, and a distinct capacity for top-down decisions. We witnessed hard-ball personnel choices, in particular in Matsushita's handling of its Motorola acquisition in the United States. Nothing in the pages that follow should obscure these very extensive and real similarities between Japanese and American management.

In the two preceding chapters we have made much of the

contrast between American and Japanese views of human beings, and thus of the ways in which each country's executives tend to manage them. The Japanese see each individual as having economic, social, psychological, and spiritual needs, much as we do when we step back and think about it. But Japanese executives assume it is *their* task to attend to much more of the whole of the person, and not leave so much to other institutions (such as government, family, or religious ones). And they believe it is only when the individuals' needs are well met within the subculture of a corporation that they can largely be freed for productive work that is in larger part outstanding. U.S. executives, conditioned by a society which for good reason firmly separated church from state, and later the corporation from both, perhaps naturally assumed in the early years of this century that the mandate of the corporation was much more narrowly economic. Such a view, especially given the later technologies of mass production epitomized by the assembly line, led easily to an engineer's view of individuals as primarily interchangeable parts and units of production. This view, of course, was challenged by scholars (as in the Hawthorne studies), by union leaders, by elected governmental representatives, and by religious leaders. Largely through legislation, executives have been forced to widen their view of their responsibility toward employees (and, indeed, of corporate practice toward the surrounding society). Still later, and especially in the last twenty years, the dramatic increase in demand from U.S. groups—notably for our purposes here from minorities and women, and now from family units—for greater influence upon corporate personnel practice, has been of great significance. It has been paralleled by increasing expectations of *individual* employees at all levels of the hierarchy for more variation in how individuals are treated within their groups, and thus for the satisfaction at work of a wider range of their needs.

This has produced considerable stress for some senior executives, whose conditioning in the first half of this century ill prepared them for the demands they have been facing. Yet they have been proceeding, reluctantly perhaps, but pragmatically, to institute programs for aggregates of people that might meet the law and reduce painful and costly personnel problems. One outcome has been the emergence of Human Resource Management, which is seen by many as something more than Personnel Administration (at least, as compared to how the latter was often performed). HRM is an attempt to manage productively and systematically more of the important aspects of the human flow through corporations, from recruitment to retirement. It is primarily concerned, understandably, with *groups* of people, and not so much with individuals as such. It is of a fundamental importance.

For example, it may surprise some that General Motors, widely regarded for so long as one of our most successful corporations, had almost no corporation-wide recruiting or indoctrination effort until very recently. Whereas Mr. Matsushita saw a consistent, well-orchestrated personnel policy as one of his three most important managerial levers (recall that Matsushita never relinquished centralized control over (1) personnel, (2) capital budgeting, and (3) accounting), at General Motors, in contrast, literally *thousands* of young people (the future managers of General Motors) were hired each year with no centralizing thrust to their recruitment and training. The great majority were hired by local plants or divisions, which often simply chose among those who presented themselves at the local hiring offices. There was no centralized strategy, no substructure or system to implement it, no evaluation to assure quality outcomes. The percentage of new hires with presumed managerial potential, who were educated in marginal secondary or collegiate institutions, and who were not outstanding even there, was truly staggering. Only in recent years has GM made significant strides in righting this aspect and other aspects of its programs related to aggregates of people. And done so in spite of the resistance of some divisions not disposed to head office intrusions. The point is that it had not begun until the early 1970s. Compare this to Matsushita, where nearly obsessive attention to the selection, training, and development of its future executives, in a divisionalized structure, had been firmly in place for decades. In summary, the attention the Japanese have long paid to their *staff*, and the skills employed by management to develop their human resources and pass their skills on to their successors, are two fundamental differences on which we will now focus.

It is comparatively easy to make the assertions that the Japanese do a better job in developing human resources and that they are comparatively more skilled in a variety of respects having to do with managing people. The difficulty is that these statements don't really help us know what to do differently; they don't tell us what is at the root of these Japanese capabilities. We believe that the essence of Japanese success in these areas is rooted in assumptions that are rather fundamental to life. First, the Japanese accept ambiguity, uncertainty, and imperfection as much more of a given in organizational life. Consequently, their staffing policies and skills at dealing with people in aggregates (as well as with one another) work from entirely different premises than do ours. We shall address this shortly. Second, the Japanese see themselves as far more *inter*dependent. Thus, they are prepared to make far greater investments in people and in the skills necessary to be effective with others. These latter aspects will be discussed in Chapter Six.

At 8:04 A.M., the intercom bleeped.

"Mr. Kemper," said the secretary in a lowered voice, "there are four cabin cleaners in reception—blacks—and they insist on seeing you. They seem to be angry."

Mr. Kemper paused, drumming his fingers on the stacks of papers that had brought him to work an hour early, before his day of nonstop meetings began. "Sounds like one we'd better deal with," he replied. "Send them in." For Larry T. Kemper, regional manager of United Airlines, overseer of 20,000 employees in the western United States, and eight organizational levels removed from the hourly cabin cleaners he was about to encounter, the day had begun.[2]

Cabin cleaners are among the lowest paid and least skilled airline employees. Their occupation involves hours of waiting, punctuated by frenzied bursts of activity when, working on tight turnaround schedules, they pour through the planes, cleaning out seat pockets, ashtrays, galleys, and restrooms. The grievance that the contingent wished to communicate was that their white foreman consistently assigned them the most unpleasant jobs. They wanted him to change that.

The challenge for Mr. Kemper was manifold. As a senior manager in a firm priding itself on its open-door policy, he sought to reaffirm the company commitment to having all levels of management open to communication from below. Moreover, the problem had clear racial overtones, which he needed to grasp and defuse lest the issue mushroom into something larger. Furthermore, he needed to conduct himself so as not to undercut the seven levels of management between himself and the supervisor of the aggrieved cleaners. Finally, there was a union issue. Although members of the airline mechanics union, the cleaners had chosen an independent channel outside the traditional grievance machinery. The problem had to be handled in such a way as not to offend the union or set precedents that would bring an avalanche of such grievances to Mr. Kemper's desk.

"I just had to 'juggle' it," Mr. Kemper explained, describing his response. "It was one of those situations that comprises 10 to 20 percent of what you do as a manager. Even if you are sure of the facts and are positive of the right corrective action to be taken, if you endorse any single answer you're dead. So . . . I . . . 'juggled.'" He seemed hesitant to use the word again. "I said I wanted to hear them out and asked that they, in turn, respect my need to talk to others involved to air all sides of the problem. What I needed," he continued, "was time, time to 'massage' the problem down to the level of the organization where the problem occurred so that, regardless of who was wrong or right, the system could learn from the problem and correct itself. Yet at the same time, I had to hold the problem in 'suspended animation.' I had to sustain the cabin cleaners' faith in the company's sincerity, in effect to suspend their probable disbelief long enough to get the organization moving. I had to ensure they got a fair hearing and a proper remedy while at the same time not undermining my management. It was 'juggling,'" he concluded, resigning himself to a word whose imagery of two hands and three or more topsy-turvy pins represented the best, if exasperating, way he could explain the seemingly vague method he used to deal with his latest crisis.[3]

This, essentially, is what happened. The black cabin cleaners demanded that Kemper immediately *change* the situation confronting them. Interestingly, he chose not to do so in any way, even though several obvious solutions were available. Rather, he set a process of communication in motion, the outcome of which he could not predict, but which in this case, as it turned out, enabled the foreman and the cabin cleaners to reconcile their differences and solve the matter at the shop level. But for our purposes here the outcome was less significant than Kemper's method. Listen to his words—"juggling," "massaging the problem," "holding things in suspended animation." Hardly the crisp analytical images of what rational American management is supposed by many of us to be about.

What kind of imagery most accurately characterizes the way executives "take action" and "change things"? A great many administrative actions are immediate and concrete. But in that 10 to 20 percent of management decisions Mr. Kemper is talking about, it is *skill* in the processes of juggling and massaging that probably achieves the best results.

Most of the important executive skills are intuitive—that is, they are not consciously cognitive. It is said that when a great pianist performs a Beethoven concerto, the music is "in his hands"; he doesn't have to think about the mechanics of what he is doing but only about the music. The synthesis is so complex "you just do it."

An executive's skills are rooted in (1) his personality, (2) his cultural conditioning, and (3) his specific training and prior organizational experience. Of these three determinants, the first is most difficult to change; the other two provide a much more fertile ground. In particular, stepping outside our culture helps us see more clearly those areas in which opportunities to improve skills exist. Once we identify a cultural blindspot and are convinced of the advantages of approaching a particular situation differently, it usually requires applied conscious attention for a time to develop skill, which can then be used less consciously until, like the pianist's, it is "just in the hands."

Ambiguity, Uncertainty, and Imperfection

Much of the lore of decisive, action-taking, American management practice reveals certain conditions as enemies to be annihilated. Among these "existential" conditions are ambiguity (in what someone or something means), uncertainty (in the outcomes of possible actions), and imperfection (in ourselves, other human beings, and the processes and theories available for use). The lore suggests such conditions ought to be reduced as much as possible by large doses of analytical rationality, confrontation of specificity, abrupt decisiveness, and demand for desired outcome. In many instances, these responses help, of course. But sometimes it is better to be indefinite, as in Mr. Kemper's encounter. A clear rational prescription, however concrete and immediate, could not possibly have accomplished what time and indefiniteness did. Mr. Kemper's imagery of juggling captures the dilemma nicely: any effort to grasp two pins results in the remaining pin's falling to the floor. Many managers, schooled in the supposed virtues of being firm, explicit, and decisive, spend their entire careers clutching for some pins, letting others fall, and ignoring the paradoxical truth that in some circumstances it's best to keep them all in the air.

In organizations there are several conditions in which vagueness may be desirable or intentional: vagueness in *intention* itself (reserving decision on what course of action one might pursue—the Kemper example); in *relation* (in the connection of one person to another, of facts to conclusions, or cause to effect, etc.); and in *communication* (obscuring the messages sent between persons). Each of these, as we will see, is most germane to the skill of management. We saw vagueness at work at Matsushita when product managers built acceptance time into their efforts to influence division managers—moving along with the line managers' learning curve rather than forcing the issue by asserting rank and authority to get closure.

Ambiguity, uncertainty, and imperfection, with their many shades of meaning, carry different connotations in the East than in the West. In the United States, for example, when a situation is "ambiguous," the implication is that it is incomplete, unstable, and needs clearing up. In Japan, in contrast, ambiguity is seen as having both desirable and undesirable aspects. The Japanese often seek a great deal of predictable order. But in other respects, having to do with many organizational matters, they are also willing to flow with things. More ambiguity, uncertainty, and imperfection in organizations is acceptable to them than to us as an immutable fact of life, what philosophers in the West have called "existential givens." By this they mean that such conditions just *are,* and, accordingly, the sooner we accept that they exist the better things will go. Regarding them as *enemies* gets our adrenaline pumping for a hopeless battle. Regarding them as conditions to be reduced or lived with, as appropriate to the situation, makes more sense.

Language and Mental Models

Language is a repository of social experience. Often, words and images are treated as interchangeable, when in fact they are loaded with different effects. Words like "uncertainty"—or "leadership" or "decision making"—may trigger mental constructs that inhibit one from seeing the world as it currently is. So powerful is language in limiting our view of things that a number of scientists

(Einstein among them) have urged alternating the languages in which we think to avoid intellectual myopia.[4]

The Japanese embrace an idea of the world that says, although there is "nothing" there is still something.[5] Consider this analogy: in English we often refer to an empty space as, for example, "the space between the chair and the table." In the Japanese equivalent, the space isn't "empty"; it's "full of nothing." The illustration makes this point: Westerners speak of what is unknown primarily in reference to what is known (i.e., of the space between the chair and the table); the Japanese view of "nothing" illustrates that dignity can be given to emptiness in its own right. One finds symbols of this in a Zen garden, where a few large rocks stand alone in a sea of raked pebbles. Westerners see the rocks; the Japanese are trained to pay attention to the space around them. A Tao verse explains:

> Thirty spokes are made one by holes in a hub
> Together with the vacancies between them,
>   they comprise a wheel,
> The use of clay in moulding pitchers
> Comes from the hollow of its absence;
> Doors, windows in a house
> Are used for their emptiness:
> Thus we are helped by what is not
> To use what is.[6]

The Japanese believe that by removing yourself from the picture you gain greater insight into what truly is there. We are blinded by our own egos from seeing the full possibilities of life. If we discipline ourselves to adopt periodically a "no-ego" state, we can perceptively drink in the full meaning of a situation without imposing ourselves upon it.

Another notion of interest stems from the Japanese word *ma*—for which there is no exact equivalent in English.[7] *Ma* pertains to a space in time with the meaning of an interval or pause. A very famous Japanese poem is written:

Spring (ma) *is dawn.*[8]

The Japanese treat the parenthetical *ma* as we would a punctuation mark. It is unspoken. However, *ma* directs the reader to stop and conjure up all thoughts and images of spring. Having done so, he is ready to proceed, bringing all his mental pictures of spring into juxtaposition with the poem's next words, "is dawn." Symbolically, *ma* tells the reader to pause, wait, and experience before proceeding.

Our interest in *ma* is that it is an illustration of an artifact of language that is less available to Westerners. Through a variety of such nuances and conventions, the Japanese culture instructs its members not to plunge straight ahead, but to move knowingly and deftly through time.

Respect for *ma* deters us from plunging ahead when the right time for action is still impending. Gifted actors and comedians, great speakers and leaders, have an instinct for this quality. We have all noted the *pause* just prior to an important point when participants are momentarily waiting for release from tension created in part by the pause itself. But, as in theater, so also in organizational life, the magic fusion between anticipation and execution often fizzles. We have all witnessed a flow of organizational events building effectively toward closure only to see the overeager clumsily destroy consensus with a premature plunge toward the finish line. Such haste is as disastrous in organizations as in the theater.

When to Be Vague

To be sure, most managerial actions do not benefit from vagueness. In many management situations, being explicit and decisive is necessary. When an executive has access to too much data for human processing he needs to simplify. If he has examined different pricing schemes for twelve months and weighed the viable alternatives, the time has probably come for him to cut off further search and decide. Deciding in these circumstances has the benefit of at least ending wheel spinning and resolving a lot of anxiety for all concerned. We did not see a lot of *needless* vagueness at Matsushita or ITT.

But there is another set of problems—such as merging the production and engineering departments—in which experience may suggest that the change contemplated is complicated and the data at hand are inadequate. Frequently, this dilemma arises with changes capable of arousing anxiety and troublesome resistance.

In these circumstances, Eastern notions of indefinition are helpful. Rather than forcing a final solution, it may be a better interim step to accept the lack of clarity in the situation and simply *"decide" to proceed.* As "proceeding" yields further information, the best course may be to move toward the goal through a sequence of tentative steps rather than by bold stroke actions. The distinction, then, is between having enough data to *decide* and enough data to *proceed.* If the problem and its proposed solution are perceived to involve groups of persons with different mandates (such as unions, professional groups, and middle management), and the distribution of power is such that top management lacks full control, then successful implementation usually requires tentativeness. Accepting the conditions of ambiguity, uncertainty, and imperfection helps make tentativeness legitimate even if the managerial culture still suggests quick closure is the mark of a good executive.

Indirection has several important applications for management. First, it may be useful in communicating—both orally and in writing. Vagueness in *communication* can cause problems, to be sure, but it can also serve to hold strained relations together and reduce unnecessary conflict. There is too much American trust in increasing the clarity in communication between people, especially when their disagreements are substantive. Getting a currently hopeless impasse clear is often unwise and likely to make things worse. Second, vagueness in *intention* legitimizes the loose rein permitted in certain organizational situations in which further insight is needed before corrective action can be taken. Mr. Kemper's situation called for both of these applications. He was probably wise to avoid being explicit as to what rules he would apply or what policies he would follow. What was needed was to communicate (1) that he was concerned and (2) that something would be done. To have taken an immediate stand would have overstated his grasp of the problem and gotten him on record as prematurely endorsing a course of action he might later wish to reject. Clearly, he could have been more "decisive." For instance, he might have referred the cabin cleaners to the provisions of the union grievance machinery. But was it desirable to be tied to a time-consuming · and adversarial procedure in so potentially explosive a situation? Alternatively, he might have opted to invoke the chain of command, which was as clear-cut as the company's organizational chart hanging on the wall behind his desk. But that risked pushing the cabin cleaners into direct confrontation with their supervisor, a potentially explosive situation. So Mr. Kemper chose instead, at least during the first round, to avoid commitment to a remedy until he could get a better sense of the situation. In this way, he kept his options open and established a sufficient basis of good faith to convince the cabin cleaners to accept, for the time being, a process rather than an outcome. He also utilized vagueness in relation to time. By holding action in abeyance, he provided time for the relationship between the cabin cleaners and their supervisor to evolve. No new rules of conduct were prescribed. No new procedures were laid down to ensure racial equality, for it was not clear whether this was an idiosyncratic, one-time situation or a persistent pattern of behavior on the part of the foreman involved. It could even be a systems-related issue that required a systems-wide remedy. Mr. Kemper's success in getting the cabin cleaners to "wait a while" bought the time for these possibilities to simmer a little longer, time to see if an accommodation would evolve by itself or if intervention would be needed, and, if so, what it should be.

Announcement-itis

One avenue open to Kemper was to *announce* a rule change or another personnel policy. This is a persistent affliction of American organizations; we make too many announcements, especially inasmuch as most organizational events largely announce themselves. The Japanese manager comes culturally equipped with a pair of helpful concepts, *tatemae* (in front) and *honne* (behind the scenes).[9] These roughly correspond to the Latin notions of *de jure* and *de facto*, with one important distinction. The Japanese think of *honne* as constituting as much of *real life* as does the ceremonial *tatemae* function. Thus, the Japanese see the making of announcements as half the reality, the other half being the action behind the scenes.

Said one manager, "People around here are fond of announcing things. It sets everything astir. The other day the president announced that 'henceforth John Pearson would be in charge of personnel matters.' Well, the Production Department, which has always handled its own personnel affairs, got its back up; rumors commenced as to whether John Pearson was on his way up or out, whether he was building an empire, and so forth. Why not just begin by increasingly referring all personnel requests to John Pearson? Before long, the informal organization will catch on to the new flow. Make the announcement later when it won't do any harm."[10]

In order to announce what it is one *wants* to happen, one must often state in advance what cannot yet be known. This can create a mess between "announcing it" and "getting it." If, on the other hand, the change is allowed largely to take shape first, the "announcement" can then simply report what has happened and direct the rest of what is needed. As a general rule, announcing one's intentions too early is a far more risky enterprise than announcing what is largely a developing reality.

Undoubtedly, some managers will react adversely to this approach. "It isn't forceful and direct." "It doesn't tell people where they are going." There are times, to be sure, when it *is* necessary to force or direct publicly, when the symbolic act of announcing a change is essential to overcome resistance and generate the impetus for action. But a great many organizational announcements do not fit these circumstances and would be better off postponed. This is especially true for announcements that affect how people will relate to one another when they are required to change behavior significantly. Whenever organizations significantly change, there is the possibility of great loss—in good relationships, communications rapport, understanding, and even to each individual's sense of self. Care, sensitivity, and patience are desirable if you can afford to move more slowly and thus preserve as much of what is valued in an organization as possible. As a general rule, the Japanese try to avoid ripping sinews of relationship and think carefully about what rips are necessary and what ones can be diminished or even avoided.

Instead of turning the spotlight on an intended change, parading revised organizational charts and job descriptions, Americans might better consider reassigning tasks incrementally, gradually shifting boundaries between functions and making formal announcements only when the desired changes have been effected. Instead of legislating a final change, this approach involves taking your *intention* to the key actors, perfecting your design by learning as you proceed, and, when it's almost implemented, announcing it if necessary or useful for further accomplishment or to reduce undue anxiety that remains.

Implicit Communication

As we saw at Matsushita, managerial communication isn't always indirect. Sometimes it is straight and to the point and it would be erroneous to draw black-and-white contrasts between the Americans and the Japanese. Certainly, Matsushita's handling of its Motorola acquisition looked very "American." There are *certain* circumstances, however, which call for indirectness—such as a controller's wishing to alert a division manager to a problem without undercutting him or jeopardizing their future relationship. At Matsushita, we infer that this was somehow handled more gracefully than at ITT.

Observing a Matsushita controller deal with certain delicate situations provides an opportunity to study an art form. Carefully choosing his words, constructing a well-balanced tension between the general and the specific, the opaque and the clear, he picks his way across difficult terrain. Whether dealing with a division manager before the planning group or with superintendents on the shop floor, he is always balancing. In discussing a variance or problem area, he may choose to come close enough to the point to ensure that the manager knows what's wrong, but not so close as to crowd or cause defensiveness. In this way, linguistic indirection serves to cushion heavy-handedness and demoralization, and it saves energy for work and maintains continuing cooperation. It is thus not surprising that the Matsushita controllers were comfortable with the usage of "wife," associated as it is with the skills traditionally associated with women in many cultures. It is hard to imagine a similar metaphor being used by an American controller.

The Japanese conduct their dialogues in circles, widening and narrowing them to correspond to the other's sensitivity to the feedback. The controller might say, "I'd like you to reflect a bit further on your proposal." Translated into Western thought patterns, the same sentence might read: "I think you're wrong and you should come up with a better idea."[11] The first approach, as opposed to the second, allows the recipient to exist with his self-esteem intact. To the Japanese mind, such etiquette is like the sliding screens in Japanese homes. Made of rice paper and wood, they do not, in fact, block sound, but at the visual level define space. How often, one wonders, would rice paper courtesies of language serve the same function of honoring an individual's personal space rather than imposing explicit feedback that exposes naked vulnerability. This can take more time, of course, but then time is to the ear what space is to the eye, and "spending" a little more time in talk can do for self-esteem what sliding screens can do for visual privacy. The Japanese are more prone to speak in the transitive mode or to leave verbs out of sentences altogether. They have an inherent *preference* not to rely wholly on words. They are more means oriented, or process oriented, whereas Americans tend to focus more on the bottom line, on the ends. Americans are more Aristotelian. We feel if it is not white, by deduction it has to be black. The Japanese live comfortably with gray.

In the Japanese language, verbs appear at the ends of sentences, so the listener doesn't know where the speaker is headed until he gets there.[12] The speaker can change his verbs in response to the listener's expression. So pronounced, in fact, is their desire for concurrence that the Japanese sometimes avoid the definitiveness of verbs altogether. The listener's receptivity or hesitancy in responding to a few key nouns sets the stage for a choreography of consensus. The Japanese employ open discussions with generalities that leave room for movement and compromise. They have *nineteen* ways of saying no—suggestive of the extreme finesse with which their language navigates the shoals of conflict, avoiding it if possible.[13]

Cultures also differ in their sensitivity to nonverbal behavior. Even in the rational West, silences, fidgeting, and facial expressions say a great deal about how debate is progressing and how ideas are going down. It is a curious fact that across all cultures, when human beings are exposed to contradictory verbal and nonverbal messages, they trust the nonverbal signals more.[14] Nonverbal communication is less subject to the communicator's conscious control and is therefore more trustworthy to others. This being the case, it is ironic that Western management theory and education has steadfastly de-emphasized nonverbal data. Yet it is not surprising when we read our description of Geneen's managerial practice that he paid great attention to nonverbal data. Japanese culture explicitly encourages, throughout an individual's lifetime development, the ability to understand without words—not merely the situation, but the intention of others.

While the Japanese have words for logical and evaluative

matters—and we can expect that such words are widely used in pragmatic organizations like Matsushita—it is also true that the Japanese are generally suspicious of too much logic. They have a word *rikutsupoi*, which translates as "too logical." It is used in the pejorative, analogously to the way we use the term "legalistic." *Rikutsupoi* is used for people who are very bright but excessively logical and pushy. All of us have known such individuals but, lacking such a concept in the West, we have more difficulty defending against them. Japanese managers frequently use the word in reference to young people who lack the richness of experience to inform their rational arguments. We have our own words, of course, for the all-too-familiar young person who forces upon us internally consistent arguments that proceed from immature premises—but it is often necessary to delete these words in print.

Linguist Frank Gibney observes, "Japanese shuns flat commitments and dotes on double negatives. A Japanese response to a question rarely is either 100 percent acceptance or 100 percent disagreement. He prefers to examine the proposition discussed and suggest various approaches that could be made to it."[15]

"It isn't that we can't do it this way," one Japanese will say.

"Of course," replies the other. "Still, we couldn't deny that it couldn't be done, could we?"

And so it continues. An exchange has begun and the two are exploring a problem from different perspectives rather than locking horns straight out. Initially inscrutable to us as Noh dramas, and imitated no more easily, this sort of dialogue keeps an area of potential agreement or compromise open and reduces the odds of emotional escalation toward direct personal confrontation.

The English language, as we most often use it, is not quite so supple an instrument. In addition, in business we admire directness and often use language like a hammer—and treat other opinions as if they were a nail. The Japanese admire diplomats as practitioners of a very necessary and useful art. We tend to disdain them for their "convolution." And sometimes we summon wistful images of the monosyllabic cowboy whose limitations of language and lack of guile are assumed to reveal sincerity and directness, especially since his potential for violence is considerable if it comes to that. Or we imagine the aggressive, call-a-spade-a-spade, table-pounding hero whose simple, brutal use of words leaves nothing unclear at all. The "shy cowboy" seems to have given way to the table-pounders in U.S. management myth, with a new mutation developing—the quiet, cold, analytical technician whose icy precision fast-freezes others as he ticks off his points, one, two, three. All three stereotypes, and others that could be added, involve admiration for those who disdain "pussyfooting" around. Yet sophisticated managers need a sophisticated appreciation for the appropriate uses of language and conversational tactics, given varied people in different situations. Four factors are particularly important.

First, the right words help enormously. One can't communicate effectively with a thousand-word vocabulary. Command of words is essential to administrative skill; it is as much a tool of the craft of administration as the nuances of accounting are.

Second is the power to speak both concretely and abstractly, to move from the specific to the general. Look at it this way: If you are about to blaze a trail across difficult terrain, it will be useful for you to fly over the area beforehand to get your bearings. Once back on land, you will recall your general impressions and seek specific landmarks—a pile of stones, a solitary tree, a precipitous mountaintop. The same is true of language. Always communicating at the same level of specificity is like persistently playing music in the same key. Variety is not only the spice of life; it greatly facilitates communication. Communicating only in nitty-gritty specifics or only in broad generalizations rapidly bores any audience. The trick is to move up and down from the general to the specific to provide different vantage points.

The third important tool of language is metaphor. Not only is metaphor a rich and revealing way of communicating experience, it is central to the process of thought itself. There is a tension in a good metaphor—the familiar becomes strange and the strange familiar. In communicating we use metaphorical images and analogies to great advantage—flying, hiking, music making, as in the paragraph above. One recalls Anton Chekhov's advice to his brother. "In descriptions," he said, "one must seize on small details, grouping them so that when the reader closes his eyes he gets a picture. For instance, you'll have a moonlit night if you write that on the mill dam a piece of glass from a broken bottle glittered like a bright star."[16] Lyndon Johnson's great personal power as a persuader derived precisely from this capacity to use concrete images, some crude indeed, as tools to influence.

Fourth, language is generally no better than the speaker's

understanding of the situation. The Zen priest's metaphor of a full cup was powerful because it expressed a truth he was able to grasp.

Mastery of language permits us to *select* among degrees of clarity and indirection, to avoid being too vague or too blunt, too obscure or indiscreet. Observed one unskilled American middle manager, "It's tough choreographing a ballet when you've been trained as a boxer."[17]

Indirection Versus Brute Integrity

Part of our drive for explicitness stems from the Western notion that it's a matter of honor to "get the cards on the table." The assumption is that no matter how much it hurts, the "truth" is good for you, and it is a sign of strength and maturity to give and take negative feedback. No doubt there is some merit in this. But between the value of such belief and our vulnerabilities as human beings lies the actual state of affairs. Granted, in many cases it is desirable to get the facts and know where one stands. At times we saw this occurring at Matsushita as well as at ITT. But it is also human to get defensive, particularly when vulnerability is high. There is no reason to believe that Westerners have less pride or feel less humiliation than do Japanese. (A recent American Management Association survey indicates that issues involving self-respect are among the major on-the-job concerns of managers.) Eastern cultures make a great deal of the concept of "face" at all levels of organization; Western cultures tend not to. In fact, in the United States, "face-saving" is widely regarded as petty or immature. Thus, at Matsushita, though hard driving and performance oriented, division managers are reviewed privately before head office controllers in contrast to ITT's "public trials." Every manager can recall instances in which an individual, publicly embarrassed by another, has caused injury to himself and to the organization just to even the score. The evidence would suggest that for most of us being pushed *too* hard and crowded into a corner is counterproductive. Great honesty is seldom helpful without empathetic compassion, skillfully expressed in private, by someone assumed to care about the other person's well-being.

The need to "speak the truth" bluntly often masks a self-serving sense of brute integrity and macho power. Such acts of "clearing the air" are often more helpful to the clearer than to those who are starkly revealed. "Brute integrity" is not just an outcome of certain linguistic tendencies embedded in the assumptions of our culture; nor is it wholly explainable in terms of our assumptions about authority and hierarchy in relationships between bosses and subordinates. At a deeper level, it has a sexist component. In our culture, simple, straightforward confrontation —a kind of *High Noon* shoot-'em-out—is mixed up with notions of what masculinity should be. Unfortunately, shoot-'em-outs work best when the other guy dies and the movie ends. If you've got to work with the person again and on a continuing basis, overly "straight" communication can complicate life immensely. In contrast, "devious ambiguity," in reference to sensitivity and feelings, is alleged to be female in the Western world. But if we set aside the historical stereotypes and contemplate the current consequences of these two modes of behavior on organizational life, reflection may suggest that primitive notions of masculinity work *over the long term* no better in the office than they do in bed.

Ask yourself: How often are brute integrity and explicit communication worth the price of the listener's goodwill, open-mindedness, and receptivity to change? Explicit communication is a cultural assumption; it is not a linguistic imperative. Skilled executives develop the ability to vary their language along the spectrum from explicitness to indirection depending on their reading of the other person and the situation.

Performance Feedback

Performance feedback, especially negative feedback, is an illuminating area in which to study indirection. Our culture stresses clarity in communication. The reality of most declining performance situations, however, is that they are messy and often fraught with uncertainty, imperfection, and ambiguity. There is, in effect, a disparity between cultural expectations and messy reality; bosses are often forced prematurely to extremes, either providing direct feedback (which raises the risk of demoralization) or, alternatively, avoiding the problem sufficiently until the weight of evidence accumulates and "justifies" confrontation.

When a subordinate begins to perform unsatisfactorily, it usually comes as a dawning awareness that most of us initially ignore. "People problems" are troublesome, and it is often difficult to separate inadequacy from the extenuating circumstances. The manager's first reaction is to hope that as the subordinate gains experience, the hitches in his performance will remedy themselves. If difficulties persist, a stop-go process begins—confronting the subordinate's blunders, followed by efforts to restore his confidence. Feedback to subordinates is seldom smooth and continuous; it tends to come in pulses at the spur of adverse events. And, throughout, the messiness increases. Eventually, if the situation does not correct itself, the manager may contemplate more serious sanctions—such as a transfer or dismissal. He must weigh whether he is being fair, and whether he has considered all alternatives. Ultimately, he must consider how to do what needs to be done so as not to make a bad situation worse. As noted earlier, cultural values ritualizing the "macho test" of direct action, notably the experience of firing someone at least once, encourage us to buck up and deal with these problems. And we do. Nonetheless, very few managers look forward to dealing with "messy" declining performance situations. Anger, dominance, pride, betrayal, jealousy, defensiveness—almost all of the more primitive human emotions —have the potential for being triggered in these encounters.

Studies of Americans who have lost their jobs reveal that in two thirds of the cases they were caught off guard.[18] The "punishments" (or absence of rewards) they had received along the way either had been so oblique as to be misinterpreted or had been obliterated by their own defenses. Typically, the earliest manifestations of negative feedback were pointed questions asked by the boss—or suggestions—which the subordinate could interpret in a variety of ways. Subsequent punishments were mere acts of omission, such as exclusion from meetings or withdrawal of positive strokes. Thereafter, the seemingly "foolproof" recourses of lower-than-average wage increases or bonuses and less good performance ratings were applied. But all along the way these often had been qualified by excuses calculated to soften the punch: "This was only your first year on the job." "You had a lot of personal problems on your mind." And so on.

Most reward systems get inflated over time: "outstanding" is used instead of "good," "average" comes to carry pejorative overtones. Yet grade inflation is rarely examined for its root cause. Grade inflation doesn't result from cosmic forces or just because language and performance scales are imprecise. It occurs because it is easier to be nice. For this reason, nearly all grading systems periodically need to be dismantled and started afresh, usually to reinvigorate them and to restore meaning to the grading terminology.

Once parallel meanings of words are allowed to coexist, a boss can check "average," meaning unsatisfactory, and the subordinate can read "average" to mean average. This exacerbates the ambiguity of one's "rewards." As a general rule, wage increases and performance reviews are not as clear signals as one might expect. Employees, particularly professionals, rarely compare notes in sufficient detail to be certain of their relative standing among their associates.

To be sure, the sterner forms of "feedback" are less subject to misinterpretation—the task forces from the controller's office, "consultants" brought in to look into one's problem areas. But even these expedients are often billed as "part of a general study" or "resources to provide assistance." A boss' occasional outburst of anger or feistiness in reviewing a project likewise can be perceived as his "having a bad day." In short, punishment is more vague than is supposed; employees in trouble frequently misinterpret the signals; what they construe as random noise may in truth be sirens of danger.

Bruce had been serving as section head at the Bank of America for over a year. His performance appraisals had been outstanding and his relations with his superiors solid—although he sometimes found them hard to read. Early in September a staff specialist in the credit approval area had asked a suspicious question: "So you really think this loan is a sound risk in the face of a recession economy?" Bruce's answer was "Yes," and the credit analyst did not dispute it. But the question was unusual, and Bruce took note of this fact. A week later, Bruce's boss suggested that he and the credit specialist "get together" to discuss another loan that Bruce was proposing. Again, there was nothing threatening in the suggestion—but there was an apparent breach of etiquette. The staff credit analyst had always taken his questions directly to Bruce rather than involving Bruce's boss, and he assumed his boss' suggestion indicated that the credit specialist had spoken to the boss. With two incidents in a short time frame, Bruce chose to act. He set about to correct any credibility problems he might have by doing more thorough homework. He caught his problem in time. But the story illustrates the subtle nature of feedback.[19]

How can we resolve the apparent contradiction between our tendency to be too clear about some things and not clear enough about others? It appears that some people swing from one extreme to another, although most of us have a clear preference for one end of the spectrum. Our own experience suggests that those who are "too" clear nearly all of the time, and those who are "too" unclear most of the time, have a preference for their way of behaving rooted in personality rather than in socialization or culture. Both seem to us to have significant problems vis-à-vis power—one overstating what he fears he really doesn't have enough of, the other underusing what he fears he has too much of. When "bad guys" snap, they often *im*plode: When "nice guys" crack, they often *ex*plode. Simple-minded as these generalizations have to be, they suggest that too many American managers have trouble, in Rollo May's phrase, "being lovingly powerful, and powerfully loving." Instead we emphasize one or the other, power or love, and are less able to deal with the complexity of organizational life as a result.

The moral of the story is this: The inherent preferences of organizations are clarity, certainty, and perfection. The inherent nature of human relationships involves ambiguity, uncertainty, and imperfection. How one honors, balances, and integrates the needs of both is the real trick of management.

Our earlier example of Kemper revealed an astute handling of a similar situation. While he was not dealing with a performance feedback situation directly, the potential was there to pass judgment on the black cabin cleaners or the errant supervisor. But Kemper did not want to undermine the integrity of the organization—its chain of command, its existing procedures, in short, its existing *clear* policies for handling such things. Yet Kemper did not ignore, as testified by his actions, that vagueness was inherent in the situation too. He recognized that existing policies weren't 100 percent sufficient, and that more policies piled on top wouldn't make the ambiguity go away. He lived with both.

So did Bruce. Bruce might have sought clarity (or his loan supervisor might have imposed it) and the result might have been onerous. Bruce's ability to read between the lines is a skill that many managers, American as well as Japanese, employ each day. We infer what is going on and act *before* a minor irritant explodes into a full-blown problem.

Many aspects of a company's reward system are quite unclear. When feedback is really clear and bad, it's usually too late. The most crucial feedback comes at a time when the *reviewer* is still ambivalent; this is the time when there is still maneuvering room to turn the situation around. But it is precisely at this juncture that the boss finds himself in double jeopardy. In the service of fairness, he tries to couch his comments in a positive and constructive way, risking that his concerns may be not heard clearly. The alternative is to be more blunt and accentuate the negative—at the risk of frightening and demoralizing the subordinate.

From the subordinate's point of view, a convenient scapegoat is to fault vagueness and insist on "clearer feedback." But most managers know subordinates want it direct when it's positive, and not when it's negative, until it's too late and then they wish they had heard the bad news earlier and blame the boss for being unclear. The alternative for subordinates is simply to be aware of the inherent indefinitiveness in relationships and to train themselves to be more artful at living with it by searching for cues.

Bruce's ability to make timely use of the "warning signs" required finely tuned perceptual powers. And organizational justice being what it is, even though the boss is technically responsible for feedback, the subordinate almost always loses if he fails to read the signals, however unclear. The trap for our younger people is that there is little in their education or in our management culture that prepares them to cope with these nuances of the reward and punishment system, which often determine success or failure. For years in school they get promoted every twelve months for anything better than dreadful work, and their feedback is frequent, explicit, and generally well understood in that context. Our culture does not make much of subtlety; we do not place a lot of emphasis on listener sensitivity to capture implied meanings. But while we extol clarity, most of those who excel in organizations, both Japanese *and* Americans, are masters at reading the subtle signals.

Success Criteria

Another realm of organizational life that is rife with vagueness is the realm of reward systems. Organizations often talk a different game than they play. It is a curious irony of organizational life that we are paid to do a job, but are promoted for doing something beyond the job. We usually receive only routine credit for doing the expected. The real impetus for career acceleration comes from doing the extraordinary. Fast trackers inevitably favor assignments with more discretion (but not necessarily more downside risk) because they provide more leeway to demonstrate high potential.

An employee who meets his performance objectives is regarded as a "solid performer" who will progress in due course. But the employee who shows initiative by repeatedly exceeding what is expected of him, who identifies opportunities and problems not foreseen when his performance profile was established and initiates actions to deal effectively with these situations, is the most likely to be noticed and promoted rapidly through the ranks. Performance plans and MBOs are negotiated in total earnestness each year—yet both parties to the agreement are often more than subliminally aware that the procedure is a way of setting acceptable expectations for ordinary people. Yet the boss knows that the situations in which his subordinate will often make the biggest difference are unknowable at the time, and his subordinate, while agreeing to performance objectives, knows that his biggest breaks will come by doing the unforeseen. Very few professionals are content simply to compete in the race for corporate recognition. Most want to win or, at least, to place among those at the head of the pack. Mastery of an elaborate and largely unclear set of cues and standards is essential to achieving this end.

The task of coming to grips with these subtle elements of organizational success requires reading the social and stylistic requirements as well as knowing the explicit task performance criteria. In fact, Rosabeth Kanter, in her analysis of factors governing managerial promotion and success in large corporations, found that personal chemistry was the *key* determinant. In her words, it boiled down to five factors: appearance, personality, aggressiveness, executive stature, and promotability.[20] "The interesting thing about these five essential ingredients," Kanter observed, "is that they don't include professional competence."[21] Why? Because a certain threshold of performance, of competence, is taken for granted. Technical competence is established within the first few years on the job. Relative success or failure among middle managers turns on social relations—on getting work done effectively with peers, superiors, and subordinates. The more socialized the members of an organization become, the more deftly they utilize indirect means of communication. This was evident in our contrast of Matsushita and ITT. Even without Geneen's blunt style, ITT would likely require more explicit forms of communication. But then ITT did not have a long tenured management cadre and did not focus on socializing its members to an "ITT way" that was long term and multipurposed as did Matsushita.

Reading the social and stylistic requirements of success is complicated when a company's signals are mixed. One of the nation's largest timber, pulp, and paper concerns hails from a family tradition of frontiersmanship and rugged individualism. Management talk is still tough. "I'm going to fire the s.o.b." and "We need to kick ass down in the mill" are frequently heard comments in the executive office. In actuality, this firm exercises extreme restraint in taking personnel actions. Consultants are used to help managers in trouble turn their problem situations around. Poor performers are given repeated opportunities to correct deficiencies, and a great deal of hand-wringing occurs before anyone is terminated. More often, a manager in trouble is transferred to another position and given another chance.

But such double cues, even in cases where the scabbard is known to be bigger than the knife, exact a cost. Hard talk instills fear among those who do not clearly grasp the difference between talk and action within the company. Rumors of impending sanctions can demoralize. One of the most reliable findings of behavioral science is that persons who are in failure situations experience heightened tension and anxiety and are most likely to revert to past success behavior. Former President Nixon's behavior in the face of the Watergate disclosures is a case in point. Numerous attempts at a "Checkers Speech" strategy of talking apparently "straight" to the public on television, drawing inside a closed circle of advisors, stonewalling, doggedly attempting to "tough it out" were all elements of a response that had worked successfully for him before—but that ultimately led, perhaps needlessly, to his downfall. Organizations that provoke fear tend to exacerbate these tendencies, and others as well.

Citicorp offers a second provocative illustration. "FNCB is an elite institution with a considerable organizational ego," states one of its senior personnel officers. "Over the years, we have hired a great many talented and aggressive people. We have in place, of course, a great many first-class management training courses that teach not only the technicalities of banking, but the importance of patience in changing organization and the virtues of effective communications and sensitivity. But the informal system rewards aggressiveness and verbal skill. The term we use around here is 'tiger'—and it is not a negative image. The attributes sought are naked ambition, tremendous flexibility, willingness to change, and an assertive kind of 'meeting macho' where you verbally punch your points home and spear those who disagree. Problems arise, however, when an organization can't expand fast enough to absorb that kind of aggressive energy. Then the tigers turn into sharks . . . all swimming around in a confined space . . . waiting. The quicker students who attend these courses on the niceties of management are watching out of the corner of their eye to see who the managers are who are going to survive and thrive. 'Interpersonal virtue' is no match for the powerful force of role models who consistently exemplify aggressiveness and hustle."[22]

Note, again, the positive values attached to a threatening image, "tiger," and the transformation of that active jungle cat into a menacing "shark," waiting. The potential for violence is so consistently evident in the metaphors used by employees of many American "hard-ball" firms that it is small surprise that they are full of fear and seek as much self-protection as the system will allow. Such firms attract people who can't really imagine losing in a fast track game, until experience begins to suggest that they may not always be "winners." Unfortunately, they may lose more than their pseudo-innocence.

But the basic point we are making is this: A host of important organizational communications—regarding feedback, goal setting, evaluating performance, and coping with the systems of rewards—contain elements of ambiguity, uncertainty, and imperfection, however hard we try to reduce or eliminate them. Man is the conduit through which the communication flows. Why overdesign the pumping station when the limits are imposed by the pipeline? Communication, to an important degree, relies on shared understanding, which is often intentionally left implicit in order to identify those individuals gifted enough to figure the system out. The lesson to be drawn from all this is not that the vagueness surrounding these things is "wrong" or that they can be easily reduced. Rather, a certain degree of vagueness just persists, and we need to better prepare the uninitiated for coping with it, and give more credit to those who do it well in order to encourage those skills across time.

Vagueness and Decision

Our tendency to view vagueness as undesirable, even as we sometimes increase it unnecessarily, exerts a pervasive influence on our beliefs about decision making. Managers, we are taught, "make decisions." The term implies mastery. Often, of course, decision making involves a difficult selection among alternatives based on tentative facts. But, through nuance and implication, the term "decision making" conveys the image of finality and control. "Decision," deriving from the same stem as "incision," literally means to cut off further consideration. "Good decision makers," our management beliefs tell us, "have command of the facts, are cognizant of the options, and decide on the best solution."[23] Bam, bam, bam.

Eastern management lore sensitizes its managers to be wary of illusions of mastery and to suspect the notion that at any one time anything is truly "decided." Whereas Western management beliefs tend to portray a decision as fixed and final, Eastern philosophical tradition emphasizes individual accommodation to a continuously unfolding set of events.[24] This is not to say that managers in Tokyo, Singapore, or Seoul let situations "flow" indefinitely, but that their concept of the decision process (more correctly, the "choice generation process") permits them to flow with the situations longer before they are expected to evoke closure.

Behind these differences lies an insight of fundamental importance to managers. As we have seen repeatedly, our concepts guide, and to some degree limit, what we can think. Western decisions are usually bounded in time and conceived of as having a definitive point of reference. Pros and cons are weighed within the time frame allotted; before any action is taken, one alternative is selected for implementation. The word "decision" has a positive connotation. After deciding, most managers experience a sense of relief.

The Japanese dislike having to make decisions, especially "arbitrary" decisions. When Matsushita bought his technology from Phillips after World War II, his company did not have the resources to make a thorough study of the ramifications of putting most of the company's capital on the line. Matsushita made a loosely arbitrary decision. American managers might consider such "bet your company type" decisions as the kind of bold-stroke actions from which the legends of great managers are made. An American in Mr. Matsushita's shoes might have gone to Phillips, met their representatives, liked their products, and said, "Let's do it." Japanese faced with the same circumstances *can* decide on the spot as Matsushita did. But they would not feel that they were living up to or creating their legend. On the contrary, they would take great pains to explain to subordinates that they didn't like having to choose under such circumstances and thus win support in the interests of the company. Japanese executives are capable of taking great risks—and they do. But they don't value bravura, individual, "legend-making" moves as much as we do—or at least they act as if they were reluctant rather than proud. They emphasize the organization's achievements over time more than an individual's one-shot successes.

As we saw at Matsushita, the Japanese recognize as much as we do that decisions must be made. However, when they have the time, they prefer to invest it in carefully building a foundation of support. They recognize that many elements of an organization will be more committed to a decision if they take part in it. We will subsequently see that this view is shared by many American managers. The Japanese feel that not only do consultative discussions result in better decisions but that it is their *obligation* to include people. In this latter respect, there is a distinct difference. Frequently, we hear stories of perplexed American firms receiving and briefing a delegation from their Japanese business partner only to receive a follow-up delegation two weeks later which requires the same briefing as before. What appears as redundancy to the Western mind reflects the Japanese approach to getting the ducks in line and all the ingredients in place for highly reliable implementation.

When the Japanese have three or four alternatives, they allow each to be talked through and explored in terms of its implementational feasibility. Clearly, they do not let these go so far as to incur too costly a duplication, but they allow each alternative to be "talked through." Because effective implementation of decisions is viewed as requiring a reconciliation of competing interests—the assistance of all of them essential to success—the Japanese utilize this procedure to ensure a proper balance between what is substantively optional and what is feasible to implement. As the alternatives are explored, it becomes clearer which has the all-around best chance of success. The American drive for closure, or decision, on the other hand, often prompts managers to choose prematurely, based on conceptual analysis and substantive merit, but without due regard for implementational feasibility. Then they struggle to get their people on board, forcing more than would be necessary had they "decided" later and differently.

Decision-making theorists have long known that the style of decision making is influenced by two key factors: (1) degree of agreement among people, and (2) the extent of knowledge as to whether the decision will produce the desired result. When both agreement and confidence in the decision's outcome are high, the decisions are easily made autocratically.[25] Such routine decisions are made in this fashion at both Japanese and American companies. When either agreement or confidence levels are low, intermediate forms between consultative and autocratic decision styles are best suited. When disagreement exists and the basis for making a sound decision is highly uncertain, highly consultative type decisions are called for. Most organizations' decisions of major consequence fall into these three categories.

Thomas P. Rohlen, a specialist on Japanese organizations, states, "Japanese managers tend to be more savvy. This doesn't mean they wouldn't want to change things faster if they could but simply that experience teaches them that often it's necessary to change things slowly. The Japanese are regularly encouraged to reflect on their experience. Some executives even do Zen meditation with the purpose of clearing their minds so they may reflect on their experience more deeply. Reflection may lead one to push harder, another to back off."

There isn't a logical difference between how American and Japanese managers think about decision making but the weight of *experience* in decision making can be very different. The Japanese tap into their experience to inform their understanding. They regard their day-to-day corporate experiences as a learning lab from which they may acquire wisdom. Many American managers learn subliminally in this fashion, but their *learning* energies are only truly engaged when they must master substantive materials, or when they are challenged by formal classroom-type programs. That Japanese companies do not recruit their future managers from business schools, but raise them up over long experience-rich careers is but another indication of this difference in emphasis.

American managers often feel obliged to decide to change things. Perhaps this stems in part from less job security. Job insecurity tends to impose a shorter half life on one's power. Often American managers are given a short time to accomplish change, and the mandate is like a gun to the head. It drives them willy-nilly into most of the traps that result from trying to force things. The outcomes are often counterproductive.

The Japanese manager gets to his position not because he's been hired to "turn things around fast" but because he's slowly climbed up the ladder and he's *there*, and will be there. He looks at things and tries to see under the surface—as an American manager might. Ever so gradually, he formulates a plan and then he formulates the means to achieve the plan. He is not burdened by threats to his potency or to his job by choosing this careful course. No doubt, Matsushita's division manager had to produce—as did Geneen's at ITT. But one sensed from the quotes that the Japanese were more secure and less fearful and more long-term-focused and thoughtful.

The images of decision making that we have been discussing exert considerable influence on executive thinking. It is simply less acceptable for an American than for a Japanese to "flow with" a situation. His superiors and subordinates, as well as his own idea of what it means to "manage," reinforce the making of decisions, and the act of deciding seems almost to reaffirm his competence. Those who pursue a less decisive path risk being viewed as "hedging" or "playing the situation along," or even of being "wishy-washy" or "indecisive" (which is, given the cultural meanings, understandably despised).

The notion of achieving change gradually runs deep in Eastern culture. For management, it provides a context in which to think about outflanking organizational obstacles and in time letting them wither away. "It is well to persist like water," counsels the Tao. "For back it comes, again and again, wearing down the rigid strength which cannot yield to withstand it."[26] Let things flow; let events take their course. When an obstruction occurs, managers need not watch torrents of frustration and energy build up behind it. But perhaps their best solution is not to dynamite it either, but simply to trace a way around it with a light touch, enough to get a trickle flowing. Let the flow of events do the rest of the work. The trick is to embrace a concept of decision making that, in circumstances in which we have enough information to proceed but not enough to decide, permits us to seek influence upon the flow without imposing a false sense of mastery over it. In such circumstances, when it is not necessary to make a decision, it is smart *not* to make a decision.

The Japanese image of a good decision maker is the man who can resist the drive for closure until he really sees what's required. That is the ideal for the Japanese. The American ideal has more fast action. He's the type who is jumping into the sports car, climbing off an airplane, or marching into meetings. It's an energetic, kinetic image. The Japanese image is contemplative— not in a meditational sense, but in the sense that it permits deeper perception.

"The American style of management," says one observer, "conveys a metamessage. It's expressed through the energy of our executive's own activities and his own body. That's the way we get promoted. Promising managers come across as 'full-of-go,' optimistic, 'never-say-no' types. In fact, a good way *not* to be promoted is to be seen as having sat in one's office and really thought deeply about things."[27]

American managers, as a group, need to reduce their pulse rate. They need to include different managerial folk heroes. They need to drink in their organizational experience and discern more deeply what makes things work. From that, wisdom can come, which is, in the end, perhaps the greatest reward from a life of managerial work, and the quality most needed for organizations to become great ones.

Skill, Indirection, and Decision

The application of indefinition in its various forms requires skill. Our discussion identifies some of the vagueness in organizational life and suggests that more skill is needed. Our perspective is that organizations are organic, not mechanical or even hydraulic. We try our best to work within them effectively, to make decisions and implement change expeditiously when that can be done. But there is often unpredictability in the system. One solution is Geneen's. He sought to reduce uncertainty, ambiguity, and imperfection

enormously through double checks, obsessive controls, quantifica-
tion, and brute confrontation. Another approach is to recognize
that only a certain amount of what an organization can accomplish
is attainable directly, and that the rest is best obtained with a flute
in hand. One imagines Mr. Matsushita holding a flute in one hand
—and an abacus in the other. An important *skill* of management is
this "Pied Piper" capacity to live with the amount of ambiguity,
uncertainty, and imperfection that is appropriate in organizations,
rather than to assume all evidence of these conditions is a call to
arms. When management is believed to be best practiced as a military science, without the humane arts, in the service of a single
financial goal, one needs no flute. But then one's organization may
never achieve its full potential.

The difficulties American managers face that come from
their problems with the three "existential givens" are made more
complicated by the U.S. culture's fear of dependence on other
people and by the high value placed on being "independent." In
the next chapter we explore the problems related to these latter
issues, and relate them to the exploration in this chapter. With that
done, we can move on to examining some U.S. firms and executives who have devised American versions of Japanese management.

Chapter Five

Interdependence

AMONG THE powerful forces influencing how executives work together in organizations, three stand out. *First is specialized work.* Responsibility for a particular functional or other organizational unit tends to narrow the focus of those so assigned. The resulting parochial behavior can lead to unfortunate outcomes unless the integration across those separate units is well managed. To paraphrase Winston Churchill, "Each person has only to do his duty to wreck the world." *Second is organizational hierarchy.* The tensions up and down the levels of the structural pyramid can lead to distortion of information, breakdowns in communication, and considerable frustration. The resulting isolation of levels of management from one another can damage effectiveness unless the problems of hierarchy are skillfully handled. One way of dealing with such up-and-down problems was illustrated by Geneen. In addition to various staff groups that went as low as necessary to do their job, Geneen went down as far as he could through his meetings searching out information. *Third is the reward system.* Unhealthy competition between those who need to cooperate can be made worse

when there is incentive for short-term gain over long-term benefits, or when there are systems for measuring results which are
inconsistent with desired outcomes.

Much of what we saw at ITT and Matsushita was related to
their different ways of dealing with these three factors. In the last
chapter we explored how American and Japanese variations in
response to ambiguity, uncertainty, and imperfection contributed
to differences between the two firms. In this chapter we will consider how the two societies' ways of resolving certain other human
problems affect management behavior. The tensions between the
individual and the organization, between superiors and subordinates, between the need for cooperation and competitive drives,
between the short run and long term, and between tangible and
intangible rewards are ones any company has to deal with. As we
will see, how a company resolves these tensions depends on how
the profound problem of "dependency" is approached by that
company's surrounding society and culture.

A Japanese executive invites a key subordinate into his office and, after pleasantries, proceeds to tell the younger man that
he needs his help. The executive is to go to New York to meet with
a key U.S. customer; he will make a presentation on a number of
important changes in the design of next year's products. He antic-
ipates that the customer will not be pleased with one or two of the
changes, and wants the presentation to diminish as much as possible any negative response. He tells his subordinate that he is still
uncertain while speaking English, and perhaps as a result tends to
get flustered and lose track of where he is during a talk. Once this
happens, usually after a surprising interruption that may raise a
matter requiring him to think on his feet, he expects that his normal difficulty with such a situation in Japan will be much worse in
another language. Therefore, he asks the subordinate to design a
presentation that will take his limitations into account. He offers
only as an illustration the possibility of a lights-out slide show,
which is less likely to be interrupted, followed by a small panel to
respond to the Americans, which he could chair. In such an instance, he says, he would be pleased if his subordinate were to
accompany him to New York to help in any appropriate capacity.

An American executive stops one of his promising new subordinates after a weekly meeting and tells him he has an important assignment for him. He wants him to put together a
presentation that is to be made to the corporate financial staff a

month hence. (He does not mention that he is very nervous about the presentation because the last time one of the corporate staff attacked his figures and made him look bad in front of his own vice president. He knows he has only a limited grasp of the financial side of things and is determined not to look ignorant and flustered again.) He tells the young man he wants a presentation that is very well thought out, double checked with the controller of the division, and organized to conform to the general pattern of such presentations—that is, a lights-out, slide-based, tough-minded analysis, no jazz or frills. He adds that he wants the completed presentation one week before it is to be made so he can make any changes necessary. (He also intends to practice giving it at home, and to double check it with both the controller and a neighbor for financial sophistication.) He ends by telling the junior executive laughingly that "all those courses at Wharton should help you do a terrific job, and you can count on my remembering it in June" (the next regular time for salary increases). When he returns to his office, he begins to think of a way to ensure that the controller will be at the meeting so that he can refer any really difficult questions to him after the slide show.

These two hypothetical situations are greatly simplified, but they do illustrate two very different ways that executives in Japan and the United States might well deal with problems common to them. Both feel inadequate to cope with the demands that will be put on them. Each needs help from others. To succeed at his task, each must depend on another person. The ways with which they deal with that dependency are, however, significantly different. And the effects of that difference, encouraged by their respective cultures, have most important implications for the people involved and for their organization's chances of success.

As every infant is dependent on others, so every executive has known dependencies. However, Japanese and American executives by and large have emerged from that state in different ways and toward different goals. American executives traditionally have been taught to become independent of others, separate, self-sufficient. Japanese executives traditionally have been taught to become interdependent with others, integral parts of a larger human unit, exchanging dependencies with others.

In each society there is a range in the degree to which individuals proceed from being dependent to becoming independent or interdependent. Those with less success are disapproved in both societies as "too dependent." They do not tend to become executives. But whereas American executives who become unusually interdependent with others risk being seen as still "too dependent," Japanese executives generally risk disapproval for being too separate, "too independent." (The resolution of dependency embraces a fourth type, the counterdependent, characterized by opposition to any powerful figure, his behavior often fueled by a powerful fear of dependency and an unconscious wish for it. Such adults are often in reaction against the failure of their parents to meet their needs when they were dependent on them. They make great radicals, but like people who are too dependent, they rarely survive a long corporate climb to executive ranks. And they are lousy subordinates.)

One way of visualizing all this is shown below (the shaded area is where nearly all executives can be found).

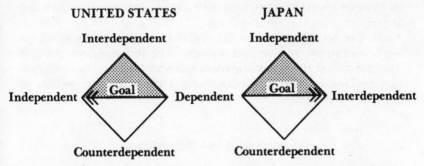

If we were to take the U.S. "executive triangle" and place Mr. Geneen and Mr. Matsushita within it, the result might look like this:

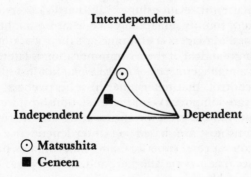

It is useful to note that each society's idealized goals for individuals are *not* precisely what corporations need to function well over the long run. American goals seem further from what companies need than do Japanese goals. But in either case the individual who is to rise to significant responsibility must adapt to his or her corporate subculture within the larger society. This adaptation requires them to become something other than what their nation's myths honor. The Japanese executive has less divergence to explain if he adapts well. With occasional apologies for his independent actions, all can be "forgiven." An American executive who achieves a good deal of *inter*dependence often has to make quite significant efforts to emphasize those aspects of his behavior which fit the *in*dependent myth of his country. Or at least he has to support the myth in speeches, and so on. The irony is that those American executives who have achieved what their companies really need from them often have to stay closeted in public to some degree.

But let us return to the difficulties posed by specialized work, hierarchy, and reward systems. The independent goals of Americans and the interdependent goals of Japanese have significant implications for how both manage these three essentials of organizational life.

Coordinated Interdependence

Chester Barnard said the creative side of organizations is coordination. "Organizations are a system of cooperative activities—and their coordination requires something intangible and personal that is largely a matter of relationships."[1] Barnard's observation, made forty years ago, sounds remarkably like what we might hear from Mr. Matsushita. Managers spend much of their working time with others, and a great deal of their communication is lateral as well as vertical. It is a manager's *span of relationships,* not just his hierarchical span of control, that determines his effectiveness. In spite of the demonstrated importance of these relationships, we are underequipped culturally in grasping their nature and force. Organizational relationships are based on interdependence. As every executive knows, peers, superiors, and subordinates provide support and assistance to one another, and they depend on one another even when they pretend otherwise.

Self

There are few concepts as deeply embedded in the Western mind as the concept of "self." Our philosophy, language, and psychology are filled with it. We see our "selves" as distinct entities, separate from all others in most important respects, with separable beliefs, talents, and experiences. In Japan each person is believed to possess a unique spirit, soul, mind, and heart—but his self (or "self-concept") is seen as an impediment to growth. People are regarded less as individuals than as collaborators in the context of their roles. One's separate "identity" is not singled out as the primary sign of personal development throughout the life cycle, as it is in the West.

Classically, a Japanese does not see his world in terms of separate categories (friends, relatives, subordinates), but as concentric rings of relationships, from the intimate (at the innermost) to the peripheral. In the innermost ring, the Japanese individual would place himself and his few "intimate others." Most Americans would place only themselves in the innermost ring. The person derives his identity in part from those nearest to him; there is a partial merging of identities. Those within the "intimate circle" are free to lay claim to the core of a person's energies and psychic resources. Farther away from the center, there are fewer claims and obligations for reciprocity.[2]

This view coincides quite closely with that of Harry Stack Sullivan, regarded as one of the few truly original American psychologists. Sullivan argued that the concept of "the individual" creates a lot of difficulty for Westerners and that it is more useful to regard interpersonal relationships—not the intrapersonal—as the smallest unit of inquiry. In Sullivan's view, it was simply not useful to talk of the individual separate from the context of his relationships.[3] Supporting this view is the conclusion that the major breakthroughs in Western psychotherapy in the last twenty years have come from working with more than one person, such as couples or families. Therapists have increasingly expanded the boundaries around the individual to encompass those relationships that powerfully affect his or her well-being, and vice versa.

Human nature may be universal but the lens through which we view and experience things is not. The Japanese perceive the drawing of lines between self and "others" as arbitrary. Their culture emphasizes reciprocal influences; ours tends to emphasize separateness. Westerners struggle to develop and then to retain separate identity in the face of invading influences. The Japanese tend to develop an "inclusive identity" that incorporates those close to them.

The Japanese way of looking at things is instructive in illuminating situations which confound Westerners. Erving Goffman, writing about the way in which friends influence one another's identities, remembers being with a business associate and encountering an old friend from college. The friend joined them for drinks. Goffman was ill at ease because he was a slightly different person in each of the two relationships.[4] Trying to accommodate the expectations of each friend at the same time created problems. The Japanese way of thinking would make that situation less discomforting since an incongruence would be expected to arise, and if possible it would be avoided. Westerners are more apt to attempt such encounters assuming they are the same persons all the time and then subsequently experience discomfort. We worry because our identity isn't "wholly consistent." We assume it should have been, as if we were really one self independent of the relationships.

We Westerners think we rely principally on *one* anchor—our self-concept. The Japanese see themselves less as "anchored" than "moored" by many lines that are tied to friends, organizational colleagues, and family. We Westerners know from experience that organizations can wreak havoc with our lives and sever important relationships. Organizations are generally quite important to us in a relational sense, even though we often tend to deny this, or to pretend it doesn't matter really.

Our ambivalence toward organizations is natural, but nonetheless troublesome. It signals one of our cultural "blind spots." Japanese culture permits a clearer understanding of these issues; organizations provide a web of relationships with peers, subordinates, and seniors which are acknowledged as important. When a Japanese loses or is unable to establish these ties, he experiences acute psychological pain—just as most Westerners do. But in the United States we often say, "He hasn't found himself" (as if his "self" was lost). The corollary in Japan is "He doesn't belong." (It is no wonder that, seeing ourselves at the center of our universe, we suffer more and more from narcissism, and it's no surprise that our therapists have trouble helping us, since they too often think the same way we do about "self.")

Because one's place and status matter so much in Japan, the Japanese have evolved an elaborate system to attend to these things. Its corporate expression is a lifetime commitment to a company, which helps to ensure the most important kind of *social* security. At an operational level, there are as well day-to-day observances that secure one's position. When one employee bows to another, the lowest bow affirms the other's right to have things his way, while the one who receives the bow accepts certain responsibilities.[6] Through such small details of conduct, the system of interdependence is reaffirmed continually. This allows a Japanese to be less fearfully concerned with how his performance is regarded by others *at the moment* because security stems *also* from who he is in his role. Specific accomplishments, one's role, and as well one's links with others, are all seen as appropriate sources of one's self-esteem.

Interdependence

A great deal is made of independence in America. Young people are encouraged to move away from home to establish adulthood. Parents, often suppressing their regret, prepare their children to "stand on their own two feet," yet suffer from the separation when it occurs, and the process of preparing for it as well. For the Westerner, the roots of independence run deep. A psychologist, James F.T. Bugental, suggests that we invented the idea of the individual about five hundred years ago, and it has been a growing force in the West ever since.[7] Locke, Hobbes, and Adam Smith contributed to our modern ideology, stressing the primacy of the individual and the wisdom of a society built on self-sufficiency.[8] In America, the frontier movement (much glorified) has exalted these values. Granted that self-sufficiency and independence are valuable qualities, it can be argued that too much of them contributes to isolation and dysfunctional rivalry in organizational life. For the Japanese, independence in an organizational context has negative connotations; it implies disregard for others and self-centeredness. When Japanese must refer to independent actions or judgments, they generally employ circumlocutions, such as "the power to act independently," or "self-direction." These signify temporary autonomous *activity* rather than a lasting *condition* of isolation or separateness.[9] The notion of "independence," so much a given in Western managerial thinking and so commonplace in our performance evaluations (e.g., "capacity for independent action," "independent judgment," etc.), is simply not a salient dimension for the Japanese. They value persistence, care, judgment, attention to detail, but if asked about independence by a Westerner, one gets a puzzled response. While the word for independent exists, it is uncommon and not relevant to the way a Japanese manager thinks.

Clearly, the American system of management, with its emphasis on independence, has strengths. But it rests on the historical needs of a frontier society that provided more than enough entrepreneurial opportunity to go around. In fifty years, we have changed from a society in which most people lived on independent farms to a nation of cities, from a time of "unlimited" resources to an era of pervasive scarcity. Today most Americans work in large, complex organizations, in close contact with other people. In these circumstances, our traditional values, especially when held in extreme form, may be inappropriate to our needs. The American West may have accommodated thousands of rugged individuals spread over the vast frontier. But millions of lone rangers employed under a few thousand corporate roofs may not much longer prove workable.

Psychologists tell us that the development of individual identity in the West begins in the ways Western mothers raise children. This occurs through the importance that mothers attach to their children not growing up dependent on them. Clearly, all human beings experience loss of maternal attachment. In the West, it is acknowledged, sometimes facetiously, by references to fantasies of "returning to the womb" and by sometimes admitted yearnings for the idyllic state of trust and oneness with another associated with infancy. Westerners, in developing a sense of selfhood and independence, are taught fairly early to turn their backs on this phase of life.

While Westerners seek to repress or disparage this common experience of infancy and dependence, the Japanese openly embrace it. Indeed, they build a great many aspects of organizational life around it. The readiness with which they accept their dependence on others stems from this source. Extensive studies of the rituals of bowing and other elaborate courtesies in Japan trace these conventions to this root. These matters are just as appropriate to Japanese society as the firm handshake, directness of speech, and eye contact are to the West.

Westerners cannot be expected to internalize a radically new orientation toward dependence. However, most of us have an experiential basis on which to build different attitudes toward this issue. In our closest relationships, most of us have experienced a level of trust that enables us to rely on one another in some deep sense. Most Americans seek such relationships with a few carefully chosen people. When we don't have such relationships, we ache in ways we have trouble naming.

For cultural reasons, dependence is a disquieting word for Westerners; for practical reasons, excessive independence is, too. Counterdependence and a cultural preoccupation with "doing your own thing" is a persistent problem for many Americans—achieving the appropriate level of independence is often as loaded and troublesome as dealing with feelings of dependence. The dichotomization forces upon us a kind of psychic Scylla and Charybdis. The either/or extremes interfere with our ability to perceive—and peacefully accept—reality. What is needed, conceptually, is a clearer notion of *inter*dependence that permits us to *preserve the best of independence and dependence without getting the worst of both*. The Japanese accomplish this through the concept of *wa*.[10] Technically, *wa* means group harmony. But its full meaning encompasses a range of English words—unity, cohesiveness, team spirit.[11] Westerners tend to experience *wa* as members of an athletic team or as close-knit social groups. We have all known such situations when everyone is in tune with the group spirit and effort is made to ensure that the aura of good feelings is maintained. This is *wa*.[12]

The Work Group

Concepts of self and attitudes toward interdependence play a vital role in the Japanese work group. The work group is the basic building block of Japanese organizations. Owing to the central importance of group efforts in their thinking, the Japanese are extremely sensitive to and concerned about group interactions and relationships. They regard group phenomena primarily in terms of morals and emotion rather than role and function.[13] Their view of groups is mostly closely analogous to that toward marital relationships in the West—and, interestingly, the Japanese recognize the kinds of problems and concerns in work relations that we focus on in marriage concerning trust, sharing, and commitment.[14] Like a Western marriage, the Japanese work group imposes task roles which are not always clearly delineated, tend to need revision, and require a constant investment of emotional capital.

The prime qualification of a Japanese leader is his acceptance by the group, and only part of that acceptance is founded on his professional merits. The group's harmony and spirit are the main concern.[15] Whereas in the West work group leaders tend to emphasize task and often neglect group maintenance activities, in Japan maintenance of a satisfied work group goes hand in hand with the role. Group members expect a lot from their leaders, for grave problems can arise if group maintenance is neglected (which is true of American groups, too, of course). The Japanese realize they are creating a potentially troublesome force when they establish a group. They know how easily group process can become dysfunctional. They are keenly aware of group maintenance demands. As a result, they manage groups with great care—care of the kind an American manager might invest in meeting his end-of-year profit goals. While a great many American firms have adopted "team approaches" in recent years, success has been mixed. The reason, we believe, is that American managers don't quite realize that what they are creating requires a lot of energy and attention from them to sustain.[16]

To the Japanese, the birth of a group entails many of the concerns and worries attending the birth of a child. Groups require stroking and nurture and attention. Group participation increases the burdens of the manager as well as the participants by requiring that extra time be put in at meetings, at thinking about issues, at making arguments skillfully, at attending to rituals, ceremonies, and relationships. Unless this investment is rewarded by improved options and increased power over outcomes, the result will be disillusionment and demoralization. The leader must balance carefully his use of arbitrary authority one moment with a readiness to be highly responsive the next.[17] Finally, the Japanese know that groups, as they increase in size beyond eight to ten people, have increasing difficulty in preserving personal and emotional connectedness. It is small wonder, in light of these considerations, that the Japanese invest as much as they do in groups, and that many Americans who dabble carelessly with groups do so with very mixed results indeed.

Because performance is valued less for its own sake than for the sake of the group, it is easier for each member to accede to the will of the majority. Even Japanese industrialists, while possibly as strongly motivated by profit and self-interest as any others, pursue self-interest *in the name of* the collective interest. Japanese organizational charts show only collective units, not individual positions or titles or names.[18] In identifying himself, a Japanese manager stresses his group identification rather than his personal job title or responsibilities. Loyalty to one's group is a most respected personal attribute—comparable to personal integrity in the West. The reality of everyday life is embodied in group routines and is reaffirmed through interactions with others.[19] Individuals whose advancement is blocked, who have low aspirations or work commitments, often respond to group social recognition and sanctions and thus remain bound to the group norms. Work groups provide social bonds of great importance; Japanese don't want to be left out. When workers retire, they rarely miss their work, but invariably they miss their group.[20] (Perhaps this is true of American retirees, too.)

Maintenance of a healthy work group requires steady personal contact. Typically, for every twenty-five hours spent at work, a Japanese spends one socializing after hours with his group.[21] After-hours activities go a long way toward mending conflicts that arise on the job. Japanese use social interaction much as Americans use complaining to colleagues. It heals on-the-job psychic injuries.

Such emphasis on group matters might seem more curious and odd than it does were it not for one important fact. There are increasing indications that the reality (not the myths) within many U.S. corporations corresponds quite closely to what we have just described.[22] Numerous studies indicate that middle managers spend one third to one half of their time in group activity, and top managers spend 60 percent. More surprisingly, many managers spend as much time on after-hours social contact as do their Japanese counterparts.[23] In short, many American managers live in a world that corresponds quite closely to that of the Japanese. The difference, primarily, is that we have a much more negative attitude toward it. Many Japanese managers are ambivalent about such matters too, and they complain about having to do it. But they almost all acknowledge that such activities are necessary, given human needs and organizational goals, and their culture affirms their providing nurturance to groups, just as it does to individuals.

We often disparage our involvement with groups as a weary task that *others* require. Our language to describe our involvement is itself revealing: "Group think," "hand holding," "breast feeding," "show and tell," "another goddamn awards dinner"—all expressions implying a low regard for the group maintenance role. Note that the disparagement is often stated in language that suggests others are immature, insecure, childish, dependent, or naive. Most of our pejorative descriptions of nurturing activities at work reveal that many male managers are uncomfortable and embarrassed at having to do what has traditionally been assigned to women in our culture. It is as if nurturance is for mothers, not fathers (an attitude that may have enhanced the parental push for children's independence in our culture). The traditional father sets goals and standards for his kids, and approves when they do well. But he doesn't offer much loving acceptance of his offspring whether they perform well or not. That relatively unconditional acceptance was the task traditionally reserved for mothers.

In this light, it may be worth noting that the introduction of more women into the ranks of management has been difficult for them as well as for males, partly because of women's traditional roles, and thus the resolution of dependence culturally prescribed for them. It seems to us that women were "taught" to accept more dependence in the past, and to aspire to interdependence at home. Recently, the many competent women coming into positions of corporate responsibility not only have the problem of freeing themselves from whatever dependent prescriptions still influence them, but also the problem that they often have a greater developed capacity for interdependence than do the men they work for and with. As they achieve middle management positions, they often experience the isolation that men's independence involves as particularly painful for them. In addition to freeing themselves from residual traditional dependency, they have to accept all too often the diminished relational satisfactions that their independent colleagues take for granted. That managerial women often seek and achieve a higher development of interdependence than do their male colleagues is thus not very satisfying for them. Male colleagues may view their willingness to exchange dependencies in a supportive relationship as culturally prohibited, threatening to sex role differentiation, a sexual come-on, or a potentially dissatisfying invitation for them to take care of another demanding dependent person. It is our guess that many younger women at the forefront of their gender's achievement of executive rank may well "burn out and drop out" as a result. If they are aware that they wish to exchange dependencies and nurturance in the context of valued ongoing relationships at work, and that they are rejected, they get the satisfactions neither of giving nor of taking. Our hunch is that they give, in fact, a lot more than they take. And *that* is what burns them out. They are expected to nurture, but not to expect nurturance in return. Perhaps it will occur to some readers, as it has to us, that the most important contribution many women might make to corporate life would be to role-model the forms of interdependence that many men need to learn. That may be a troublesome pill for many executives to swallow, but research on the inclusion of other "strangers" into companies suggests that those companies which include minorities are better managed in general than those which do not.[24] It appears that the inclusion of different "cultures" in a corporation widens its repertoire of behavior, which in turn makes it more effective generally (and not just in meeting affirmative action quotas). Whatever the case, it is our suggestion to younger female executives who sense their *need* for interdependence that they seek employment in those companies where more interdependence can be identified and, if possible, where it is explicitly honored to some degree. Later, with their technical and social and interpersonal skills more developed, and presumably their lives outside work more stable and mature, they might consider opportunities in settings less congenial.

Self-Restraint

In a culture in which group effectiveness is so prized, razzle-dazzle individual performances are discouraged. Success means success within the group. Not surprisingly, the Japanese have evolved a value system to reinforce individual behavior that is consonant with harmonious group functioning.

Most Americans have been exposed to the aesthetic of Japanese design.[25] There, we see a highly cultivated value discouraging phony contrivances and favoring naturalness.

Ostentatiousness and ornamentation are disdained as vulgar, while simplicity and understatement are esteemed as signs of sophistication. This Japanese taste for elegant simplicity extends far back in time and contrasts starkly with the continental tendencies toward opulence and complexity. Japanese architecture, for instance, is appreciated as much for the finish or texture of a pillar as for its overall design.

In a similar vein, modesty and self-restraint are highly valued in Japanese organizational life. While the Japanese may not conspicuously draw parallels between their aesthetics and their models for personal conduct, high value is placed on a style of behavior that is practical, devoid of frills and unassuming. We see this in the quality of Japanese prime ministers, whose style invariably is understated as compared to that of American presidents or Western European leaders. In baseball, as well, neither the spectacular batter nor the brilliant infielder is recognized as truly valuable until he acquires this capacity to blend into the harmonies of the team. There are no Reggie Jacksons. Great stock is placed in a person's acting as circumstances require, simply and without fuss. This helps explain the aforementioned behavior of the controllers and product managers at Matsushita—powerful members of the organization who intentionally played out their roles in the shadow of the division managers. Skillful managers, both East and West, recognize that nothing facilitates harmony, and thereby accomplishment, so much as not being regarded as a serious contender for power or credit. Those who adopt a low profile are often better able to accomplish things than are their more nakedly competitive colleagues. However, the Japanese value system which explicitly rewards this kind of behavior increases the likelihood of smooth internal organizational functioning.

Meetings: The Cultural Litmus Test

Culture asserts its invisible presence on patterns of day-to-day communications in Japanese as in American organizations. Its influence probably is nowhere more evident than in meetings. In the West, considerable effort goes into making meetings more efficient—shortening their duration, avoiding certain ones altogether. Meetings run against the grain of many deep-seated Western prejudices. Yet meetings persist; in the last analysis, they are the best known mechanism for efficient information sharing, for accomplishing collective problem solving and coordinated action.

We have referred to the fact that cultures differ in the degree to which they emphasize explicit communication and rationality. English-speaking cultures, in particular, attach importance to precision, to problem solving, to clear, logical presentation. They prize rational discourse. But too often "rationality" becomes an end in itself. Survivors of academic seminars know how readily intellectual imperialism can dominate capacities to listen and integrate new information creatively.

In much of the non-Western world, group discussion and decision making gets done without choosing sides; it is unusual for people to press their differences by magnifying them. Recall how Matsushita's managers viewed "conflict" as something requiring mutual adjustment, whereas at ITT it took the form of win–lose competitiveness.

Consider now the following scenario. A meeting has been under way for half an hour. Its ostensible purpose has become lost in an exchange of conflicting concerns and hidden agendas. A participant with marked needs for "air time" embarks on a lengthy exposition, taking what seems an inordinate amount of time to get to the point. You listen to your inner voice as much as you listen to him. For a while courtesy dictates attentiveness. This requires an expenditure of energy in the form of eye contact and facial expression of polite if not earnest interest. But as the exposition continues, your eye contact wavers—a prelude to your mind's disengaging and wandering off on its own. Alternatively, in an effort to minimize fatigue, your mind searches for shortcuts— some means to grasp whether the speaker is on the right track or not. Presently, he cites an example and you seize on it. You think you agree. The image is sufficiently ambiguous to allow you to interpret it in your own way. Your mind disengages again, taking comfort in the belief that it knows where the speaker is going. But a further example triggers disagreement, and your mind begins to contemplate a rebuttal.

Studies of the listening process in such situations reveal that we comprehend only 30 percent of what we hear.[26] The reason is that listening is so tiring. Most listeners are fully attentive only for the first few minutes of a presentation. Once they catch the drift, they partially tune out. Only when the speaker's voice and cadence indicate closure is near do they revive to interject a phrase or facial expression that is skillfully ambiguous enough to conceal how very little comprehension has taken place. And this process occurs dozens of times each day in the life of a typical executive.

While shortcuts to minimize listening fatigue are universal, cultures differ considerably in their recognition of the problem and in the ways they hinder or facilitate comprehension. A number of the cultural "filters" discussed in this chapter are pertinent here. For example, we mentioned cultural values about individuality. Westerners tend to believe that people should act "in character." One's character development is linked to abstract values: it is deemed a sign of maturity, for instance, to have a well-defined, separate sense of self. But what are the consequences of this Western tendency to differentiate self from others? For one, the "listening process" is impeded, for a sense of separation often is accompanied by a judgmental stance toward what the other is saying. The extent to which we "agree" or "disagree" with the other, and the extent to which that affirms or diminishes our sense of self, determines what we will hear and how we will respond to it.

The Japanese, by contrast, embrace a situational ethic, and practice "less-ego" listening. They hold "principle" in abeyance, regard themselves as one among others in the situation, and thus achieve an easy accommodation with the circumstances of the meeting and absorb ideas less evaluatively. In so doing, they allow a unique reality to evolve in each situation. This situational ethic enables the Japanese to air different views without falling into a duel of personalities. They discuss issues thoroughly. But once all perspectives have been expressed, they more willingly let a consensus decide.[27]

The difference between situation oriented behavior and individualistic behavior is crucial in determining how people will experience meetings. The Westerner's sense of self is consistently torn between loyalty to his own identity and deference to the group. A Japanese experiences such conflict, but to a lesser degree, and the distracting inner dialogue that can accompany group discussion is correspondingly diminished. Japanese cultural values reward those who promote harmonious exchange. Western cultural values do not always, although harmony is most often desired. We resist suppressing our individuality and often feel the need to score points in a win–lose game. Yet almost all of us have found ourselves in minority positions and, having pressed our views as forcefully as we could, have deferred to majority rule. The catch is that without cultural values to legitimize this behavior, we are left with the clammy feeling of "having sold out" or "lacked conviction" or argued "ineffectively" or "lost the game."

We are not suggesting that Americans abandon their sense of self and the responsibility associated with it and shift to "other-directedness," even if they could. But our ways of thinking and judging ourselves need to be broadened to accept the not infrequent good in "going along" with some outcomes not fully congenial to us. Success does not require group "chameleonism" in the service of harmony all the time. Even the Japanese express dissent in discreet ways. But they know when to go with the flow and do not judge themselves negatively in such circumstances.

Consider those Westerners we know who are highly effective in meetings. Odds are that their effectiveness stems from flexibility. Individuals who are *repeatedly* persuasive in meetings are rarely those who come armed with prepared speeches. Rather, they are individuals who can see other points of view and create compromises or new solutions, who can hold their views in suspension while permitting themselves to remain a part of the process —then intervene at the right point to guide the discussion to shore. They tend to choose words and images that *integrate* concerns in the group's thinking. The key is to find common ground and take others' points and use them creatively.

If you're trying to catch a runaway car, the worst strategy is to dig in your heels and grab for the door handle. The best approach is to run beside the car, try to get into the driver's seat, grab the steering wheel, apply the brake, and gradually bring the vehicle under control. Intervening in group discussions is no different. Those who move along with the flow tend to sense the best time to intervene and choose words and images that are in keeping with the group's thinking. Only rarely does one *have* to stop the flow forcibly and redirect it.

Costs and Benefits of Cohesion

There is a delicate line between the benefits of restraining one's preconceived notions and the dangers of surrendering to a process of "group think."[28] Group think occurs when the pressures for conformity overwhelm objective discussion. For example, group think can lead to a premature rush to agreement or to only *apparent* concurrence. Group think and the diminished exercise of self-expression may account in part for the dearth of inventions in Japan despite its industrial eminence. However, the most careful scrutiny of Matsushita does not reveal either a prevailing of defective decision making or excesses of group think.

Objective group decision making can be imperiled in two ways: (1) by the biases and prejudices of individuals who obstinately insist on *their* point of view and disrupt collective decision making, and (2) by group norms that suppress differing views even when such expressed differences would be constructive. Western cultures tend toward the first; perhaps Eastern ones tend toward the second. But, ironically, many major U.S. organizations suffer from both. One task of a manager running meetings is to avoid both extremes. And it takes considerable skill to limit the loudmouth while encouraging differences of opinion.

The Sempai–Kohai Relationship

Different assumptions about interdependence and reciprocal obligations substantially affect modern organizational life. As noted, the Japanese's particular concept of self fosters closer collaboration; his energies (deriving from a sense of obligation, interdependence, and belonging) appear to be more fruitfully employed as a force for cohesion in organizations. The keystone in this arch of interdependence is the *sempai–kohai* (senior–junior) relationship. Corresponding to the mentor–protégé relationship in the West, it is probably one of the most constructive forces for productive and harmonious working relationships in Japanese companies. The Japanese have made an institution of it.[29]

In contrast to the Japanese, Western organizations communicate on two levels. The most explicit communications are operational ones and encompass the substantive information essential to performing everyday activities. The second level is the "metamessage," concerning the process of how business is done. At ITT this metamessage was: "know your facts," "be confronting," "make your profit plan." At Matsushita it was: "meet your goals for society and the team." The metamessage encompasses guidelines about informal organizational rules (e.g., what waitress service may you legitimately ask your secretary to do?), knowledge of roles (e.g., do you call more senior people by first or last names?), and behavioral patterns (e.g., how is conflict handled?). These are largely communicated indirectly—by nonverbal signs of approval or disapproval and stories about the organization's history, mythology, and major actors. Each employee internalizes these messages to some degree. Through them he learns what is expected above and beyond the description of his job, what sanctions exist, what the clues of success and of failure are, and what kinds of behavior are apt to trigger what kinds of response.

It has been shown repeatedly that the higher one rises in a corporation, the more one's success depends on one's ability to read these process signals. At the entry level, *technical* skill is essential, and the newcomer's behavioral style needs only to indicate promise. At the middle level, *interpersonal* skill—at meetings, in getting things done with peers, in relating effectively with superiors and subordinates—plays an increasingly dominant role.[30] At this level more social skill, broadly defined, is required because of the relative lack of structure and job description and because the more senior the manager, the more he is apt to be managing other managers, not the technology itself. At the highest level neither interpersonal nor technical skills, in and of themselves, are sufficient. One must have and display a *style* that is consistent with what the organization thinks its leaders ought to be like.

When we learned to dance the foxtrot and the waltz, we were taught "technical" competence—put the right foot here, the left there, bring them together, shift weight, turn, and so on. And it took weeks of practice, playing the instructions over and over again in one's head, to master these movements. Today young people learn variations of disco dancing so complex that it would take hundreds of hours of observation to articulate the motions. But we don't attempt to learn such a complex skill by a focused cognitive process. Our intellect goes largely on "hold" in the face of that much complexity. We learn instead through unfocused attention—we absorb by watching the whole and imitating what we can.

Teaching a subordinate how to be effective in an organization—coaching a presentation for the proper balance of ambiguity and precision, negotiating for resources, getting one's ducks in a line before moving ahead with a program—all these things are at least as complicated as disco dancing. Yet many managers, steeped in a pert-chart mentality, try to break these activities down into intellectually comprehensible steps by charting them as in an army training manual. Yet you don't learn to wage war by studying a manual. You don't become an artist by painting someone else's dots. There are some complex human activities, and management is one of them, in which it is the aesthetic fit (i.e., the form and harmony among things) that matters most. Division and subdivision of tasks and intellectualizing and verbalizing will never accomplish the learning that experiencing, watching, feeling, sensing, and imitating will.

In Japanese organizations, the *sempai–kohai* relationship helps achieve this kind of learning. The Japanese focus on the relationship, whereas the West's boss–subordinate terminology tends to focus on each individual in his role. The Japanese unabashedly acknowledge that the *sempai–kohai* relationship is made up of emotional as well as functional ties and they harness both. Senior and junior are seen as inescapably linked; one's failure or success necessarily affects the other. The *sempai–kohai* relationship is not a hierarchical imperative to be endured, but something of mutual benefit—a force that binds.[31] One's *sempai* in Japan is usually outside of one's direct reporting relationships. In this respect, one's mentor is like an organizational "godfather." However, the pattern of behavior is so deeply embedded that it influences the manner in which direct reporting boss–subordinate relationships are conducted. They are generally closer and more supportive than in the West.

The ground rules of the boss–subordinate relationship do not always oblige the Japanese manager to act as if he is "in command." He is not called on to sum up all meetings in a masterly way, to be on top of every issue, or to be forever "exercising leadership." On the contrary, he is more likely to reveal his weaknesses and idiosyncrasies to his subordinates. (In fact, many Japanese managers feel that by revealing their vulnerabilities they are better able to enlist assistance.) Contrast this to subordinates in the West, who often have to discern a superior's weakness through a veneer of pseudocompetence. We are often inhibited from directly offering to help a boss because we are supposed to accept the "superior" image he is trying so hard to portray.

A crucial difference between East and West is that the Japanese boss reveals what goes on behind the persona. By spotting what his subordinate's strengths are and by revealing his own deficiencies, he draws on the subordinate in a way that benefits both.

When we are counterintuitive—when we share what our culture tells us to hide—not only are we able to be more open and less guarded and defensive, but both parties are able to help each other more and both are more likely to grow. Bosses grow because the problem area is on the table where it can be addressed directly. Subordinates grow because they are accepted into a kind of mentor–protégé relationship which relies on their strengths and enables them to learn how to handle their own deficiencies by observing how the boss compensates for his.

At first glance, such a working relationship may seem to many the most perplexing and foreign of the Eastern conventions introduced so far. In fact, one helpful way that Westerners can envision what such relationships are like is to reflect on the relationship between boss and secretary.[32] While the boss–secretary relationship is different in important respects, it is characterized by strong mutual dependence and reciprocal loyalty. The fates of boss and secretary are often bound together and acknowledged to be so. Managers from the middle levels up frequently take their secretaries with them when promoted. The status of the secretary derives from the status of her boss, and she derives her power indirectly through control of his calendar, his reading pile, and his priority setting, and as a conduit to office gossip. Like the *kohai,* the secretary is uniquely privileged in knowing the boss' idiosyncrasies and foibles. One's secretary is often one's lone outpost of the personal in an otherwise largely impersonal organizational world.

Clearly, the boss–secretary analogy is an imperfect one. The Japanese *kohai,* unlike a secretary, is expected one day to take his place in management. Further, the *kohai* has more legitimacy in making substantive contributions, whereas secretaries, while they may compose a meeting's agenda, rarely can reveal that they have done so without reflecting on their boss' competence. But these differences aside, what enables the boss–secretary relationship to thrive are factors similar to those underlying the *sempai–kohai* system: (1) status is firmly defined; (2) the senior and junior in the relationship are not in competition with one another; and (3) their fates are bound together.

Ironically, the boss–secretary relationship, as we know it, does not exist in Japan. There, managers rely on a clerical pool and the interaction between managers and clerical personnel is much more transactional. A Japanese manager comments: "You

Americans overload the boss–secretary relationship with all the caring and mutual help that is denied in your boss-to-subordinate and peer relationships. In Japan the reverse is true. We meet our emotional needs and develop our strongest ties with colleagues within the professional ranks. We don't need to burden the clerical people with that." [33]

Extensive research into the nature of boss–subordinate relations in the West by Harvard's John Gabarro reveals that an American boss wants to know three things about those who would work for him: (1) can they be trusted?; (2) are they competent?; and (3) are they consistent, or dependable? Note that the first and third concerns extend beyond task to assessments involving the chemistry of the relationship itself. The subordinate likewise weighs the clues that provide him with data on his boss: (1) does he have integrity?; (2) is he competent?; (3) is he open?—does he tell subordinates what they need to know in order to get the job done? As before, personal chemistry is a major factor. [34]

In Japan, the *sempai* (senior) expects the *kohai* (junior) to understand *him*. If the *sempai* doesn't always perform well, the *kohai* is expected to compensate for him and not to judge him except as a total human being. The *sempai*, in turn, is expected to display a wider breadth of understanding than normally exists in Western enterprises. These expectations lead to more humane and nurturing hierarchical relationships.

There is a fine line, of course, between knowing how subordinates are feeling and becoming engaged as a counseling psychologist. But to make too much of this dichotomy misses the point. Americans, every day, in all sorts of situations, tread the fine line between concern and nosiness, between propriety and indiscretion. Managers do find ways of staying in touch with their employees' emotional well-being without becoming preoccupied with this issue. When we attempt to separate feelings from facts, we impose a distinction that is misleading. In almost all matters of consequence in organizations, feelings are as important as facts— if not in making decisions, surely in securing wholehearted implementation of them.

These observations apply quite directly to the *sempai*'s role in giving feedback. When it's positive, subordinates want it to be very clear. When it's negative, although they may need it, they are unlikely to want to hear it. The senior thus has to decide if the cost of a subordinate's not getting feedback and not changing is apt to hurt him later on. Only knowledge of the person and his emotional construction enables the *sempai* to package and time his feedback in the most helpful way.

Most Americans can recall situations in which boss–subordinate relations complicated organizational life, in which the subordinate experienced the frustration of seeking feedback from a boss who was not forthcoming, of needing to know where he stood vis-à-vis the boss' expectation and his own performance. Because Western culture emphasizes primarily the *task* dimension of the boss–subordinate relationship, we downplay relevant interpersonal data. It's like attempting to drive a car without depth perception. That collisions occur would not surprise us. Human beings rarely engage in the complex professional assignments of modern organizations without some emotional spillover. Fear, hope, anxiety, exhaustion—all play into the calculus of work. Attempting to mask or deny emotional relations as an inescapable part of hierarchical relations is like trying to remove wetness from water.

Managing Upward

Of the mass of material written on superior–subordinate relations in the West, virtually all tends to look at the subject in terms of what managers do wrong, could do differently, and should do better. The topic is invariably treated from the standpoint of the managers, who do (or should do) the managing. When we read books on management, we tend to consider how to apply new ideas to the domain under our control. Many books on management adopt this top-down view and point out how organizations create a climate that helps or hinders employees in carrying out their roles. The prevailing assumption is one of influence flowing downward.

Nevertheless, many readers will readily agree that a large part of a manager's job is managing upward. Clearly, communication is a two-way street; for superior and subordinate to work effectively, communication must flow both ways. And as communication flows, so does influence. Ironically, so pervasive is our assumption that superiors should do the influencing, leading, and decision making, that subordinates, where they have the privilege of guiding their bosses, often feel resentment that *they* are not the boss. The reason is that this major and often very time-consuming function of the subordinate goes largely unrecognized. Subordinates find themselves living out a role in shadow governance and often doing so with vague irritation. Rarely do they obtain legitimacy and therefore fulfillment for their supportive efforts, even though by Eastern standards such efforts are openly valued as intrinsic to the relationship's success.

Because these support activities are exercises of the left hand, few managers stop to consider how the process really works. Managing from the top down, we operate with full legitimacy. All of the instruments of leadership are at our disposal—the chain of command, deeply ingrained beliefs about authority, and a variety of symbols, such as carpets, corner offices, and other perquisites. When one manages upward, none of these clear and unambiguous symbols pertains. Yet each day in thousands of offices subordinates do succeed in managing their bosses through indirect means.[35]

Recent surveys in the United States have concluded that middle managers regard two out of three of their bosses as inadequate.[36] The most common failings: "spotlighter," "underdelegator," "crisis maker," "overcontroller," and "stoic." How does one deal with such bosses? If a stoic boss doesn't tell us where we stand, we seize on the organization's "management objectives" to negotiate specific criteria for next year's performance rating so we can monitor our performance accordingly. If the boss is a crisis maker, we establish lateral relationships that send branches upward so we can determine whether the crises are real or manufactured. We respond to overcontrol by working out of the office a lot, by magnifying procedural obstacles, by seizing opportunities to advertise that the job will get done if the boss just assigns it and stays away. Managing upward relies on informal relationships, timing, exploiting ambiguity, and implicit communication. And the irony of it all is that these most subtle skills must be learned and mastered by younger managers who not only lack education and directed experience in benign guerilla warfare but are further misguided by management myths which contribute to false expectations and a misleading perception of reality.

Applications to the United States

The tragedy in many corporations in America is that conditions are often unsupportive of constructive mentor–protégé relationships or, worse, that the deck is significantly stacked against them. The individual orientation of Western culture encourages people to look out for themselves, stay separate, and regard boss–subordinate relationships as primarily task oriented.

Consider this example: Ron had worked for William in the controller's area. William had been an excellent mentor and when he was promoted after eighteen months, both acknowledged that their working together had been a satisfying and productive experience. Several years later, William asked Ron to work for him again—this time as his assistant in directing the Marketing Division. William expected to be at the job for another six months and noted that "if they played their cards right" Ron would be his successor.

Two weeks after Ron arrived on the job, William was suddenly promoted to a new position. William's successor brought none of his predecessor's personal interest in Ron to the position. Exacerbating matters, he was less competent technically and apparently threatened by having William's man working as his next in command. On the surface, it was just a "routine transfer." But, for Ron, the experience taught a hard lesson about American organizational life. "I trusted William and I trusted the organization to think about things like relationships between people. But the reality was that no one pays attention to those things. Relationships in organizations exist like illicit love affairs; when the going gets tough they are not recognized as legitimate. In trusting William, I left a job I would have preferred to remain in. I inherited his successor, who, at best, had difficulty relating to me and, at worst, was scared enough to injure my credibility in order to advance his own. To make matters worse, William (perhaps feeling responsible for the predicament he left behind) has distanced himself from me. I guess I've learned to discount personal attachments here— but the sad part is that this cuts people off from one another. I'm more cautious and less trusting than I was before."[37]

Ron's example illuminates an everyday occurrence: job rotation tears apart relational ties. The moral is not, of course, to stop moving people. Nor is it to overprotect cliques by never separating their members. As in most things we've discussed, it's not an either/or. What is called for is sensitivity to the issue—on a case-by-case basis. When the inevitable job rotations occur, people need ways of staying tied to one another, if possible, and ways of mourning their losses to whatever degree they exist.

Giving legitimacy to the mentor–protégé relationship would do a lot for many Western organizations. For example, if William had felt it was legitimate to remain a mentor to Ron, that alone would have helped Ron weather a tough new situation. Had the organization encouraged "sponsors" or "godfathers" higher up in the system, that too would have provided Ron with a steadying hand from above during the period when his day-to-day relationships were shifting beneath him.

Recognition: The Lever of Change

Three forms of reward exist in most companies: *remuneration, promotion,* and *recognition.* Of the three, the first two are less flexible than the third in the everyday scheme of things. Contrary to myth, most bosses have limited discretion in assigning dollar rewards. Job grading systems, time in grade, and inflation guidelines compound the constraints. Similarly, promotions occur only after considerable lengths of time. Thus, wage hikes and promotions are not particularly accessible as rewards in the *daily* ebbs and flows of organizational life. Moreover, the effect of such rewards is well understood to be quite short. More likely than not, recognition is the most available and effective form of ongoing positive reinforcement. It is noticed and sought after on a daily basis. In fact, in a recent survey of several thousand American managers, 49 percent indicated that recognition for what they were doing was their *most* important reward (since most managers accept the relative infrequency of more tangible rewards and expect they will be forthcoming to an acceptable extent). It is thus useful to enrich our understanding of recognition and the role it plays.

Celebrity and Reputation

We are all acquainted with "celebrity"—the big prize that organizational contestants vie for. "BLT" is the celebrity sandwich: "bright lights and trumpets," that is. And when you achieve the "BLT" kind of celebrity, everybody knows about it. And the resulting fame can contribute to one's long-term image, if tended carefully.

But there is a second possibility, which is "reputation." Reputation is acquired gradually and is more enduring. In its positive form, it accrues from being trustworthy, having skill at making things happen, and being able to achieve goals through people. Its negative form is being regarded as one who uses people, cuts corners, is out for one's self . . . a hustler. The rewards of positive reputation are realized in a variety of ways. Having our opinion sought communicates respect; being invited to participate in a significant meeting, being trusted with confidential information, being thanked for the role played behind the scenes are ways which people use to tell us we have built a reputation.

Reputation plays an important role in organizations that operate smoothly. Problems arise when organizations overemphasize public and material incentives, which rivet attention on celebrity and undermine regard for reputation. The result is a "team" with everybody trying to grab the ball and nobody blocking. Such teams seldom win consistently.

Celebrity and its attending monetary rewards lack staying power. The length of time that a bonus pleases is short. Every year you've got to get another hit, another "sweepstakes" performance that wins the trip to Bermuda. But after six trips you usually want something else. If not, you are regarded by others as amusingly immature.

Successful managers in a healthy organization tend to focus on and acquire celebrity early in their careers. Extrinsic rewards, and growing maturity, build confidence and self-esteem. Later, most executives reduce their need for celebrity and replace it with a desire for reputation. Increasingly, they want to be valued for wisdom, reliability, a good track record, and trustworthiness. At the same time, they become willing to relinquish celebrity to those junior to them, indeed to provide it to them.

Most people in organizations develop uncanny sensitivities to what's going on in the recognition game, so that, paradoxically, in giving up celebrity they gain increased power to change things. You expand your reputation by sharing celebrity. People are generally willing to change if they receive something they want in return—and celebrity is one of the most available rewards that can be given to those who still need it.

A danger of celebrity is that some people get addicted to it —individuals whose overt drive for recognition is obsessive. The symptoms are preoccupation with celebrity at the expense of reputation, seizing on another's error as a vehicle for self-aggrandizement, keeping too many options open simultaneously for fear of missing out on the "big one." Many managers so afflicted tend to remain organizationally immature. They have to have celebrity, and in their drive to get it they often deprive subordinates of what they need for their own development.

To be sure, for some people in some occupations, these generalizations do not hold. Successful politicians have to excel at establishing both celebrity and reputation. (The tawdry image of politicians may imply that it is difficult to pursue both of these things simultaneously and come across as authentic.) Einstein had both celebrity and reputation, but his reputation came first and as the result of long labors. He did not seek celebrity. *It* found *him*. And he always viewed his celebrity as would an amused spectator.

Certain kinds of temporary organizations, especially political campaign ones, tend to emphasize celebrity. Perhaps this is because there is no "tomorrow," no time frame in which reputation will pay off. Celebrity is like speculating in commodities, whereas reputation is like cultivating an apple tree. It takes years to bear fruit and needs constant care to keep doing so. It is not accidental that job-hoppers generally value celebrity over reputation. Reputation is valuable where a long-term relationship is presumed to exist.

Credit Transactions

There are few problems that vex younger American managers more than the dilemma of how to advance the boss' credibility while retaining their own. This is made harder in a society that attaches great weight to what is plainly visible and that is not attuned to thinking very much about what goes on backstage. Borrowing from the Japanese again, their notion of what subordinates do for their seniors is different from ours. On the one hand, they expect a subordinate to assist his senior in such a way that he leaves to his boss all credit for outward appearances. On the other hand, it is wholly understood that whatever a boss achieves is the result of the subordinate's efforts and support backstage. The Japanese simply can't imagine giving sole credit to the person in the spotlight. Think how different American organizational life would be if this more complete perception of where credit belongs were widely accepted.

Joe's boss was new to his job. The senior executive conference had been scheduled months before. As the deadline approached, Joe found himself taking more and more responsibility for the event, while his boss was engaged in other matters. Joe selected the setting, established the agenda, wrote the speeches, and spent weeks preparing the presentation materials. A day before the meeting his boss was briefed. The latter, unsure of his standing with the senior executives attending the conference, made clear that he would run the show. Joe moved to backstage, the boss gave "his" speech, the agenda flowed, and the conference came off without a hitch. The boss got the credit; Joe appeared to be a functionary who saw to the housekeeping. At first glance, the spotlight-hogging boss seems the villain. Or is he, too, the victim of a culture that pays too much attention to the explicit and ignores what goes on behind the scenes? For the boss knows that he got credit for what he didn't do. That may make him feel more insecure, guilty, and defensive.

The biggest weakness of organizational relationships in the West is not coming to grips with what makes superior–subordinate relationships tick. The imperative of success seems to be: If you are not seen to do it alone, you don't get credit for it. And this axiom, which motivates millions of actions each day, produces an equal number of incidents of frustration, hurt feelings, and petty retaliation. The value of the Japanese word *hosa*, which means "assist," is that it constantly reminds Japanese managers that, for every actor on the stage, others are working behind the scenes. The playwright, the set designer, the wardrobe lady, all get credit. It establishes a basis for understanding that those who labor like Joe do not do so without recognition.

The Montessori Method of Management [38]

One of the major departures in education in this century was a shift of focus from teaching to learning. Maria Montessori, an Italian educator working in Holland, was the first to advocate this point of view. She demonstrated that schools were designed to ease the burden of teaching at the expense of learning. She embarked on an inquiry that led to a number of discoveries about how people learn: First, images are better than words. If a learner can see, feel, touch—in short, bring all five senses to bear on the acquisition of knowledge—learning is increased. Second, showing is better than telling. Third, too much instruction is worse than too little. Fourth, when the stakes get too great and anxiety is high, learners tend to avoid experimentation and openness to new experiences and revert to previous success behavior. Finally, positive reinforcement of what is done right is far more effective than sanctions when things are done wrong. [39]

Montessori's insights apply to management as well. How often today do we find managers whose handling of their jobs facilitates "management" at the expense of outcomes? Systems are put in place to spare managers from dealing with problems, but they diminish what subordinates can learn and contribute. Guidelines for time management are enforced ruthlessly; iron-clad calendars and iron-willed secretaries police their bosses from interruption—and accessibility. The "case method" of learning, so amply proven as highly effective for the kind of skills required in management, is ignored in the interest of "making the manager's job easier." But what of "getting the job done"? You can't delegate mentoring to the Personnel Department.

Peter Drucker observed that bosses never realize that their job is to enable subordinates to learn how to do theirs. [40] Bosses make the wrong demands of subordinates—by structuring the relationship to "test" them rather than to help them do their jobs. Such bosses are like teachers who kill creative spirit in their students by insisting on blind recitation, the endless naming of things, impersonal rationality.

The Montessori method of management doesn't entail the intense cultivation of interdependence we have depicted in Japanese firms, and especially in Matsushita's training philosophy. But there are a number of things U.S. firms can do to utilize the constructive potential of interdependence rather than forever tearing it apart. For one, rotating people less often (every three years instead of every eighteen months) helps preserve emotional ties. (It also keeps managers around long enough to permit accountability for what was accomplished in their tenure.) Another is simply to encourage managers to coach their subordinates, to take them to lunch, to bring their juniors along to meetings and presentations where the junior can see them in action, to talk out problems. In general, the boss needs to select opportunities to move from the "persona" to the "person" in settings in which formal role behavior is not demanded. As our earlier disco dancing analogy suggests, role modeling is a most powerful teacher.

One of the most effective instruments for coaching and mentoring (and vastly underutilized) is the "role rehearsal." In it, the boss chooses a problem situation. The subordinate assumes the role of one party to the problem, and the boss asks him to role-play how he would deal with it. The value of this approach is that, rather than communicating in vague abstractions, boss and subordinate are coming to grips with something which might actually happen. By reversing roles with the subordinate, the boss can communicate to him how he himself would handle the situation. Above all, the role rehearsal establishes a give and take in coaching/mentoring. It avoids the stilted and abstract communication that characterizes many efforts by bosses to "teach" their subordinates how to do things. For much of what we really do we are embarrassed to say out loud, although we are more willing to have it seen.

According to Jerome Bruner, one of the strongest motives for learning is a deep need to respond to others and operate jointly with them toward objectives. Role modeling enables subordinates to *see* what the bosses' concept of management really is (rather than being told what the boss *says* it is). If accompanied by post facto discussions and feedback sessions, role modeling as a means of developing younger managers is unsurpassed in effectiveness. Learning flourishes when trust is established and risk levels are lowered, when it is legitimate to ask questions and expose the ignorance of both parties.

An enormous potential source of energy—for good, for evil, for apathy or advancement—exists in the interdependencies that modern organizations create. These can be ignored, extinguished, or managed. Why not harness them to productive use?

In this chapter we have explored some of the ways in which American fears of dependency and myths of independence contribute to less effective organizational functioning. The secret weapon that Japanese culture permits and encourages managers to use, interdependence, gives them significant organizational advantages. This is so because interdependence quite simply is a more appropriate response to the facts of corporate life, and to the needs and aspirations of the people who live there.

It can be said that Harold Geneen's overemphasis on his own independence too often left others captured within such constraints that they were unable to develop the kind of skills they would need when he retired. Such subordinates cannot replace the leader when that time comes. When subordinates can't grow, institutions do not develop long-term viability. Without good mentors, the next generation doesn't mature well.

The ubiquitous problems raised in all cultures by specialized work, hierarchy (i.e., what organizations need), and reward systems (i.e., what individuals need) are better met in those societies that value interdependence as a goal. Moreover, the derivative problems of superior–subordinate relationships, cooperation versus competition, and short-run *and* long-term focus (the resolution of which is central to success for organizations and individuals) are significantly reduced where interdependence is achieved. The Japanese, thus, have still another important cultural advantage in our commercial competition.

When we add this advantage to that considered earlier (resulting from their response to ambiguity, uncertainty, and imperfection), we get a keener sense of just how deep our cultural and managerial disadvantages go. And how difficult it will be to improve our position. For a good part of our difficulty lies in our views of the nature of reality, of relationships, of self, and of our prescribed roles. Our perceptions about how things actually are and our assumptions about how things ought to be are both seriously dysfunctional for organizational life and success. Our feelings are aroused whenever our assumptions or our perceptions are challenged, because these views affect our concept of self, which we do all we can to protect, maintain, and enhance. When that "self" is supported significantly by all the force of history, culture, and society, is extolled in legend and myth and popular culture, is the basis for our ideologies, political system, and dreams for ourselves—we can see the wisdom of Pogo's conclusion, "We have met the enemy, and they is us."

Happily, a good many committed, inventive, pragmatic U.S. executives have already gone a long way toward finding more effective American ways of managing "like the Japanese" in this country. We will turn next to exploring what they have to teach us.

Chapter Six

Bridging the Differences

WE HAVE seen how much of our problem as managers stems from
our culture's emphasis upon independence as the most valued way
of resolving the problem of dependency. And we considered how
our culture's coordinate overemphasis upon the separate, self-sufficient individual confounds much of our managerial behavior. In
this chapter we will begin by considering a particular style of independence that is valued in our corporate subculture. For the
"separate" individual in corporate life the concern with power is
acute, since he is on his own and must protect and advance himself
without "depending" on others. This leads to open and frequently
crude displays of power that rival the animal kingdom. It also
leads often to a constant expression of competitive aggression,
which has become a valued style of behavior among many businessmen. Buttressing the direct displays of power and expressions of aggression is a highly developed analytical skill. Originally
based upon the understandable value attached to logical reasoning, it is often carried to such extremes that it is patently *un-*

reasonable if frequently still "logical," in the narrow sense of that word.

Then we will turn to examining an American manager who in large part avoided the pitfalls of our general managerial assumptions. Ed Carlson at United Airlines will help us see an alternative way of proceeding, and will permit us to examine alternative styles and skills that would not seem too alien to many American managers and that are quite familiar to the Japanese. We should add that a number of managers in a variety of companies would serve equally as illustrations of an alternative approach to management (Boeing, IBM, Delta Airlines, and 3M come to mind). The point is that, while we have selected Carlson, he is by no means unique, and many well-managed firms parallel his example.

Harold Geneen has become one important archetype of the successful American manager. He was aggressive, competitive, and forceful, downright threatening, hard, and decisive. Nothing soft or yielding or dependent or (God forbid) "female" about him. That he remains such a respected executive and is often used to support arguments for similar behavior is significant. Geneen represents in high relief a modern version of a historical approach to management. He is Mr. Theory X^2, if you will. And for many executives, just calling him to mind is satisfying. *Imagine* having that much power, control, intellectual ability, skill, and getting those bottom-line results! It needs to be admitted that most of us at times wish for that kind of impact. Such wishes are probably a residue of the powerlessness of childhood, and a recognition of the complex limitations we most often are forced to accept as adults. Occasional fantasies about omnipotence are not necessarily harmful. Trying to act them out consistently, in our view, usually is harmful.

Nonetheless, the archetype persists, and certain firms are famous for maintaining it. One company's senior officer states: "One dares not talk soft in the board room. If you're going to bring up a problem, you damn well better have a solution. Intuitive and feeling statements are pretty much out of place." [1]

Tough talk and tough action are the stuff of management style in a great many American firms. A manager's capacity to face down challenges at meetings, assault others' positions analytically, roast subordinates for substandard performance, and, above all, fire people can positively affect his image. Too frequently in

America these actions become executive puberty rites, complicating relationships that are, at best, already complicated enough.

Harvard's Michael Maccoby, after extensive interviews with 250 managers, concluded that "many executives believe that developing a style which encompassed compassion and empathy would bring them into conflict with corporate goals. . . . One was flabbergasted," he wrote, "by the very idea of sensing his subordinates' feelings and developing an ear that listens. 'If I let myself feel their problems,' he said, 'I'd never get anything done. It would be impossible to deal with people.' "[2] Belief systems are usually in part functional. Sometimes they help us rationalize things that are hard to do. Sometimes they protect us from too much understanding or feeling. One motivating force behind such styles of management may be precisely that they diminish the discomfort of some of the most emotionally troublesome aspects of managerial activity. Highly paid executives frequently operate near the critical point in terms of their tension and frustration levels. When anger or hostility is vented upon them, there is often little reservoir to absorb it. And because internalizing the anger exacts a personal cost, the expedient course is to pass it on. Instead of one person's feeling angry about a problem, a half dozen get afflicted. The energy consumed in interpersonal friction might have been channeled more productively into solving the problem.

Fortune recently listed the "ten toughest managers" and the article's avowed purpose was to select the CEO who could take Geneen's legendary place.[3] Just good journalistic fun? Perhaps. But *Fortune* knows what many executives want to read, and we think many would act even more like Geneen if they could. And while they may not be able to do so, it is apparently satisfying to read of contenders for his black belt much as it is for the sedentary to watch bone-crunching football on television. Something deep inside, something primitive and barely restrained by the cerebral cortex, seems relieved by vicarious violence acted out within rules in a win–lose game of short duration. The problem occurs when this is transferred to organizational life where it does not fit with people weighing less than 235 pounds, and where the "game" is not of short duration and where the "losers" are part of one's own team.

Power, Aggression, and Analysis

American assumptions about power are important in shaping managerial style. One such assumption is that an executive needs to get all the power he can, needs to use it openly, even blatantly, to keep it, and should not act in any way that reduces his capacity to impact others directly. "Once a superior surrenders his will and tries to give his responsibility to his subordinate," says one management expert, "he cannot seem to take the power back. . . . He is forced to be a bystander helplessly viewing the ensuing disaster."[4] Another echoes this theme: " (Senior executives who) play down their authority . . . fail sooner or later. . . . [h]is subordinates join in gleefully by stripping his status and authority to the point where he becomes immobilized."[5]

It is worthwhile to examine these statements carefully. They have the value of unusual directness in stating a common theme in managerial literature and belief. First of all, note the language. If one "surrenders his will," "tries to give his responsibility," "plays down authority," then dire things happen. Of course. Who would suggest that any adult do any of these things? No executive in his or her right mind would be so inclined. But "surrender" or "give away" are emotionally laden verbs that are likely to repell anyone acculturated to the American way. To compound the emotional charge, these warnings have one losing one's "will," "responsibility," "power," "status," and "authority." The very idea is frightening.

Then the statements warn anyone so stupid that the additional costs are that one can't get "power back" and is "forced to be a bystander," "helplessly viewing" what is sure to be an "ensuing disaster." One will be "immobilized" as one's subordinates "gleefully strip" one. "Failure" is sure. Telling an American executive that he is going to be "forced," "helpless," "stripped," "immobilized" sounds suspiciously like the humiliating and terrifying experience of an abused child, convict, prisoner of war, or attacked woman. Good Lord. No wonder, with advice like that, executives search for even more ways to maintain obvious chest-pounding dominance over others. The alternative sounds remarkably like personal abuse of the worst kind.

It is illuminating to contrast these admittedly extreme (but far from rare) statements about power with the attitudes revealed in our study of Matsushita. The Japanese manager, while no less aware of power than his American counterpart, isn't as preoccupied with his own personal power or as fearful about "losing" some of it. Because his power is an outcome of his prior accomplishment, his current position, his age (i.e., his experience in lifetime employment in one company), and, above all, *in his network of relationships,* the Japanese manager is not particularly fearful that sharing his power with others will undermine him, and subject him to humiliating dependence. The sources of his power are multiple. His American counterpart in many firms has mostly his last accomplishment in his current position to sustain him, and the resulting insecurity drives him to protect himself against negative judgments from above, aside, and below. "What have you done for me lately" is the rueful reminder such executives hear ringing in their ears. It is not surprising that in organizations where top executives subscribe to the power assumptions revealed in the quotes above, that each level of management often alternates between beating and being beaten, from fear to anger—a kind of "managerial S&M." And it is not surprising that the result is an organization where most of the managers down the line look and act like adults who have suffered child abuse. They grow up all too often to repeat the behavior of their parents, alternating with periods in which they are victims fearful of asserting their rightful authority.

Hundreds of studies have been conducted in the United States into how the exercise of power affects leadership competence. While the findings fill volumes, the consistent picture of the effective leader is one who adopts the style of a "superfollower," who serves with his followers' blessing and consent, and who is able to inspire because he is first able to respond to their needs and concerns. Power, in this context, means the ability to get things done, to mobilize resources, and to draw on what is necessary to accomplish goals. Power is thus more akin to "mastery" than to "domination" or "control."[6] These findings contradict the earlier quotes which struck such a fearful tone. Contrary to myth, people who use power best use it directly only as necessary to get the job done. They do not worry much about it as an end in itself.

Interestingly, the nature of competition for senior management jobs in Japanese companies induces this kind of behavior. In Japanese companies, competition among managers becomes fierce at about age forty-five. There is nothing comparable in U.S. firms, although it is something like the competition to become a general or an admiral in the U.S. military. At this age, it is essential to position yourself to become a division general manager, then director, managing director, and onward to the board. Each promotion becomes more difficult, and if you do not make it, as in the U.S. military, you retire. Substantive contributions to company goals are important, but "political" power, maintaining the loyalty of those you have mentored, and being skilled at interpersonal relations are essential. In short, Japanese managers are "unaggressive" and low key (in our view) not solely because they chose that style, but in part because the nature of the competition to become a top manager requires it.

Chester Barnard once argued that employees delegate upward to management the responsibility for organizational decisions, and in so doing make legitimate the need of those above to command those below—providing the commands do not greatly exceed the leader's mandate.[7] (In case of emergencies, those below expect those above to take whatever actions are necessary to protect the whole and, while ambivalent about it, tend to accept such "excess" as necessary or at least useful.)

A vice president of one of the largest American corporations said, "I'm feeling like hell, that's why I look like hell! [My CEO] had me in this morning, and he ranted and raved and stomped around, and banged his desk, and called me a stupid son-of-a-bitch, and threatened to reduce my bonus, and told me the investment he had made in my project was worthless and . . . he said I belonged as a *schoolteacher* someplace. *God.* I'll be glad to get the hell out of here (referring to his upcoming retirement) and once I do I hope I never see that madman again." His secretary told one of us that afternoon, "I'm glad he had you to unload on. It saved all of us another bad afternoon."[8]

A retired conglomerate president stated: "The danger starts as soon as you become a district manager. You have men working for you and you have a boss above. You're caught in a squeeze. . . . You have guys working for you who are shooting for your job. Everybody says, 'The test of the true executive is that you have men working for you who can replace you, so that you can move up.' That's a lot of baloney. The manager is afraid of the bright young guy coming up. Fear is always prevalent in corporate structures."[9]

Lending support to these comments is a recent American

Management Association survey of 2,200 managers: One third of those polled felt their subordinates wanted their job and ranked "envy" as the biggest cause of their problems. We can appreciate their fear better when we recall that envy is one of the seven deadly sins, which involves wanting what someone else has, assuming you can't get it for one reason or another, and thus attempting to *bring the other down* to your level. Viewing power in primitive ways encourages primitive feelings and behavior, which in turn, when honored as appropriate, and respected as a sign of strength, reinforces in corporate life a macho style of management that is a major cause of our problems.

Ed Carlson's Teamwork

Ed Carlson's managerial methods at United Airlines differed dramatically from those of Harold Geneen at ITT. As we have seen, Geneen's careful system of checks and balances was founded on his scheme of multiple channels of information—no single individual was trusted to provide an "unshakeable fact." Carlson's teamwork approach, like Matsushita's, counted heavily on the trustworthiness of his managers' motives, actions, and information. In Carlson's view, managers could and would, under the "right set of circumstances," behave in the best short- and long-term interests of the company. In accordance with this theme, Carlson focused on *initiative*, forever pushing responsibility and accountability out toward those closest to the problem and the information relating to it. Whereas Geneen's system was concerned with "hard copy" *control*, with the flows of communications reports, and with decisions emanating from or near the chief executive officer, Carlson relied primarily on social control as far from him as possible. Finally, while at ITT the paramount concern was bottom-line financial *results*, Carlson sought multiple goals, both results and the satisfaction and development of the *people* who produced them.

To be sure, growing a multinational conglomerate and welding it together is far different from rejuvenating an ailing, overcentralized airline. The key business factors to which each enterprise had to attend were at least as relevant in determining the appropriateness of the manager's method as was his managerial style in determining his organization's ultimate success. Still, UAL, Inc., is not child's play. With 65,000 employees, the firm is heavily diversified into hotel chains and food service businesses in addition to its core airline activity. In 1970, Carlson took command as chairman and CEO of United Air Lines and its holding company UAL, Inc. By 1976, when he brought in Richard Ferris to take over as CEO of the airline, total revenues were $2.9 billion.[10] Carlson has remained as chairman and CEO of UAL, Inc., until the present.

When Carlson was called to the rescue at United Airlines, the company was about to close its books on a $46 million annual loss, the biggest in its forty-six-year history. The company was losing market share; for instance, its flights to and from Hawaii were being decimated by competition. The firm had 47,000 full-time employees on its payroll, 18 percent of them administrative, and some 380 jets flying more than 1.2 million air miles each day over a 19,300-mile system.[11]

Under Carlson's predecessor, the mammoth system had become a staggering bureaucracy. Decisions were made from the top of a long vertical chain of command. Employees down in the ranks were often discouraged from making suggestions. "The company was very centralized," recalls a former customer service manager in Boston. "It took so long to justify something that by the time you could get it justified, you didn't need it any more."[12] These kinds of experiences could not help but damage employee morale: It had sunk so low by the summer of 1970 that United's pilots, ground crews, passenger service agents, and stewardesses didn't even try to hide their listlessness. "Things were going to hell in a hurry," one senior pilot recalls.[13]

Carlson determined to cut through the red tape that was strangling the company. He wanted to breathe initiative into the organization and, at the same time, get on top of it. He did not insist on Geneen's tight control with overlapping spheres of information centered on himself. Rather, he sought to be informed without becoming pivotal to the conduct of operations, to be exposed to different points of view without unleashing divisive forces among his subordinates. Though Carlson, like Geneen, wanted eminently pragmatic decisions, he sought them through more harmonious means. He needed to improve United's organizational structure—but he avoided going to a structured extreme. He dismantled the top-down organization he inherited and developed a new one in which he was first among equals.[14]

PEOPLE ORIENTATION. Carlson's managerial method was first of all people oriented. Carlson had no airline experience before joining United; he had been the president of Western Hotels International. While acknowledging the important differences between the two operations, Carlson emphasized that "both businesses share the critical variable of people."[15] And the "people" he referred to included both customers and UAL employees.

That Carlson should have seen his past experience as so appropriate to airline management is interesting. For at its core, Carlson's system reflected a philosophy that in any organization the chief executive officer, while influencing his subordinates, had to treat them as respected and trusted individuals. He shared the view that "authority is delegated upward." In Carlson's words, "The president of a company has a constituency much like a politician. A company's constituency of employees may not actually go to the polls, but each employee does 'elect' to do his job in a better or worse fashion. People at every level of an organization have to understand your 'platform.' If they don't, you don't get their wholehearted cooperation. In a service industry like this, if you don't have their support, you don't get the job done well no matter how tightly you try to control them."[16]

VISIBLE MANAGEMENT. Carlson's second principle was "visible management." He viewed this as the cornerstone of his system. "My belief," he said, "is that employees of the company ought to see the man who's in charge. They ought to know what I look like and that I'm listening. I think it's important for me to know what's going on and for them to know that I care about what's going on. I began traveling into the field within my first week here and it has continued. I suppose I'm in the field 65 percent of the time."[17] Visible management resulted in a direct, two-way exchange of information between Carlson and people from *every* level of the company.

Like any chief executive officer in a turnaround situation, Carlson spent much of his first year fighting fires. But, unlike many, he took his fight to the field. Traveling 186,000 miles in his first year, Carlson sought to bridge the abyss of past communications failure and to sell his goals to the employees themselves.[18] Major airlines all have the same problems of communicating timely information both down and up, over vast distances, and through many levels of command. Though a salesman might notice a softening of demand for reservations among his commercial accounts, or a station manager might see that personnel are being improperly used for their particular level of business, conveying this information to the right person with authority to act on it quickly is by no means simple. Carlson's schedule kept him (and his top officers) in the field two thirds of the time. "But in a service organization such as an airline," he observed, "there is no quality control at the warehouse door to screen out errors in production." "Personnel who produce the 'product' (e.g., the pilots, flight attendants, ramp service and ticketing personnel) also deliver it to the customer. 'Controlling' employees to do a good job, at best, sets a minimum threshold of performance. Attainment *above* that threshold requires high morale and motivation."[19] Carlson's style reinforced this, through his allocation of time, his symbolic acts (informal chats with baggage handlers on the runway, etc.), and his obsessive focus on the small details that add up to excellent service.[20]

Carlson embarked on a two-pronged attack. First, as we will see later, he decentralized decision making so that the persons closest to problems could resolve them. Second, in an effort to tie the many separate parts of United together, he embarked on a communications program that was to become his trademark. Meeting with station personnel, he answered anonymous questions submitted on cards by the audience of employees. He hosted cocktail parties in each city so that employees could talk to him personally and in a relaxed atmosphere. Employees asked tough questions; he gave straight answers. If he didn't have the answer, he would say so, and then drive the headquarters staff to distraction insisting on quick follow-up.

One senior vice president said: "The dilemma for Carlson when he first came here was how do you change the structured nature of the place, yet maintain the operational and service discipline of this company? How do you break through and get people to initiate, yet maintain, respect for top management's decision-making responsibility and authority?"[21] In this lies one problem of the teamwork approach. Teamwork sounds good in principle, but it exacts a high price in executive time needed to develop an effective work group. It is not possible simply to order subordinates to behave like a team. Carlson had to work very long hours to build an effective team. Moreover, once a team evolves it attains an identity of its own which *can* dilute top management authority and control. Carlson, like the executives at Matsushita, was prepared to live with this risk, given the sorry alternatives.

Although Carlson's extensive travel severely limited his time at headquarters, he chose nevertheless to remain accessible to the field staff. He shared confidential daily operating statistics that had previously been regarded as too sensitive for the field to handle. His aim was to dispel rumors and suspicion. "Nothing is worse for morale," he said, "than a lack of information down in the ranks. I call it NETMA—Nobody Ever Tells Me Anything—and I have tried hard to minimize that problem." [22]

"Not only did Carlson really practice visible management," said one senior executive, "but he made it a requirement for all who worked for him. As a result, we didn't have many of our top people sitting in their offices. We traveled a lot, listened a lot, and what we got was more uninhibited communication with our employees." [23] Another executive said, "Within a year after Carlson's arrival, the walls began to break down and people began to pull in the same direction. It motivated the hell out of our middle-level people. They saw they really could influence things. And, above all, it worked because it was not just a phony meet-the-people campaign. Carlson conveyed genuine respect for the different jobs people do. When they saw that they mattered to him, their jobs started to matter to them." [24]

Among the executive group, Carlson's style of visible management resulted in a corollary tactic, dubbed MBWA—Management by Walking About. "It made a difference here at headquarters," one senior vice president said. "Before, we had much too much layering. After Carlson, if you had a question for a division head or vice versa, we didn't go through staff layers; we went direct. Before, we used to send memos or call people on the phone; after Carlson came, there was more of a tendency to go down and see a person face to face. Carlson didn't go for starched-collar delegation. We didn't just give a job to a person and wait for results. We became involved, concerned, asked questions. Acknowledging the significance of people on a man-to-man basis was a key factor in making this philosophy work. It took us a long way toward eliminating the stagnation that had persisted around here."[25] Through a variety of such devices, Carlson succeeded in flattening UAL's organizational pyramid. The positive result was fewer levels and better communication up and down the line; the potential drawbacks were a wider span of control and diminished central authority.

A policy that is centered in people and a highly accessible top management are not, alone, surefire formulas for success. Other firms have tried the approach and failed. The key, it appears, for any successful management approach is that there be a coherent system, an underlying logic to the whole. At United Airlines, concern for people and visible management were very important, but they were only parts of Carlson's scheme for turning the company around.

DECENTRALIZATION. Decentralization was a third and essential ingredient of Carlson's management approach. He had seen it work for Western International Hotels. The problem was that decentralizing an airline contradicted the "conventional wisdom" of the industry.

True to a form that would be repeated again and again throughout his tenure at United, Carlson did not issue an edict to decentralize. Instead, he loaded his twelve senior executives and their wives aboard a jet in early 1971 and flew them to Los Angeles for a weekend of low-key meetings. "The time had come to step away from the crisis atmosphere of the executive offices and take a more detached look at some of our alternatives," Carlson recounted later. "Besides, some of the wives had never met, and most of them were complaining about the long hours we had all been putting in."[26]

Though the meetings were loosely structured, Carlson said, "I wanted us to think through this idea of setting up some profit centers to get around the dilemma of why it took so long for a decision to be made."[27] The idea of forming a handful of centers was kicked around for two days. By the time the meetings ended, a map dividing the United States into three decentralized divisions had been drawn. Working with the proposal, the executives then argued out the parameters of what is UAL's present system. Marketing would be decentralized under a line vice president with direct access to top management. Staff authority would be downgraded and flight operations would work under a matrix type of organization, with a direct chain of command running to headquarters but with several key operational activities, such as maintenance and food service, reporting also to the new regional vice presidents and their individual airport station managers. The effect of redesigning the organization's structure, as time would demonstrate, was to turn a monolithic organization into three very successful, medium-sized airlines, each competing with other airlines for passengers and with one another's results.[28]

The comparison here to the organizational structure at ITT and Matsushita is illustrative. United's dual lines of authority and competition among operating units were in some ways similar to those of Geneen's and Matsushita's systems. The organizations shared some common structural elements. However, Carlson's way of developing his management (inviting executives to a retreat, hashing the plan through slowly to ensure full commitment) was much more like the Japanese's. The comparison suggests the manner in which a manager's skill gives life to the *system* and *structure*, and gives pattern to his style of leadership.

BASE TOUCHING. Consulting subordinates in informal face-to-face meetings was another important element of Carlson's management style. As we saw at Matsushita, such dialogue serves not only as a conduit for information, but as a means for sounding out new ideas in advance of implementing them. And there lay the fourth principle of Carlson's style—"base touching." According to one executive, "Base touching was stressed around here; it was part of Carlson's way of doing things. . . . A lot of ground work was done; we sounded people out not at just one but at several levels." Note how congruent to our earlier discussion of Japanese images of decision making and implementation these descriptions sound.

Base touching became a precondition for most decisions at United. Given Carlson's decentralized system, this was the "velvet glove" through which top management exercised guidance without undermining line authority. "The trick was to work through people," says one senior executive, echoing the Carlson philosophy, "not by giving orders, but by selling people on the merits of the program and its logic and its goals. There were times, of course, when you had no choice but to give an order because it had to be done *now*. And as you relaxed centralized control, the organization became less responsive; that was a real tradeoff. But you can only order compliance—not wholehearted support. In a service business, the distinction makes one hell of a difference."[29] It is striking how much this quote parallels the world view of Matsushita's controllers and production engineers, who are *not* in a service business.

A DRIVE FOR INFORMATION. Carlson, like Geneen and Matsushita, had a craving for information. He also had a sense for situations that took him into the interior of problems. Although interested in general principles, he almost always pressed toward action. As a former business associate recalls, "Carlson had a rare ability to focus on his target and head, step by step, toward it."[30] "As a result of his 'visible management,' he met lots of people and got swamped with information," another observer says. "But he retained it, synthesized it, bugged us constantly to follow up on questions that had been raised, or suggestions that had been offered."[31] His methods were costly in their demands on executive time and may have overloaded him with information and followup requirements, but there was less chance under such a system that subordinates were screening out criticisms, alternatives, or information.

Carlson was by no means dependent on one information channel. He used his staff to prepare background studies to supplement line proposals. "We did an awful lot of prestudy before making a decision," says one staff officer. "And we always got a number of inputs."[32] For example, when Carlson suspected that the accounting system needed an overhaul, he created a task force of sixteen people, including line and staff representing a variety of organizational viewpoints. Their assignment: to get the background and make a report. It took them a year. But the report led to a significantly changed accounting system, and it was workable. "The key to an implementable decision," one controller summarized afterward, "is not only to track down the facts, but to get the key people in agreement on what those facts mean and what should be done about them. In the accounting study, everybody was on board and ready to go."[33] The example has a distinctly

Carlson flavor: touching base to facilitate line acceptance; detailed staff work to ensure that the whole picture is presented.

PARTICIPATIVE PLANNING AND CONTROL. United Airlines' planning and control system was the sixth major feature of Carlson's approach. It gave spine to his method of management. Soon after taking command, Carlson realized he would need to focus his managers on revenue and costs and to develop accountability for those items at the lowest possible operating level. Carlson created three task forces to do the job—groups in which line managers had considerable say. Their proposals provided United with the tools to operate three decentralized divisions, yet hold them to the overall pace and purpose of the company.

An executive in United's Planning Department says, "Carlson's first move, of course, was to decentralize. Then he needed a management information system to keep on top of it. We devised that system with heavy line involvement. It pinned accountability down to 1,700 cost and revenue centers across the United States; that is, the individual station managers at the airports."[34]

To close the loop of the planning and control system, Carlson gave bonuses to managers according to their performance against plan. These rewards stimulated competition among the executive team and evidently had a positive impact. According to one middle manager, "It gradually became apparent that things were changing. First of all, I understood more of what was happening. Secondly, Carlson and his team were more sophisticated on tracking performance. Our aspirations and commitments were established from the bottom up so you really were on the line. If you originated your own projections, you were held responsible for them. In the old days, you didn't really have control over things and you could always talk your way out of being responsible for your results. Now if you didn't make a plan, you got penalized."[35]

It is instructive to consider the management information systems of United, Matsushita, and ITT side by side. Like the other two, Carlson's planning and control system was highly detailed. It involved a year-long, 120-step cycle of written plans and meetings and resulted in one- and five-year plans. A parallel set of reports and meetings then tracked results against plans. Also, like its counterparts', United's control system focused on key factors, such as profitability (of individual flights) and productivity indices (passengers boarded or cargo loaded per employee hour). Key comparisons of these factors were presented in monthly reports.

Outwardly, the similarities among these three companies are striking. But differences emerge as we examine the planning *process*. "What made Carlson's planning process work," said a United senior planning officer, "was that it was constantly massaged. The mechanism wasn't nearly as important as the dialogue. First, the plan was built on data and proposals that came from the line people in the field. This process required sufficient specificity to ensure that points of contention were raised. These were dealt with on a face-to-face basis. It led to some poker playing by the divisions now and then—and some were better at it than others. Plane scheduling, in particular, was a contentious issue. Sometimes we were still trying to get an agreement ironed out when the calendar overtook us and we had to arbitrarily cancel flights to make schedules flyable. It was not a perfect system."[36]

The quote reveals a process that was similar to Matsushita's and in important respects different from Geneen's. United, like the Japanese, raised points of contention in an atmosphere in which peers tried as a team to resolve their differences. There were pitfalls: the compromises and "poker playing" that occurred were not in the "best" overall short-term interests of the company. By giving subordinates more influence, UAL became heavily dependent on their acting in the best short- and long-term interests of the firm. And, while similar to Matsushita in some respects, United did not yet have the deeply ingrained spiritual values and meticulous socialization process to unify its members.

Under Geneen's system, poker playing among subordinates probably occurred less often. Geneen, with ITT's system of checks and double checks, was more in control; individual employees had less power. At ITT the parallel information channels and Geneen's quest for unshakeable facts ensured that all players had their cards on the table—an exceedingly important factor for a far-flung conglomerate. Carlson's system was probably not as efficient in guaranteeing that all the facts were on the table all the time. But in a service business such as United, the lower efficiency of the decision system may be the price of better employee morale, presumably central to customer satisfaction. And it seems that in nonservice businesses, the same "cost-benefit" analyses could be applied.

For United's purposes, Carlson's planning and control system provided a reliable stream of reports. Variances were noted and flagged to management's attention. Most important, the system served as a conduit for the dialogue between line and staff, which is essential to the teamwork approach to management.

SUPPORT FOR SENIOR EXECUTIVES. A seventh element of Carlson's approach involved his relationship with his senior executives. Carlson trusted his managers. United's turnover of top executives was low; many of Carlson's executives have been at United for twenty years or more—statistics that rival those of Matsushita, with its lifetime senior management cadre. This, of course, can lead to resistance to change and to stagnation, a constant concern. "The problem with many senior executives," Carlson said, "is that they get programmed; they stop listening. They come up through the ranks, learn the way things are done, and get inured to them. It's a natural enough process. As you get older, there is a tendency to withdraw. You begin by seeing only the people you're comfortable with, avoiding bad news. That's the beginning of what I call corporate cancer."[37]

To combat this tendency, Carlson rotated his top executives. "Before Carlson," said one executive, "there were functional domains. If you were the head of the marketing domain, you were a baron in a fiefdom. You didn't talk to any other areas except at relatively formalized senior-level meetings. Decentralization changed that, and so did the innumerable planning meetings which occurred at the lower levels. But it also helped to have people rotated so there was more of a generalist outlook among the senior guys. The cross-fertilization helped us break out of the 'status quo thinking' that you saw so much of in our airline's management."[38]

Carlson deliberately sought a diversity of styles and ideas in choosing the managers around him. His feeling toward people had taught him that personalities of advisors affect the way they convey facts. He chose executives who had extensive airline experience and others who did not; some were old-timers, others were young professionals. Immediately after taking over UAL, Carlson installed an "advisor," and later several, to support the one executive vice president on whom his predecessor had solely relied.

Carlson perfected a number of tactics in his skillful balancing of personalities. Despite the differences in his staff, there was no serious clash of interests and egos. Carlson was accessible and played no favorites. In the view of his senior management team, there was a lot of rapport among Carlson and his top executives. One said: "His mixture of pressure and praise commanded loyalty. He was informal without being chummy, hard driving but easy-mannered, interested in his aides as people without being patronizing. He treated us more like colleagues or associates than employees."[39]

Carlson put in sixteen-hour days and expected his top officers to do the same. Like Geneen and Matsushita, Carlson also had an obsession. He aspired to nothing less than the complete reinvigoration of a demoralized and overbureaucratized organization. When a CEO strives to achieve the extraordinary, there is no substitute for focus, willpower, and time. But when work ended, Carlson did not impose additional constraints on officers' time. In fact, Carlson excused his management team over the Christmas holidays only three days after he had taken over the firm. "Christmas," he said, "is the time for families. So let's have time with them and come back here and go to work."[40]

Carlson's feeling for people undoubtedly helped him maintain his brand of teamwork. "He was highly sensitive to people's 'wounded egos,' " one senior vice president said. "He controlled a meeting so skillfully that there was very rarely an outburst. When one occurred, he was apt to take the injured person aside and say, 'You did a good job today in helping us bring out the pros and cons of an issue.' He did it sincerely."[41] There are risks, of course, in diminishing open conflict. Often, substantive and interpersonal conflicts are intermingled and differences should not be papered over until their basis is known. More seriously, United was reputed to have "old guard" parts of the company where Carlson's unwillingness to force a showdown prevented him from introducing new ways of doing things.

TEAM HUDDLES. A final characteristic of Carlson's system of management was its stress on committee work and consensus. United had two basic committees, the Operations Management Committee (OMC), which dealt with operation matters, and the Corporate Policy Committee (CPC), which dealt with corporate strategy. More important than their names was their function. The

OMC and CPC together were the pinnacle of United's decision-making system. Most top-level decisions were made at these committees' meetings and the detailed minutes included specific action steps that were agreed on, along with designation of the person responsible for carrying them out. One officer said, "It was hard to bury an issue at management meetings. The action assignments were picked up in the minutes and you were hounded by the follow-up brigade until your action step was done."[42] The follow-up system was simple enough. Junior staff kept elaborate track of all decisions and all actions pending. Their responsibility was to stay in touch with the executive responsible for each action until it was implemented. The extensive contact among United's executive office personnel greatly facilitated this follow-up process and the personal touch eased what might otherwise have become an onerous and bureaucratic control system.

Carlson's conduct at meetings was an important factor in making the sessions successful. He would say, "I'm throwing this subject on the table and let's have a good discussion. We don't have to resolve it now, but let's see if we can focus on it and raise some questions and develop a few answers."[43] Carlson usually did not sit at the end of the table or preside as the "cross-examiner." He asked questions. He listened carefully. "He was more like the coach of the team than the captain," said one executive.[44] Team emphasis was a frequent theme in Carlson's repertoire—including his tendency to use "we" in all his letters rather than "I." The approach resulted in a far more cooperative spirit than was found in many other companies. The danger, of course, was that a prevailing harmony could insidiously dull the sharp edge of problem solving.

When Carlson was in accord with his advisors, he might play devil's advocate to see if he could support the opposite side with logic. "He sought the difference of opinion among his executives," said one observer, "and anyone in the group was expected to disagree loudly if he felt so disposed."[45] Carlson's only rule: Disagree without being disagreeable. Carlson valued substantive conflict but tried to keep personal conflict to a minimum.

Despite its size (which makes it a natural target for the unions for pace-setting wage settlements), United did reasonably well during Carlson's tenure, avoiding serious strikes and work stoppages. Most of the rank and file characterize the Carlson period as one of harmonious union/management relations, and attribute it to him. "Carlson was a real person," said one airline mechanic. "He got out to see us and took the time to know what our problems were. Sure, when it came to wages there were the inevitable negotiations, but there was less of that pent-up bitterness and anger that often leads to a strike vote."[46]

In 1976, Carlson moved from the position of chairman and CEO of United Airlines to become chairman and CEO of UAL, Inc. His successor as CEO was a younger man, perceived as more aloof and less accessible, especially by the rank and file. Interestingly, the highly disruptive strikes at United since Carlson have been attributed by government mediators to breakdowns in communication rather than to substantive roadblocks in the negotiations themselves. Herein lies a major difference from Matsushita —where organizational continuity was maintained during Matsushita's gradual retirement—by the traditions instilled in the management team and by his persistent questions and occasional personal interventions.

Unlike Matsushita, Carlson did not believe it was appropriate to interfere in his successor's handling of the airline. Even though as chairman and CEO of UAL, Inc., he had the hierarchical legitimacy to do so, Carlson viewed his management style as an "idiosyncrasy." "No two managers are alike," he said. Thus, he did not attempt to impose his way of doing things on the thirty-three-year-old man who took his place. Under Carlson, employees were convinced that they really mattered as members of the team. They were shown by example over the years that management was accessible and would listen to their grievances and suggestions. This created a formidable set of expectations. Carlson's successor, imperfectly indoctrinated, began to behave differently. The repercussions were expensive, and at times near explosive. Carlson's teamwork had achieved remarkable results through greater levels of cooperation. But when the basic premise of trust and caring on which it was built starts to fall apart, the backlash of disillusionment can undo in a few months an organizational climate that has taken years to create. Here we see a troubling similarity between Carlson and Geneen. Neither man succeeded in instilling within his company a set of values and a managerial approach that would carry on after he was gone. We contrast this to Mr. Matsushita who was constantly fine-tuning the means of training and indoctrinating staff, lecturing on the "Matsushita style" and reaffirming the superordinate goals (or shared values) that would continue to hold the institution on course even in his absence.

In some respects, Geneen's, Matsushita's, and Carlson's management methods had a lot in common. All three men were very visible to key subordinates, working long hours, but demanding the same commitment from them. All three valued face-to-face contact (although in very different ways). All were involved in their organizations' information networks, through their strong drives for information, and all used multiple sources of that information. All employed formal structures to achieve their purposes; all developed systems, notably planning, control, and financial reward systems, to direct behavior within the designed structure. All used meetings of senior executives to hammer out decisions, although Geneen's meetings were more often symbolically staged in a show-trial format, using negative motivation, whereas the other two used small, problem-solving meetings that were more informal and supportive. All three men were single-minded in pursuing their goals.

Geneen, Matsushita, and Carlson also shared a tendency toward obsession. While priorities of the three men differed greatly, each was extraordinarily persistent in enforcing what he valued. Studies have shown that most leaders with extraordinary impact on organizations tend to share this attribute.[47] Single-mindedness—whether it be Sloan's emphasis on strategy at General Motors, Thomas Watson's concern with customer service at IBM, or Chairman Mao's commitment to the purity of an ideological system—is a common denominator of great managers. For an executive to know what he wants is not enough. He needs to have the will of an Olympic athlete.

In a way, Carlson's achievements were as dependent upon him as Geneen's were. Their successors couldn't really replace them. Geneen had extraordinary *skills* that few others could match. In Carlson's case, it appears that the problem was a broader one of *style*. We will turn in a moment to a consideration of skill and style, but first let us comment on what it seems to take to build a great corporation that persists across time, especially after its builder is gone. We saw what it takes at Matsushita. It takes, first, *a long time*. Second, it takes *constant socialization* of new people and *constant training* of those who keep moving higher. Third, it takes endless articulation and reinforcement of *what the institution honors, values, and believes.* Fourth, it takes *obsessive attention* from the CEO. And, fifth, it takes *careful planning* for succession long in advance.

Geneen had a relatively long time, but his subordinates had to fit to him, and when that unique man left, none were of a kind to replace him. Carlson had less time, and needed a lot more to institutionalize his contribution so that it was second nature to his people, especially his successor. Carlson had to swim upstream in his surrounding managerial culture much like a salmon. As such, we suspect he would have required not only many years, but constant support by a series of successors, to mold United into an organization that would persist. The end result would remain a fragile creation, far easier to destroy than to create. Only constant support from the top would ensure its continuity, much as vigilance is the price of liberty in world affairs.

"Style" is often assumed to refer to the superficial. Contrasted with substance or content, its value seems slight. It conjures images of fashion and trendiness. In business, though, the style of an executive's behavior is a matter for comment and taken more seriously, although here too it often seems so vague as to be without much practical use. One thinks of looks, clothes, cars, planes, houses, articulateness, presence, charisma, intellectual talent, sense of humor, social skills, values and beliefs, personality and God knows what else. The great number of things mysteriously lumped together (in ways somewhat unique from person to person) that we generally call style leaves us with a *sense* of what the word refers to, but without concepts to grasp it more firmly. Since it includes so much, it is difficult to think about its many parts in relatively simple fashion without leaving out something that could be important. And yet, without an attempt to do so, we leave almost wholly intuitive our understanding of a central element in any organization's functioning. The style of a CEO, and its impact upon others, is as important as are a company's strategy, structure, or systems. The latter certainly influence behavior, and in ways that are increasingly understood. The style (and skills) of the top executive are equally potent and yet not very well understood so far. We want to make a venture into this largely unexplored area since we believe an executive who wants to build a great corporation must "have" a style that strongly encourages patterns of experiencing and behavior in others, which in the end are so internally reinforcing that they persist when the CEO withdraws. It is then that one can metaphorically describe his *company* as having a style which is self-perpetuating.

Style isn't really something one "has." It is, rather, something *other people attribute to a person*. They observe that person and his behavior, and from many pieces of data they get reactions to him. They search for patterns and clusters among the bits and pieces so they can account for both their reactions and the data they perceive. Over time they organize the clusters so they get a sense of the whole, and their reaction to it. Often the words used to describe the whole are value-laden, emotionally charged metaphors. Sometimes several words are used, which are likely to be more descriptive and less evaluative, such as "perfectionistic, impeccable, and detail oriented." A less involved observer is likely to be more concerned with carefully labeling the *clusters* or patterns that comprise the whole. Thus, from our data one might describe Geneen as an executive with amazing intellectual gifts, great energy, and stamina; with high needs for dominance, control, and power; who relished confrontations, fact finding, and analysis of quantitative data; whose life was largely work; and who had low trust in other people's willingness to do what he would do if he were there.

Of course, if one had access to more data, one might construct another picture. At whatever level of abstraction, based on whatever variations in data, people are able to construct a picture of a senior executive which they then *use* in several ways. They can identify *with* him, seek to be like him, move closer to him, go where he wants to go, do what he wants them to do—in short, try to *become more like him*. Or they can compare him to others negatively, reject him as a "role model," move as far away from him as his power permits—in short, reject him as *their* kind of leader, even if they have to accept him in his role for the time being.

If the first leader has this positive effect on most people in his organization he will be called charismatic. If the second leader has the effect described on too many people in his organization, he will be called swear words.

In short, an executive's style is what other people say it is. What an executive *does* have some control over is *certain of the bits of data* (his *content*) that people use to form their reaction. Before we look at how executives *can* influence others by deliberately altering some of the data he presents to them (and thus, hopefully, altering what they make of him and his style, and how they respond to that), let us try a way of thinking about at least some of the major elements that comprise the executive content that others configure into style.

It seems to us, after years of observing American executives, and hearing their subordinates from top to bottom talk about them, that there are three major clusters of variables that constantly are used. People look at an executive's *person* (e.g., appearance, intellect, personality, values, reputation), at his *role behavior* (e.g., goals, expectations of self and others, preferred methods of managing), and at his *skills* (e.g., in communications, in participating in process—at meetings, in problem solving, in displaying his person and role behavior). If we were to detail all the separate variables that come to mind in each of the three clusters, we would have another book—at least. The bits of content that people observe are truly staggering in number. But people do seem to be seeking answers to the following questions:

WHAT KIND OF PERSON IS HE?

Does he *look like* I think a leader should? (appearance)

Does he have enough of the right kinds of smarts? (intelligence)

Is he the kind of person I can relate to? (personality)

What does he really care about? (character)

What has he done, and how have others seen him before he got this job? (reputation)

What does he know? (competence)

How does he treat others? (consideration)

WHAT KIND OF BOSS WILL HE BE?

What goals does he want to accomplish?

What does he expect of me and others (and himself)?

What are his management techniques, assumptions, procedures, methods?

Does he have the intellectual and other skills necessary to do the job?

Does he structure with clarity what he wants us to do, and how he wants us to do it?

Is he fair in his judgments, rewards, and punishments?

HOW SKILLFUL IS HE "SOCIALLY"?

Can he speak well to large groups?

Can he talk and listen well in small groups?

Is he effective one-on-one?

Is he good at running meetings?

Is he good at symbolic displays that move people to action and reinforce those valued beliefs which give meaning to their work?

Can he articulate and behave so as to support the meanings his people value?

These questions are posed and answered at certain times, not only in our general culture and in our particular society but in geographical regions of our country, and within the industry and company involved. In a society as pluralistic as ours, there is no overwhelming central tendency in preferences for style, although much has been made of the "Eastern Establishment Style" at times. At the level of corporate CEO, such wide variety exists, in much of executive content (and attributions of style) that it seems clear that little danger exists of stylistic analysis becoming another technique misused mechanically. Rather, it appears that the possible variations are infinite, which means that we have the need for art more than science at this point. It is also worth noting that few CEOs would ever achieve the most positive answers on *all* the above questions from an overwhelming majority of their people. Nor do they need to. But what they "do poorly" must *not* be central to the organization's functioning at the time they are in charge. Both Geneen's and Carlson's successors appear to have had that problem.

In discussing Geneen, we were able to be rather explicit about those *skills* he had that contributed to his *style* as seen by others. His entire way of managing was largely dependent upon those personal skills, which were by any measure extraordinary. As listed before, his amazingly accurate memory, his capacity to process vast amounts of information, his speed-reading ability, his attention to detail without loss of the big picture, his gifts at interrogation, his ability to "read" nonverbal data, and his expertise in confronting people as well as problems were central to his way of working.

It is interesting how many of these same skills were possessed by Matsushita. He too had a terrific memory, a capacity to process and use a wide range of information, an ability to focus on detail in the context of a larger view, a capacity for direct confrontation of people and problems. Like Geneen, he too "invented" organizational forms to suit his purposes. Thus, both had skills of insight and design. What distinguishes Matsushita from Geneen is not so much skill as the other elements in their respective styles. On a number of those elements, Geneen had a position on each spectrum while Matsushita had range across the spectrums. Some examples:

1. Matsushita behaved as a tough shop foreman, a demanding father, *and* a gentle, philosophizing, allowing grandfather.

2. He alternated a hands-on approach and visits to the shop floor, nighttime phone calls, and intrusions to "rescue" the firm in troubled times, with the more aloof, semiretired, delegating, removed, chairman-of-the-board approach.

3. He slashed costs, demoted poor performers, retired his adopted son, extolled a Darwinian survival of the fittest philosophy, *and* focused upon developing people, with a Socratic approach to teaching managers, patience, and a high consciousness of the surrounding society, invested in a spiritual vision.

4. He was very facts-oriented, numbers demanding, insistent on systems development, *and* highly intuitive in most of his major breakthroughs (e.g., markets, organization design, choice of key managers, product design) as well as comfortable with phenomena of persisting indefinitiveness.

The "inconsistency" that many Americans would perceive in Matsushita's behavior would trouble them. But we can see how his *range* in behavior can be regarded as appropriate to his *several* long-term goals. Consistency, or narrow range, is likely to be more appropriate to single shorter term goals—that is, a narrow vision. Matsushita's ability to present his people with a wide range in behavior made it possible for them to fashion a view of his style that directed their attention to productivity, satisfaction, and growth: complex outcomes that he valued.

When a CEO's content/style is well fitted to his goals, and to his organization's needs in both the short term and long run, and to his employees' expectations and desires, and when this fit persists across long periods of time, it is possible that a great many people in the company will come to possess similar contents and be seen as having similar styles. Then outsiders will observe the similarities among people from that corporation and attribute style to the organization itself. In addition, they will refer to the corporation as having certain skills. When all that happens, a corporation is more likely to have become a recognizable entity *which tends to persist*. IBM comes to mind.

It is interesting to reflect on both Geneen's and Carlson's failure to leave behind a company that had become one which could thrive without them. Geneen's "toughness" wasn't enough. Carlson's "people orientation" wasn't enough. Persisting great corporations, such as Matsushita, result from more than coherent strategy, structure, systems, style, and skills across long periods of time. They also require the creation of *meanings* and attention to staff in addition to productivity, satisfaction, and growth. Such "meanings" have been mentioned from time to time throughout the book—"spiritual beliefs" at Matsushita, "significant meanings" at ITT and United. These ideas can be as slippery as style, and will be explored in the next chapter. We will refer to them as *superordinate goals,* those larger meanings which are in effect the glue of belief that helps hold a great organization together and give it direction, and which indeed can make it hard to change.

Chapter Seven

Great Companies Make Meaning

IN MANAGEMENT, as in music, there is a base clef as well as a treble. The treble generally carries the melody in music, and melody's equivalent in management is the manager's style. A manager's style—the way he focuses his attention and interacts with people—sets the "tune" for his subordinates and communicates at the *operational* level what his expectations are and how he wants business conducted. Beneath these messages is a deeper rhythm that communicates more fundamentally. The bass in music—whether hard rock or a classical symphony—often contains much of what moves the listener. So, too, the "bass" of management conveys meanings at a deeper level and communicates what management *really* cares about. These messages can influence an organization profoundly. In Japanese organizations, a great deal of managerial attention is devoted to ensuring the continuity and consistency of these "bass clef" messages.

In earlier chapters, we have variously referred to these "bass" clef messages as an organization's "significant meanings," "shared values," and "spiritual fabric." For clarity, we will adopt one all inclusive term to describe these characterizations: *superordinate goals*—the goals above all others.[1] They are the seventh element in our framework. Superordinate goals provide the glue that holds the other six—strategy, structure, systems, style, staff, and skills—together. When all are fitted together, organizations tend to become more internally unified and self-sustaining over time.

Superordinate goals play a pragmatic role by influencing implementation at the operational level. Because an executive cannot be everywhere at once, many decisions are made without his knowledge. What superordinate goals do, in effect, is provide employees with a "compass" and point their footsteps in the right direction.[2] For example, at IBM that translates into never sacrificing customer service; at Matsushita it means never cheating a customer by knowingly producing or selling defective merchandise. These values permit the CEOs to influence the actions of their employees, to help the employees make correct independent decisions. These value systems act as "tie breakers" in close cases, those in which decisions otherwise might be made the wrong way.[3]

Year after year, decade after decade, Delta Air Lines has been the most consistent money-maker in the airline industry. Undoubtedly, its route structure, concentrated in the fast-growing South, has contributed to its success. But route structure alone cannot explain Delta's performance—for neither United Airlines (with its dominant position in America's busiest air terminal, Chicago) nor American Airlines (with the lion's share of the market in fast-growing Dallas/Fort Worth) has been able to match Delta's performance over the long term.

Delta considers its key to success in the highly competitive and largely undifferentiated airline industry to be *service*. (As we saw, for a time Carlson succeeded in inculcating this idea at United, where it worked equally well.) Delta considers service to be the direct result of a motivated and friendly work force. Delta's approach, which includes virtually open-door access for all of its 36,500 employees, has enabled the airline to maintain its esprit de corps and remain non-union in an industry plagued by labor–management strife. Delta's management *style* and strongly reinforced *superordinate goals* are largely responsible for this achievement.[4]

At the heart of Delta's philosophy is "the Delta family feeling." More than a slogan, it is what makes Delta different. This "family" emphasis was introduced and nurtured by the airline's founder and has been carefully institutionalized. "It's just a feeling of caring within the company," says Delta's current chairman, W. Thomas Beebe.[5]

It's difficult to find workers with serious complaints at Delta. The firm promotes from within, pays better than most airlines and rarely lays off workers. These policies are what makes the "family feeling" real. When other airlines were slashing employment during the 1973 oil embargo, Mr. Beebe told senior management: "Now the time has come for the stockholders to pay a little penalty for keeping the team together."[6] Notice how the superordinate goal of preserving the "family feeling" took precedence over near-term profits and return on investment.

Like Matsushita, Delta pays attention to the socialization of new employees. It makes sure employees embrace the "family" concept by emphasizing it in training programs and at meetings. It also carefully screens job applicants. Stewardess candidates, for example, are culled from thousands of applicants, interviewed twice and then sent to Delta's psychologist, Dr. Sidney Janus. "I try to determine their sense of cooperativeness or sense of teamwork," he says. At Delta, "you don't just join a company, you join an objective."[7]

The Delta example sheds light on several features of effective superordinate goals. First, they need to tie into higher-order human values. Second, they need to be consistent with the other six S's, especially the firm's *style* and *staffing* and *systems* practices. Third, management needs to be meticulous in respecting these values (even if it means sacrificing short-term profits) or they will be seen as empty slogans.

Kinds of Superordinate Goals

Effective superordinate goals should be (1) significant, (2) durable, and (3) achievable. Most tend to fall into one or more of the following categories:

1. *The company as an entity*

Here the whole organization is reinforced as an entity one lives within and should identify with and belong to, and which is deserving of admiration and approval from employees and society (e.g., Delta's belief in the "family feeling").

2. *The company's external markets*

Here the emphasis is on the value of the company's products or services to humanity, and on those factors important in maintaining this value—that is, quality, delivery, service, and customers' needs (e.g., Matsushita's belief in advancing the standard of living in Japan by distributing reliable and affordable electrical products).

3. *The company's internal operations*

Here attention is focused on such things as efficiency, cost, productivity, inventiveness, problem solving, and customer attention (e.g., Delta's emphasis on "service" and Matsushita's dedication to first-class production engineering).

4. *The company's employees*

Here attention is paid to the needs of groups of people in reference to their productive function, and to individual employees as valued human beings in a larger context—that is, human resource systems, growth and development, opportunity and rewards, individual attention and exceptions (e.g., Matsushita's commitment to developing employees not only for the firm's benefit but to contribute to each employee's personal growth over a lifetime).

5. *The company's relation to society and the state*

Here the values, expectations, and legal requirements of the surrounding larger community are explicitly honored, such as beliefs in competition, meritocracy, the necessity of obeying the law, or being sensitive to other nations' customs (e.g., Matsushita sees itself as a major contributor in restoring Japanese status and prestige).

6. *The company's relation to culture (including religion)*

Here the underlying beliefs about "the good" in the culture are honored—beliefs in our own case largely derived from Judeo-Christian tradition, and including such things as honesty, and fairness, e.g. (the strong influence of religion in shaping the Matsushita philosophy—which reinforces many Confucian and Buddhist values including harmony, solidarity, discipline and dedication).

IBM, Then and Now

IBM has for many years been one of our most successful and effective U.S. corporations. It is known for its remarkable devel-

opment of strategy, structure, systems, style, skill, and staff, and
the fit among them, *and* for its equally advanced development of
superordinate goals.

In a 1940 *Fortune* article describing the company and its
president (Thomas John Watson), the author's imagery is initially
surprising. For example, he describes the young Mr. Watson as
having the appearance and behavior of a "somewhat puzzled di-
vinity student" who "began to confect the aphoristic rules of thumb
that have since guided his life and policies. 'Ever onward,' he told
himself. 'Aim high and think in big figures; serve and sell; he who
stops being better stops being good.' . . . Mr. Watson caused the
word THINK to be hung all over the factory and offices. . . . Generally it is framed, sometimes graven on pediments in imperisha-
ble granite or marble, again embossed in brass, yet again lettered
in gold on a purple banner, but always and everywhere it is there.
. . . Whether you particularly agree with [what Mr. Watson is say-
ing] you listen. . . . Mr. Watson's monumental simplicity compels
you to do so. . . . Let him discourse on the manifest destiny of
I.B.M., and you are ready to join the company for life. Let him
retail plain homilies on the value of Vision, and a complex and
terrifying world becomes transparent and simple. Let him ex-
pound the necessity for giving religion the preference over everything else, and you *could not help falling to your knees*. . . . Everybody
in the organization is expected to find the ubiquitous THINK sign
a constant source of inspiration, as the weary travelers of old
found new strength in the wayside crucifixes."[8]

That the author found such images useful to *his* purpose
does not necessarily mean, of course, that such images captured
an important truth about the company. They could have been
useful mostly in capturing the writer's *reaction* to IBM and Mr.
Watson. But three senior executives quoted in the article add
weight to the "religious" impression. One said: "Mr. Watson has
spread his benign influence over the earth, and everywhere it has
touched, people have gained, mentally and morally, materially and
spiritually."[9] Another remarked: "I think that we do not always
count our blessings. Every so often we should all of us stop and
think of the many things that have been done for each member of
this organization."[10] A third echoes a similar theme: "Mr. Watson
gave me something I lacked—the vision and the foresight to carry
on in this business, which from that day forward I have never had
any thought of leaving."[11]

There is an implied reference to cultural values of gratitude, faith, and commitment. There is repeated reference to the beneficial impact of Mr. Watson on *individuals*. The tone is evangelical. In the 1930s, society's acceptance of various absolutes was not yet much undermined by existential beliefs and moral relativism, and there was still widespread acceptance of the use in business of explicit, usually Christian, religious metaphors.

It was then not uncommon, and even recently not unheard of, for secular enterprises to express their organizational fervor in fundamentalist religious ways. The development of "creeds" which employees were expected to hold, of "cults" of membership differentiating employees from outsiders and identifying them with insiders, and of "codes" of behavior that reduced uncertainty and prescribed right action and attitudes was an important part of the early years of some companies. The use of company songs, dress codes, sales meetings that Elmer Gantry might have staged, ubiquitous displays of "the leader" in photographs, oils, and bronze statues, slogans presented in expensive and long-lasting materials, an often-referred-to book of the leader's speeches and essays (Mr. Watson's was *Men, Minutes, and Money*), and a house organ to reinforce values and educate were all part of early IBM. The rah-rah sales orientation of that time reminds us of the zealous proselytizing of some churches, and the ways of reinforcing the developing creeds, cults, and codes also seem similar. (It is not accidental, we think, that pushing a new product line is often referred to as "missionary work" by businessmen.)

But Mr. Watson's role certainly was not confined to devising those methods. He also created superordinate goals based on the beliefs of his society. The average person's belief in the Horatio Alger story, and in the dream of "getting ahead," probably accounted for the following remark from the same article:

> There is a careful selection of all employees, whether
> for the factory or the sales department. Mr. Watson
> never hires an office boy, but always a potential
> leader, or at any rate a potential assistant. Everyone
> addresses every man as "Mr." The company publica-
> tions never refer to any man without prefixing a
> "Mr." to his name.[12]

That attention to selecting employees, the respect expressed by the prefix "Mr.," the numerous employee programs, as well as efforts to assist employees in growth and development, indicate that Mr. Watson was aware of the power of honoring within his organization the values and beliefs of the surrounding society.

In addition, Mr. Watson attended to the developing conflict in Europe by having PEACE join THINK all over the company; he also commissioned a symphony on an important company occasion to express the longing for international cooperation, and gave and reprinted speeches on that theme. IBM was aligned with the *world* situation in employees' minds. (War was dangerous to mankind, as it was to IBM's developing international business.)[13]

The article includes far more than attention to what we call superordinate goals. It includes fascinating and detailed descriptions of all the Seven S's. But for our purposes here, it is interesting to note how the great corporation IBM has become is related in part to conscious attention over time to superordinate goals as well as the other elements.

In the years since 1940, IBM's expression of its beliefs, and its ways of honoring them, has become what seems fair to call "more sophisticated." The approach is much more analogous to the best functioning of some of our established formal religions. There is less obvious conformity required, more subtlety in technique, more complexity acknowledged in goals, and thus more skill required to behave "well." Yet the more recent statements of IBM's superordinate goals, the basic beliefs reinforced within the present firm, can be seen as having evolved from the first Mr. Watson's original efforts. And that IBM has been at it so long gives the present beliefs the enormous advantage of a successful and shared history. A recent statement of IBM's basic beliefs is as follows:[14]

Basic Beliefs

A sense of accomplishment and pride in our work often go hand in hand with a basic understanding of what we're all about, both as individuals and as a company. IBM is fortunate to have a timeless statement of its purpose—in its basic beliefs.

The underlying meaning of these beliefs was best expressed by Tom Watson, Jr., in his McKinsey Foundation Lectures at Columbia University in New York in 1962, when he said: [15]

I firmly believe that any organization, in order to survive and achieve success, must have a sound set of beliefs on which it premises all its policies and actions.

Next, I believe that the most important factor in corporate success is faithful adherence to those beliefs.

And finally, I believe that if an organization is to meet the challenges of a changing world, it must be prepared to change everything about itself except those beliefs as it moves through corporate life.

In other words, the basic philosophy, spirit, and drive of an organization have far more to do with its relative achievements than do technological or economic resources, organizational structure, innovation, and timing. All these things weigh heavily in success. But they are, I think, transcended by how strongly the people in the organization believe in its basic precepts and how faithfully they carry them out.

What is this set of beliefs Watson was talking about? There are three:

Respect for the individual. Respect for the dignity and the rights of each person in the organization.

Customer service. To give the best customer service of any company in the world.

Excellence. The conviction that an organization should pursue all tasks with the objective of accomplishing them in a superior way.

In addition to these basic beliefs, there is a set of fundamental principles which guide IBM management in the conduct of the business. They are:

- To give intelligent, responsible, and capable direction to the business.
- To serve our customers as efficiently and as effectively as we can.
- To advance our technology, improve our products and develop new ones.
- To enlarge the capabilities of our people through job development and give them the opportunity to find satisfaction in their tasks.
- To provide equal opportunity to all our people.
- To recognize our obligation to stockholders by providing adequate return on their investment.
- To do our part in furthering the well-being of those communities in which our facilities are located.
- To accept our responsibilities as a corporate citizen of the U.S. and in all the countries in which we operate throughout the world.

Note that Mr. Watson, Jr., says he believes that a corporation's survival and success are dependent upon beliefs, sound beliefs, from which it acts, and to which it is faithful. He says everything else may change, but not the beliefs. They remain "absolutes." Given that last observation, the basic beliefs are naturally stated at high levels of abstraction, and in "high-minded" language. Respect for the dignity and rights of the individual; the best customer service in the world; accomplishing tasks in a superior way. The individual, the customer, the *ways* of working. At least the first and third are not likely ever to require altering, although the ways they are applied may well change.

Notice, too, the statements of fundamental principles, expressed at lower levels of abstraction, and in somewhat less high-minded language. They refer to:

management competence
customer service
technical progress
employee opportunity development

stockholders' return
community well-being
national and international responsibilities

It will be clear immediately that, over time, the tradeoffs and balance will require a lot of managerial skill applied constantly in order to confirm these principles and their modes of application in the minds of thousands of people. If one assumes, as we do, that IBM really works at living up to its basic beliefs and principles, and if one assumes, as we do, that such effort has a powerful effect on the company's success, then it becomes possible to set aside the skepticism often reserved for high-minded pronouncements of top executives. If it is *not* just fluff, then it is a powerful and positive force indeed. One signal that IBM has been practicing what it preaches is the criticism it has received in the past related to employee "commitment and conformity." Those white-shirted, polite, competent, hard-working employees of twenty years ago were often regarded as corporate "fanatics," or even corporate "fascists," because they appeared not to display in superficial ways their "American individuality." White shirts were mistaken for laundered minds. The shirts are now colored, but it appears that their wearers are still politely service oriented, highly competent, and hard working (everything may change but the beliefs). And in our culture, any evidence of a reduction in obvious "individuality," which naturally accompanies increases in organizational commitment, will produce criticism from those who *overvalue* individuality. We have a suspicion that IBM executives in the early 1960s recognized the criticism for what it was, and smiled politely on their way to the bank. In any event, it seems to us that IBM has long attended explicitly to its superordinate goals, and that they have played an important part in its being a remarkably successful, self-renewing, profitable company with a very strong internal culture.

Mr. Matsushita may have been quick to grasp the value of strategy, structure, and systems, but the Watsons were not naive about the "soft" S's and "the arts of Japanese management." (In the 1930s, Mr. Watson, Sr., visited Mr. Matsushita in Japan and presumably was influenced by what he saw there.) In the forties, IBM was functioning very much like Matsushita. From company songs to employee recreation, from careful selection and indoctrination to employee "uniforms," from pictures of the CEO everywhere to slogans, the two companies seemed more alike than different. Each has continued to fashion its internal culture to reflect changes in the society outside, but both still pay a lot of attention to articulating and honoring superordinate goals.

Superordinate Goals and Changing Employee Values

As noted, superordinate goals tie the purposes of the firm (e.g., goods, services, profits) to human values. We believe that this linkage to human values is growing in importance. The vast majority of Americans who work today do not view their jobs as "the only alternative." Fifteen percent of all people who work are in skilled blue-collar occupations; 45 percent are white collar. Sixty percent are employed by firms with over 1,000 employees, and 47 percent work for organizations with over 10,000 employees.[16] What these statistics tell us is that most people who work today are highly skilled and/or white collar, and employed in relatively large institutions. In these kinds of environments, all sorts of factors cushion employees against the occupational hazards that plagued those employed only three or four decades ago. First, the job market itself, while never as hungry as we might wish, offers backup employment opportunities for most people with qualifications who wish to work. In addition, there are financial cushions of various kinds—unemployment insurance, a spouse's income, the opportunity to moonlight, and the capacity to save enough over a period of time to handle a transition between jobs.

These factors have moved us a long way from the circumstances that shaped employment attitudes in the nineteenth and the first half of the twentieth century. The implications of these changes are profound. The majority of people who work don't have to for economic *survival* in the short term. Increasingly, they seek, *in addition* to pay and career opportunities, other kinds of income from their jobs, including work they enjoy, colleagues they like working with, and *meaning*. Far too many generalizations are made about work on the basis of the automobile assembly-line stereotype. For the vast majority, work is a far different and far more fulfilling experience. For people in these new circumstances to be satisfied, it helps enormously if they can see the link between what they do and a higher purpose.

When the linkage between human values and a firm's objectives is unclear, employees often seek to create meanings of their own which reconcile what they do on the job to higher purposes. Curiously, we may have seen some evidence of this at ITT.

Geneen inculcated in his organization a belief in the importance of "unshakeable facts" in the service of "bottom-line results." These narrowly envisioned meanings were reinforced constantly and few managers failed to internalize them. Yet there are indications that some of Geneen's executives were unwilling to view their endeavors exclusively in terms of such bottom-line results. Their comments suggest that they created larger meanings. They told us they took pride in being a part of such a demanding, fast-moving, successful company, that they saw themselves as stimulated, accomplished, fast-track executives, a kind of corporate pro ball team. In short, they created *a larger meaning* to give value and dignity to their work lives. They were the outstanding, hard-ball pros in an economic game, no quarter given or taken. Tough, lean, mean. A winning-is-the-only-thing, best-of-their-kind elite.

Like ITT, many Western organizations pride themselves on having made a virtue of bottom-line results and other similar measures of "efficiency." If anything, the emphasis has intensified in recent years as companies have sought to produce profits during a period of slowed growth and world economic uncertainty. The problem with efficiency is that it is a little like white bread and refined sugar: Taken in isolation, it becomes bland and vaguely unhealthful—all the life-supporting nutrients seem to get refined out. Obviously, organizations need to be somewhat efficient in order to accomplish their tasks. But the problem is that people can end up performing instrumental functions as if they were truly interchangeable parts in a great machine.

Superordinate Goals Focusing on Employees

Earlier we listed six kinds of superordinate goals. One category, of particular interest, focuses on the firm's relations with its employees. Generally speaking, people want to identify with their organization; they want to trust and depend on those they work with and invest through their labor in the organization's success. But, as we have seen, the tendency of Western organizations to deal at arm's length, to neglect coaching and mentoring of subordinates, to abruptly transfer (rather than carefully *transplant*) people from one job to the next, to reorganize by decree and provide brutally direct feedback without regard for the grace and pace necessary for successful change—all these things teach employees to be wary. Most American executives think only in macroterms about "morale." They do indeed worry about massive layoffs, or gross inequities in pay or major contradictions in policy. What the preceding chapters have argued is that many far more subtle things are equally important and commonly neglected.

Employment involves a psychological contract as well as a contract involving the exchange of labor for capital. In many Western organizations, that psychological contract, while never explicit, often assumes little trust by either party in the other. If the only basis for the relation of company and employee is an instrumental one, it should not be surprising that many people in our organizations do what they must do to get their paycheck but little more. While there can be all kinds of superordinate goals, those that concern themselves with the development and well-being of employees can play a particularly important role in establishing the moral context for this psychological contract. If such superordinate values are consistently honored (as we saw at Delta during the 1973 oil embargo), then employees tend to identify more fully with the company. They see the firm's interest and their own as more congruent and tend to invest themselves more fully in the organization—including looking for ways to improve how they do their job. (we will talk about that later with the quality control)

Most consultants will confirm that they have been called in to solve a client's problem only to discover in the course of conducting interviews that someone in the client organization already had the solution. But because communication channels were blocked, or, more often, because the individual with the good idea was "turned off" and convinced that the organization wouldn't listen, no initiative was taken. The potential initiator hesitated to invest himself, in the last analysis because trying is linked to caring and history had taught him that the firm was not worth caring that much about.

Without a doubt, the most significant outcome of the way Japanese organizations manage themselves is that to a far greater extent than in the United States they get everyone in the organization to be alert, to look for opportunities to do things better, and to strive by virtue of each small contribution to make the company succeed. It is like building a pyramid or watching a colony of ants thousands of "little people" doing "little" things, *all with the same basic purpose,* can move mountains.

A recent study of product innovation in the scientific instruments and tool machinery industries indicates that 80 percent of all product innovations are initiated by the customer.[17] The majority of ideas doesn't flow from R&D labs down but from the customer up. To be sure, customers don't do the actual inventing, but their inquiries and complaints plant the seeds for improvements. Given these statistics, it matters a lot whether a company's sales force and others operating out at the tentacles of its field system are vigilant. They need to be open to new ideas *and* willing to initiate within their organization. Here is a key to success of many Japanese companies. We saw this at Matsushita, where they rarely originated it but had an unerring ability to do it better. This formula is not inconsistent with most of the major corporate success stories in the United States. Careful scrutiny reveals that despite the exalted status of "strategy" in the lexicon of American management, few great successes stem from one bold-stroke strategic thrust. More often, they result from one half-good idea that is improved upon incrementally. These improvements are invariably the result of a lot of "little people" paying attention to the product, the customer, and the marketplace.

To be sure, the case for superordinate goals can be overstated. Innovative firms tend to have a *style* of management that is open to new ideas, ways of handling *staff* that encourage innovation, *systems* that are customer focused and which reward innovation, *skills* at translating ideas into action and so forth. But the ideas don't flow unless the employee *believes* in the corporation and identifies enough with its purposes to "give up" his good ideas. Further, any of us who work in organizations knows how hard they are to move. One has to really believe an organization *cares* in order to invest the energy and effort needed to help it change. Such commitment derives from superordinate goals. And if we look at outstanding American firms that have a sustained track record of innovation, we see this to be the case. Texas Instruments, Procter & Gamble, 3M, and IBM, for example, all pay close attention to the customer and each has a highly developed value system that causes its employees to identify strongly with the firm.[18] Perhaps the intense loyalty that these firms inspire is just an interesting idiosyncrasy. But we believe, on the contrary, that this bond of shared values is fundamental to all of the rest. In our view, this is probably the most underpublicized "secret weapon" of great companies.

As we noted with Matsushita, Japanese firms, despite their evident success in adopting Western technology and their skill at devising aggressive strategies, innovative organizational structure and comprehensive systems, have not followed the West in de-emphasizing the "soft" S's. They do not trade off human relationships for impersonal efficiency. Almost all of the American employees of the twelve Japanese subsidiaries in the United States whom we interviewed in this study remarked on the personal concern of these companies toward employees.[19] This concern was manifested in two ways. First, invariably, the Japanese firms made a big deal about "meaning." Whether Toyota, Sony, or YKK (a manufacturer of zippers), the senior managers stressed the importance of developing their employees and the contribution of their product to society as a whole. These were not just "ad slogan" values, but something that management deeply believed in.

We call attention to the Japanese companies' commitment to people. One Japanese manager said, "Anyone who works for a company seeks approval for what he does and acceptance for who he is." "Almost all firms give approval through the normal reward system, but providing acceptance of each individual as a unique person requires a lot more effort." Japanese firms in the United States institutionalized "acceptance" in two ways. One was by increasing the contact between boss and subordinate. Even on the shop floor, Japanese firms fostered twice as much contact between workers and their foremen as was usual elsewhere. (Fifteen employees reported to each first-line supervisor as compared to a 30:1 ratio at American firms.)[20] One manager said, "If you're striving to give employees a sense of being recognized for their unique contributions, you have to have enough supervisors to listen." Supervisors at Japanese-managed firms more frequently worked alongside their subordinates, were more extensively engaged in personal counseling, and permitted more interaction among workers than those of the American companies did. In an effort to express their commitment to people, the Japanese subsidiaries also spent an average of nearly three times as much per employee on social and recreational programs as did their American control companies ($58.49/employee/year vs. $20.79 for American companies).[21] All of these programs were presumably symbolic; but that's not all they were. Employees often commented that the programs also fostered increased off-the-job contact among employees, had the effect of personalizing the firm, and reinforced the superordinate goal that "people mattered."

Western History and Superordinate Goals

By an accident of history, we in the West have evolved a culture that separates man's spiritual life from his institutional life. This turn of events has had a far-reaching impact on modern Western organizations. Our companies freely lay claim to mind and muscle, but they are culturally discouraged from intruding upon our personal lives and deeper beliefs.

The dilemma for modern Western organizations is that, like it or not, they play a very central role in the lives of many who work for them. Employees in all ranks of the hierarchy not only "work" at their jobs, but (1) derive much of their daily social contact there, and (2) often locate themselves in social relations outside the firm through their association with their company and occupation. (One of the first questions we are asked when we meet a person for the first time is: "What do you do for a living?") Splitting man into separate "personal" and "productive" beings makes somewhat artificial parts of what is the whole of his character. When we do so, our cultural heritage not only too strictly enforces this artificial dichotomization, but deprives us of two rather important ingredients for building employee commitment. First, companies are denied access to higher-order human values, which are among the best known mechanisms for reconciling one's working life with one's inner life. Second, the firm itself is denied a meaning-making role in society, and thus pays excessive attention to instrumental values, such as profit, market share, and technological innovation.

If we trace the history of goal setting in U.S. organizations, we find that over the past twenty years management's understanding of goals has greatly expanded—from mere monetary goals (e.g., profit and return on investment) to stockholder and constituency goals (such as environmental objectives and minority hiring). The trend has been toward expanding the notion of corporate purpose. Nevertheless, recognition of an organization's role in serving higher-order human values still awaits full-scale acceptance.

We recognize that some readers will resist the specter of a merger between "the Church and the corporation." But that is not what we are proposing. There is an important difference between religiosity and spiritualism. In the West, because of the Church's monopoly on the spiritual side of man, all spiritualism was religious. That is not so in Japan, and it need not be so in the West.

There are no strong imperatives in Japan for an individual to choose among religious beliefs. People there commonly have several religions—believing in Confucianism, Buddhism, and Shintoism simultaneously. Likewise, Japanese firms can take a general spiritual position without seeming insincere or superficial. Such firms are able to work with each employee to help him flow with the ups and downs of a career and to find deeper meanings in his own development. In the West, many managers feel both the employee and the organization are culturally conditioned to an arm's-length relationship. This causes the firm to let the employee fend for himself in adversity and draw upon the problematic spiritual resources available to him from friends, family, and religious affiliations.

What is needed in the West is a nondeified, nonreligious "spiritualism" that enables a firm's superordinate goals to respond truly to the inner meanings that many people seek in their work—or, alternatively, seek in their lives and could find at work if only that were more culturally acceptable.

Western institutions are, in fact, backing into this role. Two forces are at work: employees seeking more meaning from their jobs and demanding more concern from the corporation, and legislative pressures enforcing a broad range of personal services, including employee rights to counseling. In response to these forces, most major firms now describe these activities as "Human Resource Management" instead of "Personnel"—it is to be hoped, the first step in adopting a larger perspective. Most larger firms also provide assistance to employees dealing with chronic personal problems, such as divorce, alcoholism, and stress. And, as noted earlier, some of our most outstanding companies have long acknowledged a larger role in the lives of their employees and foster greater interdependence among them. All are remarkably "Japanese" when we look at them closely. Their success may have important implications for Western organizations of the future.

Superordinate Goals and Diversification

One problem inherent in diversification is that it becomes more and more difficult to establish *one* set of superordinate goals that provides useful guidance within a particular industry, yet is general enough to be relevant across many industries. Conglomerates, in particular, face this dilemma. Most tend to conclude that it is unnecessary or impossible to fashion unifying meanings for multiproduct, multimarket portfolios. Their method of growth through acquisition tends to encourage this. They acquire successful companies and are dedicated to making them even more successful. But they often overlook the fact that a conglomerate's meanings (which are almost always largely limited to the impersonal and financial) undermine the older meanings that gave the acquired firm its former sense of purpose. Most conglomerates stress their desire to be supportive, to avoid interfering. But the absence of positive new meanings, or, at least, the impetus for continually reinterpreting existing meanings, inevitably results in atrophy and empty slogans. Subtly, the new financial control system, the corporate emphasis on profit, or ROI, visits by the controllers, and messages conveyed at quarterly review meetings (as we saw at ITT) erode the earlier "faith." Is it any wonder that vibrancy and sense of commitment frequently disappear from subsidiaries within a year or two after they are acquired? One thinks of the change at Avis. Once a spirited company that was "Trying Harder," Avis today seems just another enterprise. The meanings lost through acquisition are rarely offset by gains through superior resources and more "scientific" management.

Tradeoffs

In any particular situation requiring a decision, it is entirely possible that an executive may have to choose to affirm one superordinate goal rather than others. Let's say a firm has effectively developed goals which include "service," as well as one related to the "professional development" of managers. If an important customer's need for delivery requires a particular manager to stay on the job when he has been scheduled for a lengthy outside executive program—to which he has been unable to go twice previously—a choice may have to be made between goals. In any particular situation, it may not be possible to honor all the important superordinate goals simultaneously. They may have to be met sequentially. There are days when we need to sin bravely and make tradeoffs between one goal and the other. A "separate and related" way of thinking about superordinate goals enables us to "fire (or transfer) an employee on Thursday" in order to attain higher levels of service, successive phases in a dynamic cycle. The issue is the *balance over time* of such decisions. If delivery-installation *always* comes first, even when a specific situation may not support such primacy, then people will come to see the goals related to managerial development as mostly noise.

It seems true that top executives measure, or try to monitor, what they care about. No measurement equals no real caring in most companies, and most managers know that early in their careers. In short, effectively honoring superordinate goals requires not only managerial skill and appropriate system development but also CEO reinforcement through style. Too little skill, or inappropriate systems, or CEO indifference, leads rapidly to cynicism. And cynicism is the enemy of the trusting commitment most CEOs sincerely want from their employees. The moral: Don't claim you care about it unless you are prepared to act accordingly, for you don't get goodwill from subordinates by promising what you do not deliver, anymore than they do from you.

Strategic Eras and Superordinate Goals

An organization's superordinate goals emerge, in part, from leadership which instills values through clarity and obsessive focus. A firm's history also contributes to its enduring value system. Organizations tend to grow through stages, face and surmount crises, and along the way learn lessons and draw morals that shape values and future actions. Usually these developments influence assumptions and the way people behave. Often key episodes are recounted in "war stories" that convey lessons about the firm's origins and transformations in dramatic form.[22] Eventually, this lore provides a consistent background for action. New members are exposed to the common history and acquire insight into some of the subtle aspects of their company. Matsushita made a considerable effort to pass on his company's legacy to each new recruit.

Superordinate goals are immensely helpful at the beginning of a strategic era.[23] Setting out to build a fast-food empire, Not only did McDonald's stress price, quality, profit, and market share, but they believed they were performing a real service to Americans living on limited means. This "social mission" gave a larger meaning to operational objectives. The cooks and order takers in McDonald's franchises found higher-order goals helpful in accepting the company's rigorous quality control system. Strict standards could be met more readily when seen in the context of "helping society." As one manager put it, "The lower down you go in an organization, the more difficult it is for employees to identify with the firm's business objectives. A firm's social and humanitarian objectives are far more tangible to a dishwasher or janitor than is its goal of market share."[24]

Toward the end of a strategic era, a firm's past meanings can get in the way. In fact, this invisible force has undone late-in-an-era executives who sought to change things. Case studies of incumbents whose terms of office spanned the time periods when their organizations were moving from one era to another seem to indicate that they "failed" more often than they "succeeded." Organizational meanings can be so deeply ingrained, so fundamental to what people think and feel, and so important to their beliefs about their jobs and themselves, that when initially these meanings are challenged, there is often resistance and later dismay and a great sense of loss.

One recent example is the current transition at AT&T.[25] That company's deeper meanings were built on providing *reliable* and *inexpensive* telephone *service* to America. The firm's superordinate goal uniting managers, workers, and even stockholders has been the "social mission" of providing a reliable, low-cost phone system to America. Bell Labs and Western Electric further enshrined AT&T's pride as the "World's Best Telephone Company." But in the early 1970s competitive data processing applications began to spill over into AT&T's traditional domain. It became increasingly clear that the telecommunications fields and computer fields were overlapping. The result: AT&T was increasingly facing competitors in the computer industry; it would have to broaden its focus, change its strategy and become more of a marketing-oriented company in order to meet that competition. Ideally, its superordinate goal needed to shift to being a "marketer and innovator in telecommunications." In competing with firms like IBM, AT&T has to tailor its products and respond more rapidly to shifting market needs—in short, to make significant changes in all Seven S's.

Two of AT&T's chief executive officers saw this happening and began to move to change the company's direction. Their names are not likely to be enshrined as "great leaders" in AT&T's legends. They attempted to realign the strategy, but all of AT&T's systems were oriented toward tight operational controls—the sort that keep track of costs, operator errors and equipment reliability in the traditional phone service. They also encountered a staff of employees whose middle and senior managers had come up through the ranks as managers of telephone switching offices and repair facilities. With backgrounds in engineering and accounting, this management cadre lacked strong instincts for sales and marketing. In short, there were formidable barriers to change. Perhaps this helps us understand why the current chairman of AT&T believes that the shift to a true marketing orientation will require twenty years.

Transitional times are periods in which older meanings and behaviors are slowly and painfully relinquished, and leaders who anticipate future threat when things are still apparently going well make an important contribution that is not often widely recognized at the time or, for that matter, honored later. Not until this painful and difficult process has run its course will the readiness for new meanings permit a "great leader" to articulate them convincingly. Strategic eras impose their own destiny on organizations and their leaders.

There are, to be sure, numerous tales of CEOs who have taken an ailing company, revitalized it, and achieved great success and recognition for doing so. The key word is "ailing." When a firm is widely seen as being in deep difficulty, as Memorex was in 1971, for example, there is an obvious imperative for change and a general recognition by employees of the need to alter older beliefs and ways of doing things. With Memorex at the brink of bankruptcy, its former beliefs in "rapid growth" and "free form entrepreneurialism" were in disgrace.[26] Not only was Bob Wilson free to move forcefully, the organization was ready to receive him. The mourning for past meanings had already largely taken place.

Many of the entrepreneurial figures connected with the earlier era had already departed. Dissatisfaction with the way things were, and fears for the future, were strong. Wilson was thus in a position to build from the near-ruins. In contrast, his contemporaries at AT&T were having first to tear down monuments still standing *before* problems were clearly evident to all concerned and the costs of changing accepted.

Superordinate goals affect nations as profoundly as they do companies. Without such goals, around which a nation can rally, each constituency is out for itself and each citizen is more on his own. It appears as if the same late-in-the-era malaise is currently at work in our country. We have gone through a string of Presidents, each roundly criticized in his time, each dropping low in the polls during his tenure, and each facing great difficulty in building a consensus as to what America is all about, what it is for, where it is going, how it can get there, and what its priorities should be. The heart of these difficulties, we think, is not just the quality of leadership, but the angry resistance of a nation that is still mourning the accumulating losses of more of its earlier beliefs than it is prepared to relinquish. Perhaps a new President will be able to fashion a compelling expression of an adjustment of our nation's superordinate goals and begin anew.

Misuse of Superordinate Goals

Having made the case for the importance of superordinate goals in motivating employees and sustaining an organization over time, we must note that a skillful grasp of the use of all of our seven variables *can* be directed toward truly tragic outcomes. The staggering horror of the Third Reich and the mass suicides in Guyana come to mind. It is not hard to imagine an indoctrination of people into some kind of corporate Hitler Youth Corps. Indeed, fascist imagery is often used to express our unease with enterprises that succeed in fashioning intense commitment, and our fear of the fanatical is certainly not paranoid. We have seen enough of it in our Western history to be wary. There is no reason to rest assured that we are safe from pathology, madness, or evil in leaders or social systems at any level of enterprise, from small corporations to larger religious movements to nation states.

Yet, if our fear of the totalitarian of either the right or the

left keeps us from struggling to encourage meanings that are between those extremes, that move men's hearts and compel action
within ranges acceptable to our society and culture, we risk creating the kind of corporate emptiness which invites the extremists to
fill the void. We cannot protect ourselves against such threats,
either nationally or in a corporate context, by preferring a kind of
pseudo-innocence (which suggests that our ignorance or naiveté
about such meanings is acceptable, since others are "assigned" the
function of dealing with extremists in our society). Rather, we
must accept that owning up to our power to influence meanings
imposes responsibilities to guard against the risks of its misuse. In
this, we have some advantages built into our society. The still large
separation of the state, the corporation, and the church from one
another, and of the media from all three, provides at least reasonable assurance that checks exist to achieve balance in the distribution of power and its uses. But, nonetheless, it needs to be said
that increasing our understanding of executive manipulation of
superordinate goals does not necessarily ensure benign outcomes.
Indeed, as the power and responsibilities of businessmen continue
to expand, it is appropriate that they be subjected to the kind of
scrutiny and limitations that our constitution imposed on the leaders of the nation. And if they are wise, these businessmen will not
complain too much at these constraints, for in the long run history
suggests they are useful and even necessary, even if they seem a
damned nuisance a lot of the time.

Chapter Eight

Conclusion

IT HAS been accepted only slowly by many American executives that part of our economic problems are the result of inadequate management. Since World War II, we have held a very high opinion of our managerial knowhow, and others have agreed. In the late 1960s, the French journalist Jean-Jacques Servan-Schreiber wrote that Europe was in danger of becoming our economic vassal. He saw the threat from American multinationals and conglomerates as based not only on economic clout and technological superiority, but on superior management skills. That view was not confined to Europeans. Another observer noted, "The Japanese, too, regularly came to the United States to attend its business schools and tour its factories, and they used to joke that a B.A. degree meant Been in America."[1] "Management" was viewed as one of our important competitive advantages throughout the world.[2]

But during the early 1970s our reputation abroad increasingly weakened even while our self-satisfaction remained the same. American managers were not yet obliged to consider that they might do things differently. As our competitive position softened, and our rate of productivity increases declined, we did become concerned, but for a while we managed to blame everyone but ourselves. Of course, government legislation, environmental protection costs, tax laws, labor unions, energy costs, and a number of other things did contribute, but only recently have we faced up to the fact that we are part of our problem too. There is a growing consensus—both at home and abroad—that to a significant extent the management practices which had seemed to serve America so well, and were admired around the world, were failing us.[3] Reginald H. Jones, chairman of General Electric, recently commented, "The indictment in many cases is justified. It should be taken very seriously."[4]

The general press understandably tended to report the fact of managerial failures, that is, the symptoms rather than the causes. When they did consider the roots, they tended to exaggerate the fault of "inept management," which only encouraged more successful executives to dig in and deny extreme allegations, and thereby avoid acknowledging the lesser but real extent of their own failures. For most people, reading about the decline or death of corporations has the same usefulness as staring at accident victims.

Peter Drucker wrote that management is not a mere discipline, but a "culture" with its own values, beliefs, tools, and language.[5] We have explored how this subculture (of U.S. management) lies within the nation's larger culture. Both cultures contain the root causes of our recent managerial decline. There has been an ineffective grabbing at gimmickry and quick fixes as we have felt the pinch, and that tendency has hurt us. The "enemy" isn't the Japanese or the Germans; it is the limitations of our managerial "culture." The problem isn't simple, and neither is its solution. No quick introduction of uncoordinated parts will address the whole problem. Quality control circles, "Theory Y" reorganizations, team building, two-week organizational development programs, etc., etc.—each has its uses, but unless there is an overall *fit* of all the managerial parts across time, there will be little sustained leverage and few results. Three central themes deserve a brief summary.

The Framework, and Its Use

Executives have only a limited number of "levers" to influence complex large organizations. We have explored seven—superordinate goals, strategy, structure, systems, skills, style, and staff. These terms, taken individually, are likely not to surprise anyone. We hope, however, that executives have found that our *emphasis* and treatment of those "levers" other than strategy, structure, and systems—and our way of integrating all seven into a single framework—offer some new insights.

There could well be more (or fewer) variables than the seven. We think the seven we selected are of crucial importance. More would be hard to grasp systemically; fewer would leave something central out. We chose alliteration on the theory a little vulgarity enhances memory. And a checklist is not without its uses, although we prefer to organize our view of the framework as a managerial molecule, as illustrated below:

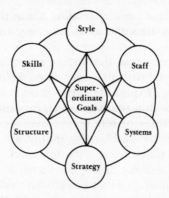

Our goal is not to advance another new "model," nor did we seek one that would primarily appeal to academic researchers. Rather, we want to help executives develop a more effective way of perceiving and cutting through the complexity of their organizations.

Each of the "levers" an executive uses, even if he uses "too few," is important, but *the central point is that the FIT among and between them has to be good to get long-term leverage.* At ITT we saw that Harold Geneen got outstanding bottom-line results over quite a number of years, as long as he was there, because of the extraordinary fit of the "levers" he brought to bear, and this was true principally because of his own remarkable skills. At United, we saw Ed Carlson emphasize additional levers and achieve good *fit*. But Carlson was unable to institutionalize his approach during the time he had, as in Geneen's case, and United's comparative advantage declined when he moved on. At Matsushita we noticed well-integrated levers institutionalized over time, and careful preparation made for succession. This led to both short-term results and long-term advantage. At Matsushita, a corporate culture was sophisticated in using each of our "levers," as well as in arranging their *fit* to one another, an achievement fully realized over six decades of effort. In Matsushita, we saw a great corporation.

Looking at these organizations through our framework induces feelings of humility, even awe. The vast intricacy of Matsushita or ITT or United Airlines affects us as does gazing at a galaxy. Or we can compare these organizations to the human body. Many managers, notably but not only younger ones, believe all one needs to do is change one or two pieces and the whole will somehow be bettered. One has only to pick up an issue of *Fortune, Business Week,* or the *Wall Street Journal* to read about some CEO slashing here, firing there, acquiring, divesting, or otherwise acting like a hack surgeon. One would be hard pressed to find accounts of similar episodes in Japan. They surely would not be honored. There are times when one must cut deep, fast and crude, but they are rare in well-managed companies, and their frequency in the United States is a symptom of our managerial malaise.

Addressing oneself to one or two of the S's is generally not sufficient. Even if the manager is aware of the need to work at adjusting the fit of the rest of the Seven S's after a significant change in one or two (say, strategy and structure), it is certain to take *effort* and *time* to achieve integration. Many executives are unwilling to work at some of the S's, or are so impatient they cannot sustain the effort for long, so they focus on those they can change by fiat—notably strategy and structure, and, of course, systems. Periodic reorganizations to "stir things up" are not uncommon among executives who will not, or cannot, manage all the "levers" at their disposal, and/or do not have the tenure, the will, or the stamina to endure long enough. Forcing still another structure on an organization is probably the most time honored refuge of the unsophisticated American manager. Lately this technique is being supplemented by the designation of cashcows in portfolio strategies, and the imposition of controlling systems of measurement which conflict with desirable long-term outcomes. Perhaps the best way to get a rough take on your own organization is the frequency of repeated changes in strategy, structure, and systems which always seem soon to need more of the same because results are disappointing. If attention to the other S's is intermittent, faddish, and if it is liable to cancellation at the first signal of reduced profits, the chances are good that your company is in classic American trouble.

The Japanese Reflection

The second major theme of this book has been to advance our understanding of ourselves by comparing us to the Japanese. We do not encourage direct copying of their techniques, or even their management and cultural philosophy. Their techniques, taken piecemeal, all too often wither in our climate; we cannot assume their philosophies whole even if we want to, which most of us don't. We want to look at the Japanese as if they were a special kind of mirror, one which might allow us to see ourselves in some new ways that may suggest directions for careful change.

What we saw was that generally we were very similar to the Japanese on all the "hard-ball" S's—strategy, structure, and systems. Our major differences are in the "soft-ball" S's—skills, style, staff, and superordinate goals. Their culture gives them advantages in the "softer" S's because of its approach to ambiguity, uncertainty, and imperfection, and to interdependence as the most approved mode of relationship. We saw that their development of language and forms of discourse, especially their indirection, permit high development of skills we seldom achieve or honor. Their careful attention to their human resources from the initial recruiting all the way through retirement made us look as wasteful of our people as we have been of our other resources. We saw how the boss-subordinate relationship encourages a degree of effective collaboration that we might envy, and how consensus is used to accomplish smooth implementation, which often eludes us. In short, we saw that by comparison we were all too often grossly underdeveloped in our sophistication about "man-in-organizations," and powerfully disadvantaged by our culture.[6]

A long and hard look into the Japanese mirror has jolted us. What we see is not much cause for cheer, but at least it makes clear what much of our problem is. And there are already many forces at work in our culture that can modify the inappropriate cultural injunctions of our past. The effort to alter our managerial sub-culture—the time it will take, and, indeed, the wisdom it will demand—is great. But we have been known to move effectively before when the need was real and the threat was great.

The shock is just a beginning for us. And in providing us with this view of ourselves, the Japanese have served us well, much like traveling abroad for the first time helps us to understand from where we come. That we should have a better view of who we are, and of what our part in our problem is, should offer little comfort to the Japanese. We have a long history of pragmatic effectiveness in addressing problems once we see them. We not only *can* meet their managerial challenge, but some of our best corporations already have.

The American Way

It is perhaps surprising to some that most of the practical solutions to our problems are not to be found in Japan, but right here at home. The dozen high-performing companies[7] identified in our study of Japanese and American firms included six that were American. The prime determinant of their success was not society or culture; it was management. United Airlines and IBM were among these firms, and in a variety of ways they outperformed their Japanese counterparts.

When we consider outstanding American companies that have sustained their vitality over decades, firms such as IBM, Boeing, Procter & Gamble, Delta Airlines, 3M, and Hewlett-Packard among others, we find many similarities among them, and between them and outstanding Japanese companies such as Matsushita. *Each* of their S's is fully utilized, and the "synch" *among* them is very good. Notably, all attend effectively to the "soft" S's. IBM, for example, pays as much attention to the recruitment and indoctrination of staff and the inculcation of superordinate goals as does Matsushita. Both companies do so in a disciplined, systematic way that is woven into their institutional fabric.

This results in staff members who have a high degree of

shared understandings and beliefs about their company, about what takes priority, about what is expected of them, and about their high value to the enterprise.

All of our outstanding companies are very advanced in their grasp of strategy, structure, and systems, but, unlike less successful firms which rely primarily on these S's, the best companies also have great sophistication on the four "soft" S's. Thus, the best firms link their purposes and ways of realizing them to *human values* as well as to economic measures like profit and efficiency. As we said earlier, it is probably the least publicized "secret weapon" of high-performing American firms. Even when journalists and academics report on such enterprises, they all too often observe them through traditional American cultural and managerial filters, and tend to assume that the "soft S" factors are just froth. That "froth" has the power of the Pacific.

Developing high levels of sophistication in each S, and among them, is not without short-term cost. Delta paid a price for its commitments during the oil embargo by avoiding layoffs and absorbing the costs. There is still no free lunch. And balancing the demands of all the S's requires even more managerial skill and effort and wisdom. Such executives are not developed overnight. There is no quick fix in sight. Rather, each company's CEO and other top executives need to recognize that it takes time, discomfort, stamina, and commitment to strengthen what is weak in their organizational development. Moreover, there is no sure blueprint for success. Every firm has to evolve its own way of being good at all the S's, and their fit to one another. Mechanistic, programmatic "solutions" that do not change what executives do and, indeed, to some degree who they are, are likely to fail. The task is not to imitate cosmetically, but to evolve organically. And each company, like each individual, has to develop in its own way.

Notes

Chapter 1

1. Charles J. McMillan, "Technological Policy and Planning in Japan," Notes delivered to lecture to Joint Center on Modern East Asia, Glendon College, York University, November 16, 1979, p. 1. For discussions along these lines, see also Norman MacRae, "Pacific Century, 1975–2075," *The Economist*, January 4, 1975, pp. 15–35.
2. Herman Kahn and Thomas Pepper, *The Japanese Challenge: The Success or Failure of Economic Success* (New York: Crowell, 1979).
3. Ezra F. Vogel, "Meeting the Japanese Challenge," *Wall Street Journal*, May 19, 1980, p. 26.
4. Ibid. See also Ezra F. Vogel, *Japan as Number One: Lessons for America* (Cambridge, Mass.: Harvard University Press, 1979), chaps. 1, 2.
5. Vogel, "Meeting the Japanese Challenge."
6. Adam Meyerson, "Japan: Environmentalism with Growth," *Wall Street Journal*, September 5, 1980, p. 18.
7. Underlying the more general treatment of Japanese management in this book are a considerable number of technical papers written by Richard Pascale and his coauthors over the past six years. Listed in chronological order, these are:

207

"Made in America (Under Japanese Management)," with William Ouchi, *Harvard Business Review*, September–October 1974.

"The Adaptation of Japanese Subsidiaries in the United States," *Columbia Journal of World Business*, Vol. 12, No. 7 (Spring 1977).

"Communication and Decision Making Across Cultures: Japanese and American Comparisons," *Administrative Science Quarterly*, April 1978.

"Personnel Practices and Employee Attitudes: A Study of Japanese and American Managed Firms in the United States," *Human Relations*, Vol. 31, No. 7 (1978).

"Zen and the Art of Management," *Harvard Business Review*, March–April 1978.

"Communication, Decision Making and Implementation Among Managers in Japanese and American Managed Companies in the United States," with Mary Ann Maguire, *Sociology and Social Research*, Vol. 63, No. 1 (1978).

"Comparison of Selected Work Factors in Japan and the United States," with Mary Ann Maguire, *Human Relations*, Vol. 31, No. 7 (July 1980).

8. For a general discussion of this period of European history see Barbara W. Tuchman, *The Distant Mirror* (New York: Knopf, 1978), pp. 25–39, 288.

9. Otto Gireke, *Political Theories of the Middle Ages* (Boston: Beacon Press, 1960), p. 86.

10. Max Weber, *The Protestant Ethic and the Spirit of Capitalism* (New York: Scribners, 1956).

11. Alfred D. Chandler, *Strategy and Structure* (Cambridge, Mass.: MIT Press, 1962), p. 29. For a succinct managerial review see Peter Drucker, *Management Tasks, Responsibilities, Practices* (New York: Harper & Row, 1974), pp. 21–25.

12. See Charles O. Tucker, *China's Imperial Past* (Stanford, Calif.: Stanford University Press, 1975), pp. 301–56; A.L. Sadler, *The Life of Shogun Tokugawa Ieyasu*, pp. 327–82. For commentary on the evolution of social conformity in the West, see Michel Crozier, *The Bureaucratic Phenomenon* (Chicago: University of Chicago Press, 1964), pp. 184f., and Amitai Etzioni, *A Comparative Analysis of Complex Organizations* (Glencoe, Ill.: Free Press, 1961), pp. 310f.

Chapter 2

1. "The 50 Largest Industrial Companies in the World," *Fortune*, August 11, 1980, p. 204.

2. For general biographical information on Konosuke Matsushita, see Togo Sheba, *Konosuke Matsushita* (Tokyo: Rengo Press, 1962); see also Rowland Gould, *The Matsushita Phenomenon* (Tokyo: Diamond Sha, 1970).

3. Seven factors will be discussed. They are strategy, structure, systems,

style, staff, skills, and superordinate goals (or shared values). While each of these variables is hardly new, they were first suggested to us as related elements by the work of Cyrus Gibson, who was using his version at that time to teach the middle-level executives in Harvard's Program for Management Development. Subsequently, in a series of meetings with Thomas Peters and Robert Waterman, both of McKinsey & Company's San Francisco office, we further developed our grasp of the interrelationships as systematic. We are especially indebted to Waterman for his original work in further explicating what we also had been exploring and call here "skills," and to Julian Phillips, who added the variable "staff" to the framework. Our work with McKinsey was of such an interactive nature that we are unable to credit Peters, Waterman, and Phillips with an academic specificity that equals our personal appreciation and respect. Suffice it to say that we owe them a lot, and want the reader to know that they and Gibson are our colleagues in this enterprise, although we free them from responsibility for our particular use in this book of the ideas we originally began developing together. See R.H. Waterman, T.J. Peters, and J.R. Phillips, "Structure Is Not Organization," *Business Horizons*, No. 80302, June 1980.

4. Peter Nulty, "Matsushita Takes the Lead in Video Recorders," *Fortune*, July 16, 1979, p. 111; see also "Panasonic Marks 20th Anniversary," *Merchandising*, June 4, 1974, pp. 122f.
5. Interview with Lee Shevel, Vice President, Matsushita Quasar, Chicago, December 13, 1974.
6. "The 50 Largest Industrial Companies in the World," p. 204.
7. Ibid., p. 204.
8. Matsushita Electric Annual Report, 1979; see also Gould, op. cit., p. 6.
9. Alfred D. Chandler, *Strategy and Structure* (Cambridge, Mass.: MIT Press, 1962), pp. 54f.; Gould, op. cit., pp. 21, 36ff., 80f., 88–91.
10. Gould, op. cit., pp. 21f., 44f., 80f.; Sheba, op. cit., pp. 56, 82ff.
11. For detailed descriptions of the Matsushita organization and control system, one must move away from the popularized biographies (e.g., Gould or Sheba) and turn to interviews or relatively inaccessible published sources. One excellent source is Yasuo Okamoto, ed., *Waga Kuni Kaden Sangyo Niokeru Kigyo Kodo* (Business Behavior in the Home Appliance Industry in Japan), Monograph, Tokyo University Economic Research Fund, 1973. Another source is a case study written by K. Takahashi and H. Ishida, "The Matsushita Electric Industrial Co., Ltd. Management Control System," Business School, Keio University, 1971. Other references are published only in Japanese. These were particularly useful: Konosuke Matsushita, *Hito o Ikasu Keiei* (Management That Activates People), PHP Kenkyusho, Kyoto, 1979; Arataro Takahashi, *Matsushita Konosuke ni Mananda Mono; Hito o Tsokuru Jigyōkeiei* (A Lesson from Konosuke Matsushita's Management of Personnel Training) (Tokyo: Jitsugyo No Nihonsha, 1979), pp. 117,

184–89, 263–66; and Takeshi Asozu, *Matsushita Konosuke No Hitozukai No Shinzui* (The Essence of Konosuke Matsushita's View of Personnel Management) (Tokyo: Nihon Jitsugyo, 1977).

12. Tohiko Nimura, "Characteristics of Personnel Management at Matsushita," in Okamoto, op. cit., p. 169.

13. Based on comparisons with organizational developments in the United States as reported by Alfred D. Chandler in *Strategy and Structure* (New York: Doubleday, 1966).

14. P. Lawrence and J. Lorsch, *Organization and Environment* (Boston: Division of Research, Harvard Business School, 1967).

15. Okamoto, op. cit., pp. 132f.

16. Ibid., pp. 88–94.

17. Interview with S. Tani, Matsushita Electric Industrial Co., Osaka, Japan, July 3, 1980; see also K. Takahashi and Ishida, op. cit., pp. 7f.

18. Okamoto, op. cit., p. 82.

19. Ibid., p. 88.

20. "Matsushita: A Non-Traditional Youth Movement in Management," *Business Week*, April 17, 1978, p. 98.

21. A. Takahashi, op. cit., p. 109.

22. Ibid., pp. 184–89; see also interview with Tani. Of particular value is K. Takahashi and Ishida, op. cit., pp. 5f.

23. K. Takahashi and Ishida, op cit.

24. Interview with Lee Shevel, Manager, Matsushita Motorola, Franklin Park, Ill., December 13, 1974.

25. Interviews with Matsushita managers, Osaka, Japan, July 1980.

26. Ibid.

27. "A Japanese Giant in Trouble," *Business Week*, November 16, 1974, p. 81.

28. In 1974–75, as part of a larger research study on Japanese firms in the United States, both Japanese and American managers assigned to Matsushita's recently acquired Motorola facilities at Franklin Park, Ill., were interviewed. Among these, interviews with B. Fujii, vice president, and Wayne Bledsoe were particularly informative.

29. Interview with Fujii, December 13, 1974.

30. See A. Takahashi, op. cit., especially pp. 117–226; see also Gould, op. cit., pp. 51ff., 88–91.

31. Gould, op. cit., pp. 52f.; see also K. Takahashi and Ishida, op. cit., pp. 10f.

32. Gould, op. cit., pp. 90f.

33. Interviews with M. Tange, Matsushita USA Personnel, August 25, 1980.

34. Interview with Onishi.

35. Mike Thorp, "Japan's Matsushita," *Wall Street Journal*, November 21, 1979, p. 48.

36. Naoyumi Tsumoga, "Accounting Functions of Matsushita," in Okamoto, op. cit., p. 205.

37. Gould, op. cit., pp. 5f.

38. Ibid., pp. 5f.
39. Ibid., p. 79.
40. Interview with senior managers, Honda Motor Co., Tokyo, July 1–2, 1980.
41. Interview with Touche Ross senior partners, Tokyo office, Tokyo, June 30, 1980.
42. Gould, op. cit., p. 91.
43. K. Takahashi and Ishida, op. cit., pp. 5–10; see also A. Takahashi, op. cit., 184–89.
44. K. Takahashi and Ishida, op. cit., pp. 5–10.
45. Gould, op. cit., p. 48; see also A. Takahashi, op. cit., p. 186.
46. Interview with Y. Yamashita.
47. Norman Pearlstine, "Blurred Image," *Forbes*, September 4, 1978, p. 29.
48. Interview with Onishi.
49. Gould, op. cit., pp. 3f., 16f., 108.
50. K. Takahashi and Y. Yamashita, op. cit., p. 17.
51. Ibid., pp. 18f.
52. Ibid., p. 19.
53. Makiko Yamada, "Soshiki to Keiei," in B. Masao and K. Masamura, eds., *Sangyo Shakai to Nihonjin* (Tokyo: Chikuma Shabo, June 25, 1980).
54. Interview with Y. Yamashita.
55. Waterman, Peters, and Phillips, op. cit., pp. 21f.
56. Gould, op. cit., p. 120.
57. Ibid.
58. Interview with Tani.
59. Ibid.
60. Interviews with Matsushita managers.
61. Ibid.
62. Asozu, op. cit., p. 26.
63. Gould, op. cit., pp. 152f.
64. Ibid., p. 153.
65. A. Takahashi, op. cit., p. 111. For a general discussion, see also Gould, op. cit., pp. 15–19.
66. Interviews with Matsushita managers.
67. Interview with T. Kojima, Manager, Planning Dept., Matsushita Facsimile Co., Tokyo, July 1, 1980.
68. Nimura, op. cit., pp. 148–66.
69. Ibid., p. 166.
70. Interview with Y. Yamashita.
71. For a general discussion of the Matsushita entry-level and career-long education programs described in this section, see Gould, op. cit., pp. 116f., 126–29; see also interview with Onishi.
72. Interview with Paul Kraus, McKinsey & Company, Cody, Wyoming, June 1980.
73. Interview with Tani.

212 / THE ART OF JAPANESE MANAGEMENT

74. Gould, op. cit., p. 48.
75. Ibid., p. 49.
76. Interview with Onishi.
77. "Matsushita: A Non-Traditional Youth Movement," p. 98.
78. Gould, op. cit., p. 24.
79. "Matsushita: A Non-Traditional Youth Movement," p. 98.
80. Gould, op. cit., p. 126.
81. Ibid., pp. 49f., 128; see also K. Takahashi and Ishida, op. cit., pp. 9f.
82. Gould, op. cit., p. 126; see also Nimura, op. cit., pp. 157f.
83. T. Kunimasa, "Matsushita Confident of Expanding in the U.S.," *Japan Times*, November 21, 1975, p. 26.

Chapter 3

1. Hugh O. Menzies, "The Ten Toughest Bosses," *Fortune*, April 21, 1980, pp. 62–65.
2. "Harold Sidney Geneen," *Current Biography Yearbook*, ed. Charles Moritz (New York: H.W. Wilson, 1974), p. 139.
3. "The 500 Largest Industrial Corporations," *Fortune*, May 5, 1980, p. 276 and July 1960, p. 132; see also N.R. Kleinfield, "End of an Era: Geneen Ceding Control of ITT," *Herald Tribune*, International ed., December 24–25, 1977, Finance Section, p. 1.
4. N.R. Kleinfield, "End of an Era—Geneen Ceding Control of ITT," *Herald Tribune*, International ed., December 24–25, 1977, Finance Section, p. 1.
5. Interviews with ITT executives, ITT headquarters, New York, April 19, 1976.
6. Harold S. Geneen, *Christian Science Monitor*, May 17, 1959, p. 12.
7. Stanley H. Brown, "How One Man Can Move a Corporate Mountain," *Fortune*, July 1, 1966, p. 163.
8. "The View from Inside," *Business Week*, November 3, 1973, p. 45.
9. "Harold Sidney Geneen," p. 140.
10. Interview with Robert Kenmore, former ITT executive, Palo Alto, Calif., January 31, 1975.
11. Anthony Sampson, *The Sovereign State of ITT* (New York: Stein and Day, 1978), p. 130.
12. "The View from Inside," p. 46.
13. Interviews with ITT executives.
14. "The View from Inside," p. 46.
15. "They Call It Geneen U.," *Forbes*, May 1, 1968, p. 29.
16. Brown, op. cit., p. 163.
17. "They Call It Geneen U.," p. 29.
18. Interviews with ITT executives.
19. Interview with Jack H. Vollbrecht, President, Aerojet-General and former executive of ITT, El Monte, Calif., February 25, 1977.
20. Interviews with ITT executives.

21. "They Call It Geneen U.," p. 28; see also "Harold Geneen—Maybe I'm Worth $5 Million a Year," *Forbes*, May 15, 1971, p. 187.
22. Sampson, op. cit., p. 133.
23. Brown, op. cit., p. 163.
24. "They Call It Geneen U.," pp. 28f.
25. Interviews with ITT executives; see also *International Management*, February 1970, p. 25.
26. Interviews with ITT executives.
27. "The View from Inside," p. 46; Brown, op. cit., p. 163.
28. "ITT: Can Profits Be Programmed?," *Dun's Review*, November 1965.
29. Sampson, op. cit., pp. 131f.
30. Interviews with ITT executives.
31. Ibid.
32. Ibid.
33. Ibid.
34. Ibid.
35. Ibid.
36. "The View from Inside," p. 46.
37. *International Management*, February 1970, p. 24.
38. "They Call It Geneen U.," p. 29.
39. Interview with Vollbrecht, p. 24.
40. Interviews with ITT executives.
41. Ibid.
42. Sampson, op. cit., p. 131.
43. Interviews with ITT executives.
44. Ibid.
45. Ibid.
46. "ITT: Can Profits Be Programmed?," p. 39.
47. "How ITT Manages Itself by Meetings," *International Management*, February 1970, p. 122.
48. Interview with Vollbrecht.
49. "The View from Inside," p. 46.
50. Interviews with ITT executives.
51. Interview with Vollbrecht.
52. "How ITT Manages Itself by Meetings," pp. 22, 24.
53. Ibid., p. 24.
54. Ibid., p. 24.
55. Brown, op. cit., p. 163.
56. Interviews with ITT executives.
57. Ibid.
58. "ITT: Can Profits Be Programmed?," p. 40.
59. Interviews with ITT executives.
60. Ibid.
61. Sampson, op. cit., p. 133; see also "They Call It Geneen U.," pp. 28, 30.
62. "They Call It Geneen U.," pp. 28, 30.

63. Interviews with ITT executives.
64. Brown, op. cit., p. 83.
65. Interview with Vollbrecht.
66. "The Radical Shake-Up That Will Alter ITT," *Business Week,* June 16, 1980, p. 77.
67. Interviews with ITT executives.
68. Ibid.
69. Ibid.
70. Ibid.
71. Ibid.
72. Carol J. Loomis, "Harold Geneen's Moneymaking Machine Is Still Humming," *Fortune,* September 1972, p. 220.
73. Interviews with ITT executives.
74. "Geneen's Fast Ax," *Newsweek,* July 23, 1979, p. 60.
75. "The 50 Largest Industrial Companies in the World," *Fortune,* August 11, 1980, p. 204.
76. Ibid., p. 204.
77. "The Radical Shake-Up That Will Alter ITT," p. 77.
78. Ibid., p. 77.
79. Robert H. Hayes and William J. Abernathy, "Managing Our Way to Economic Decline," *Harvard Business Review,* July-August 1980, pp. 67f.
80. Fritz J. Roethlisberger, *Training for Human Relations,* Division of Research, Graduate School of Business Administration, Harvard University, Boston, 1954.

Chapter 4

1. Interview with Taizo Ueda, senior economist, Honda Motor Co., Ltd., Tokyo, July 1, 1980.
2. The account is drawn from an interview with the western divisional manager of United Airlines, San Francisco, October 10, 1974.
3. Ibid.
4. There are several readily available sources on the role of language and metaphor in human thought. See Benjamin Lee Whorf, "Language, Mind, Reality," in Robert E. Ornstein, ed., *The Nature of Human Consciousness* (San Francisco: Freeman, 1973), p. 328; James L. Adams, *Conceptual Blockbusting* (New York: Norton, 1974), pp. 28, 63.
5. There is a fascinating literature on these ideas. Good starting points include R.G.H. Siu, *The Tao of Science* (Cambridge, Mass.: MIT Press, 1957), pp. 74–77; Koichi Tohei, *Ki in Daily Life* (Tokyo: Ki No Kenkyukai, H.Q., 1978), p. 21; Arthur F. Deikman, "Bimodal Consciousness," in Ornstein, op. cit., p. 76; and T.S. Lebra, *Japanese Patterns of Behavior* (Honolulu: University Press of Hawaii, 1976), pp. 48f.
6. Witter Bynner, *The Way of Life According to Lao Tzu* (New York: Capricorn Books, 1944), p. 30.

Notes / 215

7. For an excellent discussion of *ma,* see Takehiko Kenmachi, *Ma No Nihon Bunka* (Tokyo: Kodanoha, 1978). For briefer treatment in English, see *A Hundred Things Japanese,* Japan Culture Institute, 1975, p. 30; see also "Japan's Art of the Moment," *Newsweek,* April 30, 1979, pp. 100–104.
8. Sei Shōnagon, *The Pillow Book,* in Kenmachi, op. cit., p. 6.
9. Rokusaburo Nieda, *Honne to Tatemae* (Tokyo: Diamond, 1973). There are several similar concepts in the Japanese language, including *uchi* (in) and *soto* (out), *abo ura* (intimate or behind the scenes) and *omote* (ritual, in front). For a discussion of these terms, see Lebra, op. cit., p. 112f.; Takeo Doi, "Some Psychological Themes in Japanese Human Relationships," in J.C. Condon and M. Saito, eds., *Intercultural Encounters with Japan* (Tokyo: Simul Press, 1974), p. 24f.; Helmut Morsbach, "Some Characteristics of Japanese Interpersonal Relations—A Western Viewpoint," paper presented at the Conference of the British Psychological Society, London, December 1977, p. 12; and M.K. Kobayashi and W. Warner Burke, "Organization Development in Japan," *Columbia Journal of Business,* Summer 1976, p. 6.
10. Interview with managers of Zenith Television Division, Chicago, November 1974.
11. Frank Gibney, "The Japanese and Their Language," *Encounter,* March 1975, p. 33.
12. Doi, op. cit., p. 23.
13. Kobayashi and Burke, op. cit., p. 22.
14. John C. Condon, "Introduction," in Condon and Saito, op. cit., pp. 8f.
15. Gibney, op. cit., pp. 32f.
16. Siu, op. cit., p. 66.
17. Interviews with managers of Wells Fargo Bank, San Francisco, April 10, 1974.
18. Interviews with division managers of Wells Fargo Personnel Dept., San Francisco, October 1975.
19. This account is drawn from interviews with managers of the International Division, Bank of America, San Francisco, August 1979.
20. Rosabeth Kanter, *Men and Women of the Corporation* (New York: Basic Books, 1977), pp. 47–55, 177.
21. Ibid., p. 177.
22. Interview with vice president of personnel, Citicorp headquarters staff, New York, May 29, 1978.
23. Some of the most insightful discussion of Western style decision making appears in these four classics: Chester I. Barnard, *The Functions of the Executive* (Cambridge, Mass.: Harvard University Press, 1938), pp. 14–18, 184–99; R.M. Cyert and J.G. March, *A Behavioral Theory of the Firm* (Englewood Cliffs, N.J.: Prentice-Hall, 1963), pp. 149ff.; Henry Mintzberg, *The Nature of Managerial Work* (New York: Harper & Row, 1973), pp. 55–99, 186–89; Leonard Sayles, *Managerial Behavior* (New York: McGraw-Hill, 1964), pp. 207–14.

24. Thomas P. Rohlen, *For Harmony and Strength* (Berkeley: University of California Press, 1974), pp. 28–31, 97f., 107f., 114f.; Lebra, op. cit., p. 11. For a managerial discussion see Peter F. Drucker, *Men, Ideas and Politics: Essays* (New York: Harper & Row, 1971), pp. 704–11, and Michael Y. Yoshino, *Japan's Managerial System* (Cambridge, Mass.: MIT Press, 1968).

25. See, for example, V.H. Vroom and P.W. Yetton, *Leadership and Decision Making* (Pittsburgh: University Press of Pittsburgh, 1973).

26. Bynner, op. cit., p. 74.

27. Interview with managers of Toyota Motor Sales, Compton, Calif., March 1974.

Chapter 5

1. Chester I. Barnard, *The Functions of the Executive* (Cambridge, Mass.: Harvard University Press, 1938), p. 75.

2. Chie Nakane, *Japanese Society* (Berkeley: University of California Press, 1970), pp. 5–14.

3. Henry Stack Sullivan, *The Interpersonal Theory of Psychiatry* (New York: Norton, 1953), pp 3–12.

4. Erving Goffman, *Presentation of Self in Everyday Life* (New York: Doubleday, 1959), pp. 160f.

5. T.S. Lebra, *Japanese Patterns of Behavior* (Honolulu: University Press of Hawaii, 1976), pp. 12f.

6. Ruth Benedict, *The Chrysanthemum and the Sword* (New York: World, 1967), p. 49.

7. James F. T. Bugental, "The Silence of the Sky," adapted from a presentation to UCLA Extension Program on "Knowledge and Uncertainty," Lake Arrowhead, Calif., September 4, 1965, pp. 8ff.

8. F.X. Sutton et al., *The American Business Creed* (Cambridge, Mass.: Harvard University Press, 1956), p. 285.

9. Michael Y. Yoshino, *Japan's Managerial System* (Cambridge, Mass.: MIT Press, 1968), p. 43.

10. Thomas P. Rohlen, *For Harmony and Strength* (Berkeley: University of California Press, 1974), p. 46; see also Ronald Dore, *British Factory—Japanese Factory* (Berkeley: University of California Press, 1973), pp. 230f.

11. Fumio Obata, "Leadership Style," unpublished paper, March 17, 1980, p. 2.

12. Rohlen, *For Harmony and Strength,* pp. 58f.

13. Numerous sources discuss the Japanese work group. Primary sources for this section were Thomas P. Rohlen, "The Work Group in Japanese Company Organizations," Research Conference on Japanese Organization and Decision Making, Sheraton-Maui Hotel, Maui, Hawaii, January 5–10, 1973, p. 2; and M. Saito, eds., *Intercultural Encounters with Japan* (Tokyo: Simul Press, 1974), pp. 24f.; Rohlen, *For Harmony*

and Strength, pp. 1–4, 61–65. A fascinating treatment of the historical antecedents to human group behavior is contained in Richard E. Leakey and Roger Lewin, *People of the Lake* (New York: Doubleday, 1977), pp. 104, 206–12.

14. Rohlen, "The Work Group in Japanese Company Organizations," p. 3.

15. Nakane, op. cit., pp. 62f.

16. Interview with Thomas P. Rohlen, San Francisco, November 6, 1979.

17. Rohlen, *For Harmony and Strength*, pp. 117ff.

18. Yoshino, op. cit., pp. 202f.

19. Ezra F. Vogel, *Japan's New Middle Class* (Berkeley: University of California Press, 1963), pp. 147, 156f.; Nakane, op. cit., pp. 82f.; Lebra, op. cit., pp. 22f.

20. Lebra, op. cit., p. 43; Peter Drucker, *Management: Responsibilities, Tasks, Practices* (New York: Harper & Row, 1974), p. 187.

21. Rohlen, *For Harmony and Strength*, p. 65; Rohlen, "The Work Group in Japanese Company Organizations," pp. 10ff.; David W. Plath, *The After Hours* (Berkeley: University of California Press, 1969), pp. 88–93, 96–111.

22. Rosabeth Kanter, *Men, Women of the Corporation* (New York: Basic Books, 1977), p. 64.

23. Michael Doyle and David Strauss, *How to Make Meetings Work* (Wyden Books, 1976); Robert Schrank, *Ten Thousand Working Days* (Cambridge, Mass.: MIT Press, 1978); Henry Mintzberg, *The Nature of Managerial Work* (New York: Harper & Row, 1973), p. 30; Pascale and Maguire, "Communication and Implementation Among Managers in Japanese and American Managed Companies in the United States," *Sociology and Social Research*, Vol. 63, No. 1 (1978).

24. Lewis B. Ward and Anthony G. Athos, *Student Expectations of Corporate Life*, Division of Research, Graduate School of Business Administration, Boston, 1972.

25. These qualities have been tied to the aesthetic quality—*shibui*. See Kawakita Michaiki, "The World of *Shibui*," *Japan Quarterly*, Vol. 8, pp. 33, 35–42; Lebra, op. cit., pp. 20f.

26. Ralph G. Nichols, "Listening Is a Ten-Part Skill," in Richard C. Haseman, Cal M. Logue, and Dwight L. Freshley, eds., *Readings in Interpersonal and Organizational Communication*, 2nd ed. (Boston: Holbrook Press, 1973), p. 534.

27. Rohlen, *For Harmony and Strength*, pp. 28–31; *A Hundred Things Japanese*, Japan Culture Institute, 1975, pp. 102, 198; Benedict, op. cit., p. 196; Robert E. Cole, *Japanese Blue Collar* (Berkeley: University of California Press, 1971), p. 139; see also Vogel, op. cit., pp. 148f.

28. This term was coined by Irving Janis. See Irving L. Janis, *Victims of Groupthink* (Boston: Houghton Mifflin, 1972).

29. There is an extensive literature on the *sempai–kohai* relationship. See Nakane, op. cit., pp. 26f.; Lebra, op. cit., p. 51; Rohlen, *For Harmony*

and Strength, pp. 123–29. This relationship is also treated under the notion of *"oyabun–kobun."* See Cole, op. cit., pp. 196f.; *A Hundred Things Japanese*, p. 104.

30. See, for example, Kanter, op. cit., pp. 47–68. Also Roger Ricklefs, "The Hidden Hurdle," *Wall Street Journal*, September 19, 1979, pp. 1, 31.
31. Rohlen,*For Harmony and Strength*, pp. 123–29.
32. For an excellent, insightful treatment of the boss–secretary relationship see Kanter, op. cit., pp. 68–87.
33. Interview with managers of YKK Zipper, USA, Macon, Ga., June 1, 1974.
34. John J. Gabarro, "Socialization at the Top—How CEO's and Subordinates Evolve Interpersonal Contracts," *Organizational Dynamics*, Winter 1979, pp. 2–23.
35. John J. Gabarro and John P. Kotter, "Managing Your Boss," Harvard Business School Case No. 1-480-024, 1979; see also Barnard, op. cit., pp. 167, 170f.
36. Preston G. McLean and Katherine Jillson, "The Manager and Self Respect," AMA Survey Report (New York: AMACOM, 1975), p. 2; M.P. Dunnette et al., "Why Do They Leave?," *Personnel*, Vol. 50, No. 3 (May–June 1973), pp. 25–38.
37. Interview with a manager of Wells Fargo Bank, San Francisco, July 8, 1979.
38. This notion is borrowed from Peter Drucker. See Drucker, op. cit., pp. 229, 303–310.
39. W. Timothy Gallway, *The Inner Game of Tennis* (New York: Random House, 1974), p. 19. See also Harry Levinson, *The Exceptional Executive* (Cambridge, Mass.: Harvard University Press, 1968), p. 166; and Jerome J. Bruner, "The Will to Learn," *Commentary*, Vol. 41, No. 2 (February 1966), p. 41.
40. Drucker, op. cit., pp. 229, 303.

Chapter 6

1. Interviews with ITT executives, ITT headquarters, New York, April 19, 1976. See also Douglas McGregor, *The Professional Manager* (New York: McGraw-Hill, 1967), p. 23.
2. Michael Maccoby, "The Corporate Climber Has to Find His Heart," *Fortune*, December 1976, p. 100.
3. Hugh O. Menzies, "The Ten Toughest Bosses," *Fortune*, April 21, 1980, pp. 62–65.
4. Joseph DeRivera, *The Psychological Dimension of Foreign Policy* (Columbus, Ohio: Merrill, 1968), p. 287.
5. Abraham Zeleznik, "The Human Dilemmas of Leadership," *Harvard Business Review*, Vol. 41, No. 4 (July–August 1963), p. 51.
6. See, for example, Chester I. Barnard, *The Functions of the Executive*

(Cambridge, Mass.: Harvard University Press, 1938), pp. 161–84, 225; Leonard Sayles, *Managerial Behavior* (New York: McGraw-Hill, 1964), p. 215; McGregor, op. cit., p. 140; Harry Levinson, *The Exceptional Executive* (Cambridge, Mass.: Harvard University Press, 1968), pp. 3, 45, 192; Harlan Cleveland, *The Future Executive* (New York: Harper & Row, 1972), p. 92; Henry Mintzberg, *The Nature of Managerial Work* (New York: Harper & Row, 1973), pp. 60f.; Herbert A. Simon, *Administrative Behavior*, 3rd ed. (New York: Macmillan, Free Press) p. 13; Rosabeth Kanter, *Men and Women of the Corporation* (New York: Basic Books, 1977), p. 167; H. Edward Rapp, "Good Managers Don't Make Policy Decisions," *Harvard Business Review*, September–October 1967.

7. Barnard, op. cit., pp. 161–84.
8. Comments by a senior executive of a *Fortune* 500 Company to A.G. Athos, July 26, 1975.
9. Studs Terkel, *Working* (New York: Random House, 1972).
10. UAL, Inc., Annual Report, February 1977, p. 1.
11. Loving Rush, Jr., "How a Hotelman Got the Red Out of United Airlines," *Fortune*, March 1972, p. 72. See also Edward E. Carlson, "Visible Management at United Airlines," *Harvard Business Review*, July–August 1975, pp. 30–97.
12. Interviews with senior UAL executives, Elk Grove, Chicago, May 14, June 19, 1975.
13. Rush, op. cit., p. 73.
14. Ibid., pp. 72–76; see also interviews with Edward E. Carlson, Elk Grove, Chicago, December 13, 1974.
15. Ibid.
16. Ibid.
17. Ibid.
18. Rush, op. cit., p. 76.
19. Ibid.
20. For a detailed discussion of the importance of symbolic behavior, see Thomas J. Peters, "Leadership: Sad Facts and Silver Linings," *Harvard Business Review*, November–December 1979, pp. 164–72.
21. Interviews with senior UAL executives.
22. Interviews with Carlson.
23. Interviews with senior UAL executives.
24. Ibid.
25. Ibid.
26. "How United Airlines Pulled Out of Its Dive," *Business Week*, June 29, 1974, p. 67. For a discussion of Carlson's ideas about decentralization, see Rush, op. cit., p. 75; see also Harold D. Watkins, "Carlson Moves to Decentralize United," *Aviation Week and Space Technology*, May 17, 1971.
27. "How United Airlines Pulled Out of Its Dive," p. 67.
28. Ibid., pp. 66f.; see also interviews with senior UAL executives.

29. Interviews with Carlson.
30. Interview with Richard Paget, President, Cressap, McCormick, and Paget, New York, October 30, 1974.
31. Interviews with senior UAL executives.
32. Ibid.
33. Ibid.
34. Watkins, op. cit., pp. 28f.; see also Rush, op. cit., pp. 72f.
35. Ibid.
36. Ibid.
37. Interviews with Carlson.
38. Interviews with senior UAL executives.
39. Ibid.
40. Rush, op. cit., p. 74.
41. Interviews with senior UAL executives.
42. Ibid.
43. Ibid.
44. Ibid.
45. Ibid.
46. Interview with UAL ground personnel, San Francisco, February 19, 1975.
47. Peters, op. cit.

Chapter 7

1. There is a substantial literature on organizational values (superordinate goals). See Henry Mintzberg, *The Nature of Managerial Work* (New York: Harper & Row, 1973), p. 73; Michel Crozier, *The Bureaucratic Phenomenon* (Chicago: University of Chicago Press, 1964), pp. 180f.; Thomas J. Peters, "The Case for Getting Things Done," unpublished paper, May 5, 1976, pp. 16–21; Phillip Selznik, *TVA and the Grass Roots* (Berkeley: University of California Press, 1949).
2. This imagery was proposed by Alan Kennedy, partner, McKinsey & Company, Evian, France, March 20, 1980.
3. Ibid.
4. Janet Guyon, "Family Feeling at Delta Creates Loyal Workers, Enmity of Unions," *Wall Street Journal*, Monday, July 17, 1980, p. 13.
5. Ibid., p. 13.
6. Ibid., p. 13.
7. Ibid., p. 13.
8. Gil Burck, "International Business Machines," *Fortune*, January 1940, pp. 36–40.
9. Ibid., p. 43.
10. Ibid., p. 43.
11. Ibid., p. 43.
12. Ibid., p. 40.
13. Ibid., pp. 40, 43.
14. "IBM's Basic Beliefs," *IBM Orientation Booklet*, undated, p. 11.

15. Thomas Watson, Jr., "A Business and Its Beliefs," *McKinsey Foundation Lecture* (New York: McGraw-Hill, 1963).
16. Rosabeth Moss Kanter, *Men and Women of the Corporation* (New York: Basic Books, 1977), pp. 15–16.
17. Eric von Hippel, "Users as Innovators," *Technology Review*, January 1978, pp. 31–39.
18. See, for example, John A. Prestbo, "At Procter and Gamble Success Is Largely Due to Heeding Customers," *Wall Street Journal*, April 29, 1980, p. 1.
19. Richard T. Pascale, "Personnel Practices and Employee Attitudes: A Study of Japanese and American Managed Firms in the United States," *Human Relations*, Vol. 31, No. 7 (1978), pp. 597–615.
20. Ibid., p. 604.
21. Ibid., p. 609.
22. John J. Leach of the University of Chicago was one of the first to investigate organizational history as a diagnostic tool in consulting. See John J. Leach, "The Organizational History," Thirty-Eighth Annual Academy of Management *Proceedings*, 1978.
23. The term "strategic era" was coined by Thomas J. Peters, consultant, McKinsey & Company. The notion that superordinate goals impede the shift from one strategic era to the next was first introduced by McKinsey director Lee Walton, Ventura, Calif., December 5, 1979.
24. Interview with middle management, McDonald's, San Jose, Calif., June 6, 1974.
25. This example is based upon R.H. Waterman, T.J. Peters, and J.R. Phillips, "Structure Is Not Organization," *Business Horizons*, No. 80302, June 1980, p. 23.
26. These comments on Memorex based on the trial transcript, *Memorex v. IBM*, C-73-2239-SC, U.S. District Court, Northern District of California, August 11, 1978.

Chapter 8

1. Steve Lohr, "Overhauling America's Business Management," *New York Times Sunday Magazine*, Sunday, January 9, 1981, pp. 14f.
2. Ibid., p. 15.
3. Ibid.
4. Ibid., p. 16.
5. Ibid., p. 16; for original source see Peter F. Drucker, *Management*, Harper & Row, New York, 1972, pp. 17–21.
6. *Man-in-Organization, Essays of F. J. Roethlisberger*, The Belknap Press of Harvard University Press, Cambridge, Mass., 1968.
7. We are greatly indebted to the research of Thomas J. Peters into the attributes of excellent companies, which expands considerably on the insights reported here. See Thomas J. Peters, "Putting Excellence Into Management," *Business Week*, July 21, 1980.

ABOUT THE AUTHORS

Richard Tanner Pascale is a member of the faculty of the Stanford University Graduate School of Business and the author of *Managing the White House*. Anthony G. Athos is the Jesse Isador Straus Professor of Business Administration at the Harvard Business School. They are consultants to numerous Fortune 500 companies.